ON BEING LITERATE

'Literacy is neither the major problem, nor is it the main solution.'
Harvey J Graff

MARGARET MEEK

On Being Literate

HEINEMANN
PORTSMOUTH, NEW HAMPSHIRE

HEINEMANN EDUCATIONAL BOOKS, INC.
361 Hanover Street   Portsmouth, NH 03801-3959
Offices and agents thoughout the world

For
Samuel Howson
and
Benjamin Howson
in memory of
their great-great grandfather
David Ballingall
scholar

First U.S. Printing 1992
First published in 1991 by The Bodley Head Children's Books
an imprint of the Random Century Group Ltd,
20 Vauxhall Bridge Road, London SW1V 2SA

Library of Congress Cataloging–in–Publication Data
Meek, Margaret.
    On being literate / Margaret Meek.
        p.   cm.
    Originally published: London : Bodley Head, 1991. With a new
pref.
    Includes bibliographical references (p.   ) and index.
    1. Literacy.   2. Literacy—Great Britain.   3. Reading.
4. Reading—Great Britain.   5. Educational sociology.
6. Educational sociology—Great Britain.   I.   Title.
LC149.M42   1992
302.2'244—dc20   92-24785
                                                     CIP

Page 27, *East Coker* from *The Four Quartets* by T.S. Eliot, used
by kind permission of Faber & Faber Ltd.
Page 40, *Modern Secrets* from *Modern Secrets*, 1989 by
Shirley Geok-Lin Lim, used by kind permission of Dungaroo Press.

Printed in the United States of America on acid free paper
    92   93   94   95   10   9   8   7   6   5   4   3   2   1

Contents

Preface, xi

Introduction, 1
  About This Book, 1
  Noticing Literacy, 4
  Unequal Literacies, 7
  Differences, 9

1. Literacy, 13
  Speech, 13
  New Ways of Talking, 15
  Writing, 18
  What Writing Makes Possible, 23
  Reading, 30
  What Reading Makes Possible, 38
  Thinking, 42

2. Differences, 49
  Being in the Know, 52
  Being in Control, 54
  Culture and Class, 57
  Gender, 61
  Texts, 62
  Learning and Teaching, 66

3. Beginnings, 69
  What Emerges as Literacy?, 73
  The Privileges of Play, 77
  Language Play, 79
  Being Read To: Marking Marks, 88
  Beginnings – Again, 97

4. Why Are Stories Special?, 100
  Sorting Out the World, 100
  Episodes, 105

Contents

Making Worlds, 107
Reading to Children, 110
Texts – and Pictures, 115
Not Only Stories, 122
5. Schooled Literacy, 124
A Necessary Partnership, 130
An Historic Change: the National Curriculum, 134
Entitlement, 136
English in School, 138
Attainment and Assessment, 142
6. Important Lessons, 148
Informal Lessons, 152
Formal Lessons and Classroom Informalities, 155
Confident Knowing, 162
7. Literate Behaviour and Literature, 165
Learning From Written Text, 165
Textbooks and Other Resources, 171
Libraries and Study Skills, 175
Literature, 179
8. Causes and Cures, 189
Signs of Change, 189
Misalignments, 192
What Hinders: What Helps, 199
Dyslexia: a Special *Special Need?,* 202
9. New Literacies, 207
Old Habits: New Challenges, 207
Children Writing, 211
Television, 216
Computers, 222
Contemporary Journalism, 226
10. On Being Literate, 230
Postscript, 239
Notes, 240
Index, 256

Preface
The Culture Shift

As soon as you have read the first page of the Introduction of this book, you will know the most important thing about literacy: its definition depends on what people, at any given place and time, take for granted as the the usual things to do with reading and writing.

No later than the second paragraph I ask my readers to consider what happens in a post office. I chose this as an example of a spot where, in most literate societies, we see some of the common uses of literacy in a public place: 'epiphanies of the ordinary.' Throughout the rest of the book I draw attention to other contexts of literacy and to other commonly understood events, exploring and discussing them more reflexively to determine what counts as being literate in Britain at a time of significant social changes.

My invitation to read this edition has to be slightly different for North American readers. First, I have to acknowledge my great debts to friends and colleagues in the United States and Canada who have taught me a great deal. We have talked about reading and books and teaching for at least two decades. Their scholarship and generosity have allowed me to take advantage of our common language and shared concerns so as to avoid the ethnocentrism that may seem to pervade these pages. Most American teachers I know can read this text without the need for any gloss from me on the differences in our literate cultures. But I ask them, and others who are not so closely acquainted with British social life and educational institutions, to scan this text and the scene it portrays with the eyes of an ethnographer, someone whose job it is to make the unusual seem ordinary the better to notice the strangeness of the usual. Try this, and by reading about how we in Britain are learning to live with difference, you will, I hope, better understand the necessary complexity of reading and writing which most of us take for granted.

In this kind of exercise my mentors are your compatriots, Clifford Geertz and Shirley Brice Heath. They taught me that what counts as literacy needs 'systematic unpacking' of its history and its cultural functions.

Now think again about a post office. If you have ever bought stamps for postcards, or tried to mail a package (we say 'post a parcel') from the British Isles, you know that this may take time. Royal Mail establishments operate as offices of our social services. As you wait in a queue ('stand in line'), you notice that some people buy stamps not for letters but to save for a TV licence. Others are putting money into a savings bank, or taking it out. A few are filling in ('out') forms to licence a car by paying a road tax. Older people collect state pensions; parents get a child allowance. It is also possible to apply for a passport, send greeting telegrams or to discuss philately. All of these are literate activities which correspond with what we do with our time and money. Behind the operations stand other institutions: the schools where the clerks and customers learned to read and write, and the systems of laws and accountancy, the over–arching Great Literacies of a modern industrial state.

Our common experience is school, where everyone is inducted into the institutionalized forms of cultural practices, especially reading and writing. But there are marked differences in procedures, methodology, texts, expectations. Most of my examples are drawn from schools in England, where I have taught for many years in most parts of the system. England has different educational traditions from Scotland, where I learned to read and write and went to school. Each country has a long, convoluted history of literacy teaching. It is almost impossible to give a straightforward account of either of these educational systems in a short space, so I have resorted to representative autobiographical anecdotes, still without doing justice to their rich diversity. You will pass lightly over the scholars and writers whose names crop up from time to time in the text. But to make sense of what is implicit in these chapters it is useful to remember that, especially where education is concerned, England is a deeply divided society. So are most others, but in England the rifts are visible and consequential in the kinds of literacies available in different traditions of schooling. The class system distinguishes a minority (mostly males) whose private education leads, disproportionately, and more directly, to powerful cultural privileges. The rest, 85 percent of the population, go to schools maintained by public funding. In terms of literacy teaching, most 'maintained' schools are as effective as any in the private sector, but the conventional belief that there is something special about a fee-paying school remains. At present, fundamental changes are taking place which will effect all schools in this two-tier system, but there is no sign that the underprivileged, notably the poor, will benefit directly.

Whenever we have debates about education, and there have been more than usual lately, in which learning to read and write are central issues, words like 'entitlement,' 'access,' 'standards,' and 'methods' appear in the discursive rhetoric. They point out the perceived gaps in the provision of full, rich literacy for all. In a lecture about children learning to write, one of our distinguished educators, Harold Rosen, quotes the French philosopher Michel de Certeau: "to write is to be forced to march through enemy territory." This tone may be unfamiliar to those who believe that literacy, and the efforts of teachers to promote it, are largely beneficent.

Talk in Britain and North America about literacy 'in crisis' shows little sense of history. The complaint that reading standards are falling is ages old; it points, always, to changes in reading choices, publishing practices, and what people think reading is good for. The movement away from the canon of 'great literature' does not mean the end of the world as we know it, although to listen to some of the arguments presented a few years ago in a Massachusetts congress meeting you might have thought so. In England the contention of an Oxford professor, Terry Eagleton, that it is not inevitable that Shakespeare will continue to be read in school aroused much passion among those who could not foresee any possibility of removing his plays from the syllabus in the first place. I have followed, with much interest, North American debates about which books should not be read in school, wondering all the while what we mean by freedom of speech and freedom to publish. You will understand that the consciousness of every teacher of literature in Britian is coloured by the affair of *The Satanic Verses*.

Why do we, in our different ways, censor what children read and fill our bookshops with expensive ephemeralities? The answer is well known. Literacy, in the form of book sales, is as much about money as is soap powder. We tend to notice your overzealous censorship of children's books and the enormous market for 'educational sellables,' the workbooks and ditto sheets that we are glad we can't afford. From North America you may well ask of us, "Has your emphasis on teaching reading by means of children's literature really made children better readers of factual texts?" No literacy crises simply arise. They are manufactured by different groups with vested interests in how and what children should read, and, above all, how teachers should be made accountable for the so-called 'delivery' of literacy in school.

Before you go far in this book you will encounter the drama of the new English (note, not British) National Curriculum for maintained schools. (Private schools are exempt.) It is part of a wider reform of the whole education system, a change that is still incomplete, but likely to be continued. Some of the details I have included are still new to English readers. The essential point to grasp is that until 1990 schools were administered by Local Education Authorities. More significantly, the details of the curriculum were, until then, in the hands of teachers. Now the control of the system has been taken back by the central government. Its political dimension has become clear, and a uniform, mandatory curriculum with accompanying tests has been put in place. The rationale is that this will standardize schools across the whole country. What *counts* as literacy, at the various levels of attainment, is at the heart of the matter.

You may think this makes sound sense. After all, England, while populous, is not very big. Our French colleagues, whose national curriculum has just been deconstructed to become decentralised and local, are amused. They offer to teach us how to subvert centralisation. But they agree that we now have a different kind of debate on our hands, one in which the philosophers' concern with knowledge meets the literacy of accountancy, especially in the domains of history and science.

In this new climate and context, our discussions about the teaching of reading and writing are not academic tussles about rival theories of the reading process and the part played by 'real books' (your equivalent is, I think, 'Whole Language'). The debate is not about reading, nor about the proclaimed partnership with parents. It is about the kind of control to be exercised in school over both teachers and learners, about who gets what kind of literacy and who will pay for it.

Children's own experiences of literacy, their encounters with reading and writing in the world, the texts they choose for themselves, their feelings and preferences are all excluded from test scores which are taken to be indicators of performance. The most powerful literacy in education is the literacy of accountancy: Learning must balance costs, budgets, contracts, management. But in the humane aspects of literacy: parents reading to children, the enchantment of stories made only of words and the imagination, and the dawning power of writing, it is impossible to equate a number with a value. Yet this idea runs counter to the kinds of measurements that count as 'results.'

If you think this is a particularly English scene you will find its American counterpart described by Patrick

Shannon in *Broken Promises* (Bergin & Garvey, 1989). The concerns of politicians, local communities, parents and teachers all come together in a classroom where children also have their own experiences and expectations of learning to read and reading to learn. There the influence of science (rationalisation of progress in terms of basal readers), and business (the publication of 'efficient' instruction materials for profit), and psychology (the predominance of research into failure), has obscured the importance of the human interactions of teaching and learning. The important understanding, that children learn well when they enjoy what they are doing and when they want to be successful,is smothered in a mass of technology that promises 'results.' I think we are saved from some of your North American excesses because we cannot afford them, but that does not mean that we are gifted with any greater vision of what full and rich literacy for all could bring about.

One thing more: about television. You have more of it than we do, although we are rapidly catching up. British TV directed specifically at children still retains the bookishness that was part of its early history. The link between TV and children's literature is strong, and there is a growing understanding that each has its own attractions. Although there is no evidence that watching American TV programmes has a deleterious effect on children's reading, many parents still resent the amount of time that children spend in front of screens,and protest that the programmes are harmful. Children and adults whose lives seem to have a high degree of boredom or uncertainty seem to need the instant relief of television, but we still cannot be more certain about what constitutes a 'bad' effect. In defending television I have been much criticised by those who expect others to take all the responsibility for their children's viewing habits. The only solid evidence or effect I can find is that children respond with great interest to being shown how television 'works.' From their early years they are as keen to criticise presentations and performances as they are to look at them, especially when they think their views will be treated with respect. We are, of course, still guessing in this area where, as Seamus Heaney says: "our unspoken assumptions have the force of revelation."

This may also be true about what I have written about literacy. I certainly believe that literacy is not only important for everyone; it is vital if we are to respond to what is written about us and to make views known. But there is more to reading and writing than the efficiency of the post office and the getting of information. A. S. Byatt, in a novel called *Possession* says: "There are readings which make the hairs of the neck, the non-existent pelt, stand on end and tremble, when every word burns and shines hard and clear, infinite and exact, like stones of fire, like points of stars in the dark." I also long for children to discover that kind of reading because I know just how many people have had to make do with something more threadbare.

Before you reach the autobiographical piece in the last chapter you will have discovered that bringing what I care about to consciousness is the way I examine my conscience about those who never discover how the text of a book can enter the text of their lives. To those who share my concerns I offer this book as tribute.

Introduction:
About This Book

Most people, except you reading this book, rarely think about being literate. Once we have learned to read and write so that these seem natural things to do, we take our literacy for granted. Everyone else seems to do the same. A quick glance at the railway-station timetable board and we know whether the train we are meeting is late, though what we actually see may be the expected time of arrival. A hasty scribble, '*Back in 5 mins*', is enough to reassure whoever reads it about our unexpected absence. We do these things almost without thinking because we believe, and our experience confirms, that our world is organized so that people who read and write can communicate with one another by means of written messages.

Think of what happens in the post office every day. Count the number of pieces of paper, documents, that testify to our very existence: birth certificate, medical record, school register, application forms, examination results, pay slip, national insurance card, income tax return, driving licence, season ticket, passport, census return. Our names and addresses are not only in the telephone book, but also where other records are kept, in banks, or on police files. Parliament, the civil service, multinational credit companies pile up written information that affects our lives. The Public Record Office is a monument to centuries of papers from which our history is written. Less grandly, someone feeds into a computer our debts to the gas, electricity and water boards. Supermarkets are crowded with more print than anyone could read in a week. Journalists and newspapers, newscasters, television stations and broadcasting agencies—all over the globe—are counting on the fact that what is written can be read. Even such things as a shopping list and a till receipt are simple, powerful examples and symbols of how it all works.

In our print-crammed lives we are hooked into extensive networks of communications that we have learned to see as ordinary. The bonds of traditional authority, such as the law, the churches, the associations, clubs and groups that we belong to, as well as all the ramifications of our buying and selling, keep us involved with one another by means of written rules, notices and certificates. Some people put the testimonial records of their achievements into frames and hang them on walls. We bear witness to the dead by writing on tombstones and memorials. No one is untouched by the consequences of literacy. What seems natural in all of this is in fact the result of the social uses of writing, what people do with it in the contexts of the events and practices that beget it.

Literacy began when writing was discovered as a useful way of keeping records. Its usefulness was extended and its forms were changed when it became recognized as a means of communicating at a distance and over periods of time. The writer dies, but the words remain. Written texts allow readers to argue, centuries later, about events long past, and to be curious about people long dead whose languages and ideas still seem to be alive and relevant. Imagine what Europe might have been like without the Bible as a book. Writing also becomes a source of power for those who know how to use it and for those who can read.

Literacy is part of history; it also has its own particular history. The earliest examples of writing we have are inscriptions, marks cut into resistant materials, such as stone or clay, by means of pointed instruments. When archaeologists excavate the sites of ancient dwellings they find what the owners valued: pots, jewellery, hunting tools. If they uncover inscriptions, then they can interpret what the writer was thinking about. When writing implements became more handy, and writing surfaces more refined, it was easier to write more quickly, so texts became longer. We still have ancient scrolls and manuscripts we call books. A scribe could spend a lifetime making one copy of a text. Most of the later technological changes, printing, typesetting machinery and now the electronic processes that transmit documents around the world at the speed of light, have come about as the result of our ever-increasing understanding of what writing makes possible. Libraries that once housed unique copies of handwritten books now have machines that reduce printed papers to microscopic dots and other machines to enlarge them again. We have the history of writing in our hands when we use tools with sharp points, pens and pencils. But, to be literate is to learn to use the technology of our day, and to decide, in our own time, what reading and writing are good for.

Everyone knows that to be at home in a literate society is a feeling as well as a fact. We are aware that, in our history, literacy has exalted the poor to the level of the powerful. John Bunyan, the tinker, influenced the thinking and feeling of his time more than archbishops. In the lives of ordinary people across the centuries literacy has had importance beyond its usefulness, beyond its function in public networks of social cohesion and the techniques of its productions. However and wherever people learn to read and write, literacy adds to their sense of human worth and dignity. Most people agree that we extend our consciousness, our sympathies and our understanding in the ordinary processes of reading a newspaper or a novel, or by writing a letter of condolence. Because we can read we can also *question* the authority and the apparent dominance of those whose forcefully written documents urge something upon us. We can query the gas bill. We write as well as speak to register our protest against injustice. By learning to read we gain knowledge. In writing we come to ask ourselves what it is that we know and understand, so that we too can go 'on the record'. So we take for granted the fact that, in our society, we and our children need to be literate.

At the same time we should understand that literacy, so

natural-seeming to us, is not universal. There are still places in the world where people do not learn to read and write in childhood because their way of life does not depend upon it. To be 'non literate' in these places is therefore not a term of defect or of deprivation. This can also remind us that, in the history of literacy in Britain, the notion that *everyone* has to learn to read and write is a fairly recent idea. I doubt if my great-grandparents had time to read except when they went to Sunday school.

The questions this book addresses include: what does it mean to be literate? Can we tell how literate our children should be, what literacy is for and what it is worth? In a world of documentation and official print what kinds of literacy do most people need to acquire? Can we assume that, once they have learned to read and write in school, our children's literacy will last them for a lifetime? One thing is certain. We are now facing a social and cultural upheaval, a revolution, perhaps, that shapes our view of the future in ways that no one could have fully foreseen fifty years ago. It seems right, therefore, that we should take stock of our literacy, what it is and what we think it is good for, in order to decide how best we can help our children to learn the literacies that they will need.

Noticing Literacy

We begin with some everyday experiences. When, for example, do we notice that we are literate, that we depend upon being able to read and write? What do we learn when we stop taking literacy for granted and look at it?

Suppose we go on holiday, to Greece, Israel, Turkey, India or the Far East. As soon as we arrive at the airport or the station we encounter writing in a script and an alphabet that are strange to us. Our ordinary reading doesn't work, especially if the words go from right to left. As we are cut off from reading by the writing system we begin to 'read' other things: the situation, the faces of people around us, the contents of the shops or kiosks. We count on sign language, gestures and the few words we quickly learn, such as 'please' and 'thank you', to help us out. We are forced to behave as if we were in an oral culture with people whose alphabets are older than our own. We can have this kind of enlightenment without even crossing the Channel. A visit to Wales brought home to me what those who arrive from Pakistan or Vietnam experience when they first come to live in Britain. Even a daily event, like buying a ticket for the London Underground, makes me aware that one of my most powerful assumptions about being literate is my confidence about what I *needn't* read. When new ticket machines were introduced I had to read the instructions for putting money into a slot, to press buttons with signs and figures, to collect the ticket and the change, all in ways that needed concentration and effort for several days. What stayed the same was my expectation that the written instructions on the machine were there to help me. In ways such as this we make our literate behaviours into routines and habits, just as we buy newspapers and know where to find, and sometimes how to do, the crosswords inside them. Once literate, always literate? Well, we'll see.

As I wait for my Tube train I find myself, as usual, scanning the advertisements in front of me. One has a huge picture of a conventional refrigerator. Underneath are the words: 'If your machine won't run BOS software, it's probably a fridge.' I have no problem with the words, but, since the meaning seems to escape me, I read them again, this time paying attention to the fact that what they say is not wholly what they intend to convey. At the same time I notice my impatient fellow travellers. I 'read' their clothes, their tapping feet and briefcases. They are going to the City, to the world of fast information exchange between Tokyo and Wall Street. Ah! computers: so 'machine', 'run' and 'software' now slot into a different context, that of micro-technology. The copy-writers have counted on the moment of hesitation between my reading and my understanding to capture my attention. Advertising, besides being big business, is a game that literates nowadays play with each other. The readers congratulate themselves on spotting the trick and getting the message. But the real winners are the makers of the product, those who pay the writers. We all know the rules of this game. What we don't always remember is that we learned them when we discovered how to tell a story or a joke.

This introductory preamble is to make explicit two simple ideas on which the usefulness of this book depends. The first is that literacy is not natural, even though we act as if it were because we need to take it for granted. It doesn't come to us as a part of our being, like red hair, long legs, or even as speech, which is also socially learned. We become literate by behaving as the literate do, making efforts under their instruction, at home, at school and in our encounters with writing in the world.

My second axiom about literacy is that it changes as societies change. As I waited for that long-delayed Tube train, pleasing myself with the puzzle of the software advertisement, I remembered my grandfather teaching me to read from the public print that said OXO, and from the writing on the enamelled panels nailed to the wooden railing of our small seaside railway station which carried advertising messages about the literacy of that time.

> *They come as a boon and a blessing to men,*
> *The Pickwick, the Owl and the Waverley pen.*

As we lingered on the platform my grandfather would explain, rather more often than I liked, the relation of Pickwick, Owl and Waverley to a world of writing now almost out of memory. He was one of the first boys to go to his village school in 1868, just before primary education became compulsory. He was an eager pupil, so much so that for most of his life thereafter when he could choose to do what he wanted, he wrote and read till he died in his late eighties. The texts he preferred were in Hebrew and German. In his lifetime he saw the decline in illustration in novels for adults, the perfection of the fountain pen to replace the hazardous dipping of the Pickwick, Owl and Waverley nibs in clogged

6

ink-wells, and the revolution in reading glasses that gave him a serene old age. He scarcely encountered the post-war advertising explosion, and he knew nothing of the subtlety of modern copy-writing techniques.

Yet here am I, the granddaughter whom he taught to read, still taking lessons from my surroundings in ways that could not have been imagined when I went to that same village school and used the beginners' writing tools available in 1930: a sand tray for tracing letters and a slate for doing sums. In ways that had scarcely changed since the invention of printing I learned to make my fingers represent my thoughts and thus make visible the dialogue that I 'ran' in my head. I was thirty before I watched television, and then only irregularly. Literacy becomes different as times change. Sometimes we notice it more than others. As my generation is overtaken by the computer age, another chapter in the history of literacy will come to an end, although I doubt if anyone will notice exactly when it happens.

Unequal Literacies

There is always some kind of public concern about literacy. Parents are naturally anxious about their children's education, at the heart of which is literacy. Schools and teachers are expected to assume responsibility for making children literate in demonstrable ways. Governments want value for the money they invest in schooling so checks and test results make teachers and education authorities accountable. Each group—parents, teachers, administrators and public servants—holds the others responsible for the attainment of children in school, while concern about the relation of teaching methods to pupils' success produces conflicts and differences of opinion, resulting in more general worry that children are not as literate as they should be. As adults have become more impatient about their children's learning and demand more demonstrable accomplishment, the arguments about how reading and writing should be taught have been more acerbic and less helpful. Each child's progress to literacy is more complex than the test results show.

A second root of powerful unease is grounded in the nature of our society. We know well that, while all children are expected to learn to read and write, literacy is not the same for everyone. A national curriculum will make no difference to this social fact. Being literate may be acknowledged all over the world as a universal good, but there is no sign, as yet, of its becoming a universal entitlement or a universal provision. There are different versions of literacy, some much fuller than others, some much more powerful than others. *Where* they go to school seems to lead some children to positions of power in adult life even more directly than *how* they prove their competences in examinations that are open to all. Literacy is part of our class system.

No reasonable parent believes that all schools give equal access to literacy to all children. Those who pay for schooling, those who fight the local authority, or those who seek to demonstrate their children's superior intellectual powers in order to send them to selected schools are all showing that they believe some kinds of literacy acquired at school are more desirable than others. In the tortuously competitive society that ours has become, an active, democratic social concern about the availability of the fullest possible literacy for all often gives away to a more particular concern for one's own children. This too can seem natural, and can conceal from us the fact that literacy is embedded in particular systems of belief, in ideology. Being literate has long been associated in people's minds with 'getting on'. Those who have visible privileges and powerful authority over others—doctors, lawyers, bankers, scholars, scientists, entrepreneurs and priests—have, in many cases if not in all, profited from the shaping of their careers by the specialized literacies that are associated with them in school and university. Those who, on looking back at their schooling, wish they had been thus individualized (*privilege* is 'individual' or 'private law' in Latin), or had 'done better', want

8

the greatest possible literacy advantages for their children. They want to ensure these not only in terms of career success, but also in the acquisition of a richer, more continuous literacy, one that goes beyond whatever someone in authority decrees is 'basic', that is, literacy in its cheapest, meanest form. This desire is not limited to one class or to one section of the population, although it may be expressed differently in different places. The great divide in literacy is not between those who can read and write and those who have not yet learned how to. It is between those who have discovered what kinds of literacy society values and how to demonstrate their competences in ways that earn recognition. Others may have less confidence in their ability or less desire to prove themselves in this way.

There are signs of change. Some say that there is a literacy 'crisis', but this is just our modern way of drawing attention to what we think is important. Clearly, literacy is always part of any change in our culture, our way of living, our assumptions. My contention, banal as it may seem, is that reading and writing have helped us to understand the world and our place in it and will now allow us to consider the possibilities of different kinds of future. While we know from our history that literacy has not always been a benefit, has been associated with evil, wars, disease, oppression and self-regard, it has never encouraged, nor been part of, cultural despair or helplessness. On the contrary, it is also a mode of recreation, both effortful and restful. So we owe it to our children to understand as clearly as possible what we mean when we say we want them to be literate.

Differences

This book is a companion to the one I wrote about learning to read. In that volume I took reading out of the total literacy context so that I could look at some aspects of reading in school and books written for children to help parents who wanted to support their children's learning. Now I want to consider the ways in which learning to read and write are related to the wider aspects of schooling so that parents and teachers and, I hope, children, will understand something of the nature of literacy and its place in our culture.

My purpose is not a neutral one. Work both with teachers and pupils has convinced me that there are two models of literacy on offer in our schools: a utilitarian one aimed at giving people the ability to write little more than their name and address and to fill in forms, and a supercharged model which allows its possessors to choose and control all that they read and write. This powerful literacy includes the ability, the habit even, of being *critical*, that is, of making judgements, especially about the writing of others. My belief is that, until most, indeed all, children in school have access to, and are empowered by, critical literacy, including the understanding that reading and writing are more than simply useful, then we are failing to educate the next generation properly.

At the heart of this is a consideration of *differences*. Some of these have already been hinted at: the change in technologies for writing, for example. As word processors become more common, handwritten letters take on different meanings. Along with their intended message they may convey old-fashionedness, lower economic status, or intimacy with the reader. Telephone networks have increased prodigiously, but instead of an expected reduction in postal deliveries, we have more junk mail, bigger catalogues than ever, more insistent solicitations.

But there are more important and more subtle differences in the literacy scene. The first of these lies in the composition of our society itself. An ordinary school classroom shows clearly that we are now a multicultural nation. The fact is more immediately visible in the inner cities, but the implications are universal. Then, we are more aware than ever of the difference that social class makes to children's learning in school. There is irrefutable evidence that in primary schools poor children tend to be less successful at reading. We also know that boys and girls are differently located in society. Their passage through the years of school education gives them different expectations of adulthood.

They read books differently. The consequences of all these differences are not well understood or even acknowledged.

While it is possible to record the changes that occur in literacy over time—the difference between my literacy and my grandfather's—it is more difficult, but equally necessary, to take account of different literacies in use at the same time. Not every member of our society is as comfortably literate as he or she would like to be. We have a special responsibility for those whose literacy is marginal, like those who might read a redundancy notice without realizing that it is not a communication between equals. Besides, we have little idea how much literacy, or what kinds, are needed for certain occupations—storekeepers, porters, taxi drivers—or whether the literacy of nurses on hospital drug rounds is of a different kind from that of the prescribing doctors. Our normal habit is to associate literacy with social status, and then to imply the differences in terms of skill.

Some people believe that they have as much literacy as they want. The interests of a sports enthusiast are more active than those of an antiquarian bookseller. The association of literacy with 'getting on' seems to be a sound one until it becomes evident that the powerful are not necessarily bookish, and the great readers, the academics, have a reputation for learning which sometimes seems to have more to do with docility and orderliness than the moving of the mountains of the mind. Significantly, even the most sophisticated tests of literacy, those measures which are believed to indicate levels of competences, tell us nothing about the effective *use* of reading and writing skills, what the literate do with their literacy.

One thing is certain: we shall make no difference to the education of a single child by complaining that literacy isn't what it used to be. Indeed it is not, and therein lies our need to acknowledge the complexity of our subject and to face the fact that most of what we have to discover about literacy is embedded in the social practices for which we use it and in the ways which, if we are not careful, we may use it to divide rather than to unite us.

These and other matters will be considered in the pages that follow. The first paragraph of each chapter indicates the aspects of literacy, or as we shall soon say, literacies, that are dealt with. The sub-headings give some indication of how the theme is developed. If advice to parents, teachers and others who are concerned to help children and young people through the maze of schooled literacy does not appear as you expect to find it, then you must tell me. You are invited to read this book in a questioning, countering, even oppositional mode, as an exercise in critical literacy.

CHAPTER 1

Literacy

Literacy has two beginnings: one, in the world, the other, in each person who learns to read and write. So literacy has two kinds of history: one, in the change and development over time of what *counts* as literacy; the other in the life histories of individuals who learn to read and write, and who depend on these skills as features of their lives in literate societies. It is impossible to understand literacy without referring to its history, to those who are literate at any given time, and to what people actually *do* with reading and writing. So we have to unravel some of the meanings we give to literacy as a word, and some of the situations where we find it in use. This should help us to see more clearly what we understand about the nature of literacy nowadays, what we mean when we say we are literate, and why we are concerned about the literacy of our children.

Speech

Literacy is about language, and the primary form of language is, of course, speech. To talk is to be human. When we speak we know that we exist amongst others like us, and we take care to help our children to learn what we usually call their 'mother tongue'. Children, in their turn, want to join in human conversations as soon as possible. Talking and listening are so ordinary that we scarcely notice that they are ways of using language in order to learn how the world works and to accumulate shared understanding about it. We also

13

tend to ignore the other things we do when we chat busily to each other: raising our eyebrows, shaking our heads or shrugging our shoulders, tapping our feet in impatience or sighing in sympathy. Eye contact, gestures and common contexts of meanings are all part of our conversational habits. To understand literacy we have to register the fact that spoken language covers a wide range of activities, and is woven into the texture of every aspect of our lives.

Compared with the amount we speak, we read and write much less. But, because we learned to read when we were young and we live with print all around us, we find it hard to imagine a time in the past when there was no possibility of *seeing* language. Our pre-literate ancestors learned what they needed to know in continuous face-to-face encounters with family and neighbours. They were taught ways of *remembering* who they were, where they came from, how to keep alive. By talking and singing, by reciting genealogies, they handed down to their children the history of their tribe. We see traces of this in chronicles that have survived long enough to be written down, as in the Old Testament, which shows us that 'all Israel was enrolled by genealogies'. The distinguishing features of pre-literate societies were the ways by which they taught themselves to surmount the limitations of human memory. So they chanted in rhythmic and rhyming verse the legendary deeds of their heroes and invented ways of expanding memory, such as the cumulative tale. One of the best known of these is 'The House that Jack built'. The reciter learns to associate the rat with the malt, the cat with the rat, and so on, to bring back the complete string of events.

Another oral inheritance we can trace from pre-literate times is the proverb. In these pithy statements we catch a glimpse of the lives of those who handed down hard-won experience in the shortest, most memorable form. Each proverb is a little story, an event. Taken together they show us the tensions and arguments of people who lived close to each other and whose lives were interdependent. 'A soft answer turneth away wrath'; 'least said, soonest mended';

'he who hesitates is lost'. Behind 'a stitch in time saves nine' are generations of seamstresses before my grandmother who taught me the literal truth of this saying. The packed advice of proverbial wisdom, found as it is in all languages, is only one snippet of evidence that all societies are, unmistakably and fundamentally, oral.

Our understanding of literacy must begin with the recognition of that orality and its continuing presence in our lives. The most impressive aspects of it are the great formal productions, the epic poems of the Greeks, the *Iliad* and the *Odyssey*, which were clearly oral poems before they were written down and attributed to Homer. The Indian Vedic hymns, the Old Testament, ancient Chinese tales, Arabic and African epics, Scottish ballads and Welsh legends all represent powerful ways of thinking and feeling which, in their early days, owed nothing to writing for their organization and continuance, their great beauty, complexity and imaginative force. Long before *Cinderella* became the story we know, it had many forms in vigorous folk-tales found throughout the world. So, when literacy began, it inserted itself into established civilizations which already had powerful ways of talking and remembering.

New Ways of Talking

Speech has always been, and is likely to remain, our primary mode of human contact, so it is not surprising that we seek new ways of extending its range and power. The advances in technology that have influenced our lives most in the last century are related, as speech is, to sound: recorded music, telephones, radio and television. The telephone has shrunk the globe. Once upon a time important messages were announced by heralds, or written on sealed parchment carried by ambassadors who conveyed the information in them by making speeches to the receivers. Now presidents and prime ministers speak to each other across oceans by bouncing their words off satellites in the sky. Millions of people hear about natural or political disasters, or the next day's weather, almost instantaneously from radio voices they recognize as familiar, although the speakers may never be seen. When they speak, television announcers behave as if they knew their listening watchers, but they cannot see them. Computers can now simulate speech. Recorded talk is now so common that children may listen to the voices of their parents long after they are dead.

These technological extensions of normal speech are sometimes called 'secondary orality', a phrase coined by Walter Ong, because the face-to-faceness of the primary kind of conversation is lacking. When radio and television announcers and readers speak as if they were addressing a visible audience they are in fact reading what someone else has written. (The French call it *'écrit sonore'*, 'sounded writing'.) Despite the apparent spontaneity of politicians in television party political broadcasts, the words they say are rolling before their eyes as they read them from the teleprompter, an artificial memory that eliminates the natural hesitations of talk. So, these 'speeches' become 'statements' which are 'for the record'. They aspire to the status of written texts, yet they keep enough informality for the speaker to retract what was said, if necessary.

Television and radio announcers don't expect their listeners to reply, interrupt or protest. Even 'phone in' programmes, organized to seem to be conversations, are edited at the point where the caller contacts the producer before being allowed to engage with the expert. If viewers are not satisfied with what they hear they can write to 'postbag' programmes where a presenter reads an edited part of the letter. On television the viewers see the actual handwriting of the sender. But this is quite different from the usual habit of writing to one person only.

The importance of radio and television talk is that it gives listeners and viewers the illusion of being part of a wider, linked community and thus of knowing what goes on in the world. The technologies that produce secondary orality maintain and promote, for better or worse, a series of common concerns, from elections to soap operas. The radio talk operates like the lecture, which had its origins in the early universities when books were expensive. A discussion programme is the modern version of the disputation, the kind of formal argument engaged in by medieval scholars. Secondary orality, especially when experts turn prepared texts into conversations at different levels of formality, is a new form of literacy with old roots. The continuing element is the understanding that talking is a distinctive way of teaching and learning.

Modern sound media allow us to hear a greater number of languages, and many more varieties of our own language, than we could otherwise encounter in our day-to-day lives. Most people are now aware of different accents and language forms, and show little difficulty in understanding them when the speakers appear on television. British children early distinguish and imitate American accents, or the intonation of favourite comedians and singers. The arrival of the tape recorder meant that oral language could be collected, so that the efforts of linguists were both enlarged and enhanced as they turned spoken language into written transcriptions for study and comment. The enthusiasm for discussing language varieties owes much to these investigations, but more, perhaps, to the acknowledged fact that differences in spoken English are now world-wide. As English becomes a world language we learn to appreciate the worth of the plain speech of all people. We also know that forms of regional speech, dialects, are, in fact, languages. The special concern, expressed in government documents about education, that children should know *about* the English language, is the result of the demonstrations of the great variety of its uses that radio and television make possible. Written stories can be read as if they are being specially retold. So modern literacies reticulate oral language. Reading and writing are embedded in talk and surrounded by it. This we must remember when we learn, in the pages that follow, that literacy is more than just a question of reading and writing.

Writing

Literacy begins with writing. A mark, a scratch even, a picture or a sign made by one person which is interpreted and understood by others may be regarded as a form of writing. The idea is simple enough. Once we have grasped it, even the hieroglyphics of the Egyptians seem, if not familiar, then at least part of the same world as our word processors. To me, writing seems to be a perpetual and recurrent miracle.

In the history of our species, writing is a comparatively recent invention. If we assume that humankind is about 50,000 years old, then writing has been around for 5,000 years or so. We know this because the ineluctable fact about writing is that, surviving the death of the writer (provided the material lasts), it tells the story of its origins.

The earliest form of writing we know is that of the Sumerians whose civilization flourished in the eastern Mediterranean corner of south-west Asia in about 3500 B.C. The Sumerians used clay tablets on which they made marks to record the trading transactions of merchants and sea-farers, early book-keeping notes. There were also picture scripts, of which the most remarkable was the fine hiero-glyphic carving of the ancient Egyptians, their sacred writing. The skill of reading these picture-signs was lost for nearly 1400 years. Because no one could read it, Egyptian writing was erroneously believed to hold magic secrets, an idea still attached to scripts that are part of religious rites and ceremonies.

The deciphering of hieroglyphics, and our consequent understanding of writing systems, was advanced by the discovery in 1799 of the Rosetta Stone, a huge slab of black basalt, now in the British Museum. On it are carved three different scripts. Two are Egyptian, the sacred writing and a more ordinary demotic lettering; the third script is Greek. Once it became clear that these were parallel versions of the same text, it was possible to use the Greek to decipher the two Egyptian versions, and, thereafter, to interpret other

Egyptian texts. The Rosetta Stone remains a landmark in the history of writing. Every time I look at it, and I'm only a few hundred yards from it now, I think of the original carvers who, about 196 B.C., created with care and toil a bilingual text which records for ever how King Ptolemy V had 'apportioned justice to all'.

The most complicated script is Chinese. It consists of a long series of intricate picture characters, ideograms, which represent ideas and objects derived from Chinese life and culture. In ancient times the writing was practised as an art form, studied and guarded by selected scholars. It is beautiful, hard to learn, and represents the discipline of scholarship and the aesthetic devotion of Chinese writers to this day. Chinese children learn to write their language all the time they are in school, but very few of them have completed the task before they leave. Yet some literacy scholars are persuaded that no one system is more difficult to learn to read and write than any other. Whether or not this is the case, to learn to write always involves practice with a tool which has to be brought under control so that the writer can concentrate on putting together the message rather than on the formation of the signs.

When I began to write in school I formed letters in a sand tray with my forefinger. The unsuccessful attempts could quickly be made to disappear. Children still write in sand or in the earth in countries where paper and pens are expensive. But if the writing is to stay to be read, it must be retained by the surface. So the earliest writing tools were designed to bite into stone, bark, papyrus, wax, vellum and, finally, paper. My modern pencil, which looks like a Roman stylus, works in that way as I compose this sentence. Civilizations which used handwriting produced manuscripts; *manus* is the Latin word for 'hand'. They are sometimes called *chirographic* cultures; *kheir* is Greek for hand. *Calligraphy* is practically the same word. We now use calligraphy to mean 'beautiful writing' in order to distinguish those who practise hand-writing as an art form in the tradition of the scribes who copied books and ornamented them before the days of printing. Now, I wonder, will my grandchildren, who are learning to use a computer and word processor before they go to school, miss out altogether the handwriting stage of becoming literate?

The writing which, for us, counts as literacy is a system organized to represent sounds by shapes. This makes language visible, soundless, permanent; we call it *alphabetic* writing, from the names of the first two letters of the string of shapes we inherited from the Greeks. They learned an alphabet from the Phoenicians who were trading in the eastern Mediterranean around 1500 B.C. The Phoenician alphabet was the Semitic one, to which, the experts say, all other European alphabets, and those of the near East— Greek, Arabic, Cyrillic (the one the Russians use) and Roman—are related.

At first the Semitic alphabet that the Greeks borrowed had no shapes or letter sounds for vowels. (Modern Hebrew is the same in this.) The Greeks added letters for the vowels, and so created a letter for each sound in their language. They now had a *phonetic* alphabet, their distinctive contribution to the history of writing. Moreover, they showed how this supple way of marking language, and writing it down, could be used. By 500 B.C. they had established the functions of powerful writing which remain to this day: for prayers, laws and trading, where a fixed record is important. In addition, they had discovered how to make a *text*, continuous writing, something written down that could be re-read, assessed, thought about. With their restless, dramatic, querying, arguing habits the Attic Greeks made writing intellectual, logical, riddling.

What we know about the Greek views of literacy we owe, for the most part, to Plato. He gives a glimpse of how uncertainly, slowly, writing entered the lives of the most naturally thoughtful, reflective people Europe has ever known. In recording the wisdom of his teacher, Socrates, Plato shows Socrates rejecting writing as too static, too fixed for truth-telling compared with the liveliness of spoken argument. A text cannot answer a reader's questions; it just stays there. Moreover, writing seems to lessen the power of memory. Yet, the irony is, we imagine we *hear* Socrates saying these things, two thousand years and more after he was put to death, because Plato wrote them down.

Once writing had appeared, there was no going back. Slowly—not least because life was short, the materials difficult to get and to handle, and the recompense for being a composer of texts or simply a scribe was not great—writing seeped like an underground river into the lives of societies. For a long time oral and literate cultures existed side by side. The records show that the first effect of writing was to preserve what was already there, as records, rather than to change anything. As people came to live in towns they kept records of transactions, decisions in the lawcourts, plans, wills and notes of financial dealings. But when they really wanted to know what was going on and what was important, they gathered in market squares, in the streets, at fairs and religious ceremonies. They had no newspapers, only town criers to tell of taxes and wars. The literate were those whose material ends were served by learning to write, who knew what writing was useful for. The others learned what they needed, or let writing pass them by.

The problem posed by the history of writing in the spread of literacy is, what counts as evidence? How are we to judge the emergence of writing in the lives of ordinary folk? Generalizations quickly dissolve into particulars. Here are examples from the annals, or records, kept by a community of monks in St Gall in Switzerland during the eighth century.[1]

709 Hard winter. Duke Godfried died.
710 Hard year and deficient in crops.
711
712 Flood everywhere.
713
714 Pippin, Mayor of the Palace, died.
715 716 717
718 Charles devastated the Saxon with great destruction.
719

This is not the kind of public record we now keep. Yet, from this scant account, with the help of the historians, we can glimpse a community threatened by famine, flood and war. Monks had no idea of an 'author', except God, as the creator of all things. Their obligation was to guard, to copy, to pass on the holy scriptures and the commentaries to which they had privileged access.

From the manuscript literacy of the monks we come to understand the difference between composing and copying. The scribe is expected to keep the text secure; it cannot be changed as it is reproduced.

Centuries later, when Shakespeare's plays held Londoners spellbound, the written texts probably consisted of parts for the actors, or, at best, a prompt copy to help those whose memory faltered. Yet before another century passed, writing in English had reached every corner of the country so that even those who could not read had a clear idea of the power of the written word for ordinary folk. What the Reformation began in making the Bible generally available in the vernacular, the Civil War and its aftermath continued by making available for even the lowliest reader, commentaries on national affairs. John Bunyan, a travelling tinker, was writing *The Pilgrim's Progress* in jail at almost exactly the same time as Milton was writing *Paradise Lost*. Neither text is best read in solitude. In contrast, the three-volume novelist of the nineteenth century looked to readers with the leisure to read long books silently, alone. Now, the newspapers and magazines that we see every day have the compressed, short sentences that characterize our fast-moving city life, our restlessness, our impatience for news, our dread of boredom. All writing that is quickly read is done at a particular time, in a particular place by particular people. There is a *style*, a recognizable kind of writing for each period, that reflects the writers' views, or their readers', and the interactions of readers with writers.

Writing is bound to change, yet two things seem to stay the same. As it doesn't come to us all, like speech, in the common process of growing up, writing has to be learned as a way of using tools that demand almost monkish application and industry in particular kinds of contact with teachers, some of whom know about the complicated nature of composing, others of whom are mainly scribes. Then, there have always been fewer writers than readers, and amongst writers there are wide differences in skill and acknowledged success. Only a small proportion of what is written reaches the world at large by way of publication. The rest has to find its own readers. Even now, when literacy is available to all, we still do not know how much writing, what kinds of writing and for what purposes, go on in the lives of ordinary people. The kind of writing that most people read is often at odds with the powerful uses of writing which are backed by different kinds of authority. Also, there are specialized kinds of writing done by those belonging to select groups who know they are writing for readers who share their interests and their understandings: mathematicians, poets, scientists, lawyers, soldiers, merchants and moneymakers. They keep their writings almost as professional secrets and thus exclude all but a select band of interpreters.

What writing makes most visible is the relentless and distinctive human endeavour which we call thinking. Again and again, in any discussion of literacy, we run up against the multiplicity of modern consciousness that writing helped to bring about. Therefore it is worth looking at what writing seems to make possible, and to ask if all those who learn to do it can also be helped to see what it is good for, and to use it for a wider range of purposes and possibilities. What kinds of writing should children learn to do?

What Writing Makes Possible

Those who study the history of writing are convinced that it is one of the most momentous of all human inventions. It makes possible the use of language beyond speech. It makes us conscious of language itself in ways that affect both our public and private lives. It creates what is to be read, and, therefore, readers.

Public writing is, essentially, useful. All information, contracts, laws, economic operations, everything related to money, whatever helps administration and creates bureaucracies is organized in writing. Where once we had street vendors calling their wares, we now have writing on food wrappers telling us when it is to be sold, and how soon we have to eat it. The chief function of public writing is to tell many people the same things. It is organized to seem reasonable ('Do not speak to the driver while the bus is in motion'), but is also a way of establishing conformity and control in society.

The more complicated our social arrangements become, the more separate are the relations between those who compose public writing and those who are expected to read it. We have no idea who writes the fire regulations that appear on the walls of every public building. Members of Parliament don't actually write the laws they make. Specialized lawyers compose the words that go into the law books when the debates have ended. Public writing enters our lives at every point. It takes our literacy for granted and depends on print, on the machines that took over the labour of the scribes.

Print is part of the separation of writers from readers. It gives what is written a special kind of authority. The printing of bills implies we should pay them; a summons to jury service looks as if it could condemn us if we failed to attend. Public writing in print lays on us, as citizens, the obligation to read and to act without any reference to the writer. The dominance of print, its usefulness, ubiquity and power give rise to the widely-held idea that written information is, by itself, knowledge.

Advertising is a particular case for the examination of modern print and the literacy needed to deal with it. Its force is to make us buy things, but the products themselves are commonly available, and so we see ourselves as living in a world where various kinds of soap, petrol and banks are the norm. We seem to acquire a kind of secondary literacy generated by the products. The copy-writers draw on this when they offer us only *S-ssh* to read and we know by association what it refers to.

The literate response to public writing is the ability to reply in writing, and to know that we have the right to reply. Bills may have mistakes, bank statements are not infallible. There is after all, sitting at a machine, a writer-copyist whose human proneness to error is not displaced by the ellicacy of the machine itself. There are even ways of gaining exemption from jury service. The confidently literate know how to deal with public writing. They use their rights of appeal and know how to create bodies of public opinion. It is not that they are better writers than the majority; they simply know how writing operates, that Members of Parliament have to reply to letters, for instance. Those who lack confidence in their literacy are less inclined to do these things, suspecting that, even in writing, what they think or know will not merit attention. The significant shift in literacy with regard to public writing is that the confident literates know what they *needn't* read. Those who cannot read believe that if they were to learn, they would then have to read all they see.

The oldest kind of public writing is in the form of graffiti. Writing on walls is the spontaneous mark-making of those who have something urgent to say about the state of things. Roman soldiers protested about their pay in this way. Graffiti-writing is what an anonymous writer wants to say to challenge the power that official writing, itself anonymous, has over the lives of those who feel the need to answer back. The distance between the writers of official documents and the skilled composers of graffiti is the span of public literacy in a society at any given time.

While public writing has an external nature, personal writing is that which we do for purposes we define for ourselves. We may even keep the writing where no one else may see it; a journal or a diary is the most obvious kind. People still take pleasure in writing letters; they feel they know themselves better as they write. Although the general assumption is that writing is practised much less now, we know for certain that, all over the country, there are those who watch plants growing and record what they see, others who scan the stars and report to their local astronomy group, research local history, keep parish records, collect, check, write up the details that interest them. Some write plays for dramatic societies; thousands submit entries to national poetry competitions. Publishers receive hundreds of un-solicited manuscripts each week.

Our need to write, to make a mark, seems to be very strong. In fact, we all benefit from the use we make of written language to sort out our experiences, to order the events of our lives, our actions, our feelings. Writing extends our awareness, broadens our consciousness. It lets us encompass what we know and understand by bringing what we seem to be telling ourselves into a form of language that we can inspect, think about. Writing makes us reflect.

Reflection is a kind of scanning backwards, a combination of remembering and thinking, when we look at what we have written. We do this intensely when we want to be as clear, as unambiguous as possible, especially when we are concerned about our readers. We want them to believe we are efficient, logical thinkers. Yet, think of the last time you wrote a letter of condolence to someone you didn't know well enough to be informal with, or when you felt you had to make a written complaint without blaming the sales-person. Personal writing is always complicated by what we feel about any situation. We usually want to convey information-plus-feeling, so that a single, linear statement rarely seems to do the trick, and we always wish we could do it better. In speech we can prop up our hesitations with 'What I mean is . . .' or repeat some parts of our message in another form. But once we let what we have written go from us, we cannot call it back. At that point literacy seems full of threats and difficulties.

If we are anxious about writing it is usually because we believe there is a right way to do it and we might make mistakes. This comes from our memories of writing in school where 'correctness' was a large part of what we were set to learn. That correctness is the part of writing we associate with public behaviour. Writing never seems to be easy. We become more confident, we know how it goes, but we also keep making increased demands on ourselves.

Successful writers admit that writing is difficult, that it needs practice and patience, revision and rewriting. The poets are nearest to the agony of 'getting it right'. Seamus Heaney says writing is like *digging*. T.S. Eliot probably comes closest to this feeling when he speaks of twenty years of

> *Trying to learn to use words, and every attempt*
> *Is a wholly new start, and a different kind of failure*
> *Because one has only learnt to get the better of words*
> *For the thing one no longer has to say, or the way in which*
> *One is no longer disposed to say it. And so each venture*
> *Is a new beginning, a raid on the inarticulate*
> *With shabby equipment always deteriorating*
> *In the general mess of imprecision of feeling,*
> *Undisciplined squads of emotion.*

I always wonder how often he rewrote these lines before he felt they were as he wanted them to be.[2]

To look at writing is, of course, to read. But we can also look at texts to see what kind of writing they are, how they are patterned, organized as *discourse*. Part of the skill of writing is to be appropriate, to get the right tone and mood and style for the way what we write seems to need to be written. A scientific paper is a different kind of discourse from a newspaper article, even if the topic is the same.

The interaction of writing and reading is a primary fact of the literacy that we now have to learn. In the nineteenth century, when the demand for literacy for all could no longer be denied, there was no wholehearted agreement that everyone should learn to write, only to read. It was felt that if 'ordinary people', those whom public literacy would keep in their place, were allowed to say what they thought, there would be a shift in the balance of power, so popular writing was feared as 'seditious libel', the kind of writing that had contributed to the upheavals of the French Revolution. Something of this fear still remains. When countries where literacy is not widely dispersed are encouraged to increase their literacy programmes, the assumption is that reading will be taught first, despite the evidence that older people become literate quickly by learning to read what they want to say in writing. The association of writing with power is its most permanent feature. So we have to take this into account when we look at how children are taught to write, and the kind of introduction they are given to the process of using writing for their own intentions and purposes.

Nowadays we can all become writers. The tools are readily to hand; the new technologies, word processors and printshops which make our words look as good as anyone else's, are 'user-friendly'. The greatest changes in literacy are associated with writing, chiefly because the range of discourses and the means of both renewing and reinventing them have become more generally available.

But when we speak of writing as something people do for a living, we are usually referring to what writing *makes*: poems, plays, autobiographies, the nine centuries of English texts that people call literature. This is the writing we characterize by its relation to the *imagination*. It is the kind of personal writing that most people wish they could do. The relation of literacy to the kind of writing that makes artefacts generally referred to as 'literary' is interesting. Until the middle of the eighteenth century, literature and literacy meant almost the same thing. Literature was the books that a literate person read.[3] Now we keep the words apart and give them specialized meanings; literacy for social usefulness, literature for certain selected texts that, by tradition or personal taste, are considered to be well-written and that are to be read, somehow, differently. I want to bring the two words together again so that literature does not depend for its definition on private opinions of its worth but is simply the writing that people do, while literacy is about reading and writing texts of all kinds and the entitlement of all.

There is nothing intrinsic to literature that prevents a reader, any reader, from reading it as he or she pleases within the guidance of the text. When I see children of nine or ten writing stories that are 'imaginative', that is, either a reworking of an event in their lives or of something they have read or seen on TV, or their exploration of something they wish might come to pass, I see them behaving in the same way as Tolstoy, Jane Austen or Dickens, although their models may be Enid Blyton or Roald Dahl.

When I ask myself, what is it that writing does, I have to force myself to confront its obvious usefulness, the ways in which it penetrates our society, because I take for granted almost everything that print makes possible. In fact, I am inclined to think of the plays of Shakespeare or the stories that children write as more worth the effort of becoming literate than the ability to read timetables. Both are important. But the tendency to see literacy as useful has often kept the attention of teachers on the need to emphasize its controlling aspects, spelling, grammar and getting the words right, rather than on its liberating feature, the exercise of the imagination.

I test out this idea not in the current easy state of production and reproduction of modern printing, but in the tough, scribal manuscript world of *The Canterbury Tales*, Geoffrey Chaucer's masterpiece which he was still writing when he died in 1400. There are eighty-four surviving manuscripts, an extraordinary number when we consider the demands that writing with quill pens made on the copiers and the length of the work itself. The richness of Chaucer's work lies not only in his skill as a poet, but also in the depth and breadth of his contact with, and under-standing of, the medieval world of writing, the world which was already there when printing arrived.

Chaucer was a customs official. He knew the uses of writing in counting, recording and making lists. But he also knew that those who could read, and those who were read to, *enjoyed* what he wrote—a cumulative tale, a story made of other stories about a group of recognizable people: clerics, an innkeeper, a lawyer, a knight and his squire and others whose occupations have long since disappeared, who went on a pilgrimage, the medieval version of a package holiday.

Chaucer gave his characters stories to tell, some of them tales that his readers and listeners already knew: fables, sly ironies about the lives of churchmen, fairy-tales, courtly romances and legends, all of which have been retold to this day over and over again, in one form of discourse or another. As we read them, we enter both the world of the writer and the imaginary worlds of his characters. The number of manuscripts shows that Chaucer was a best-seller. I like to think that the scriveners copied with some pleasure what was, for that time, a great amount because they found the content not only more enjoyable but also more pertinent to their lives than the king's treasury accounts or the land registries of the gentry.

After the introduction of printing, literacy began to mean reading rather than writing. Writers were becoming authors rather than scribes, and their status gradually changed.

Reading

For most people, being literate means being able to read. Reading seems a natural thing to do, easier than writing, certainly. As adults we take for granted that when we want or need to read we shall be able to. The 'being able to' seems to be what counts as literacy, for readers vary a great deal in the amounts and kinds of reading they do, yet all are numbered amongst the literate. Someone who reads hardly at all, but assumes that she knows how to, would be outraged if classed with the illiterate, those who have failed to learn. Reading represents literacy in ways that seem reasonable, ordinary, 'basic' to our lives. Do we believe that reading always stays the same? Clearly, as writing changes, so will reading.

We learned to read as children in response to the expectation and encouragement of adults. Our parents, those who helped us learn to talk, probably introduced us to reading before we could use books, so that we internalized a number of processes which made signs and print familiar and meaningful. The petrol pump and the supermarket, first recognized as lights and letters, were interpreted as stopping and shopping. During our reading apprenticeship we came to expect the world to offer us things to read: images and pictures, dials and screens. Other adults, the teachers who gave us reading lessons in school, turned print, books and writing into school reading, the kind that the community pays for and expects us to be able to do. Perhaps we even earn our living by doing what we learned as reading and writing lessons. The current surveys suggest that at least 67% of adults now in employment are involved in dealing with written information.

Put to the test of what they expect reading and writing to do for them, most of those who believe they can read are correct in this belief, usually because they choose to read what they find familiar, pleasurable or useful. Difficulties arise for all of us when conditions, texts, subjects and technologies change. Then, natural-seeming reading habits have to be extended to deal with unfamiliar print, different subject matter, new ways of presenting documents. A so-called literacy crisis occurs, or, as the news media tend to say, 'reading standards go down', not when fewer people learn to read, but when the reading most of us are expected to be able to do isn't the kind we are used to.

The most significant aspects of reading are educational ones. It is in schools that the standards of success are set, the tests administered, the results interpreted, the certificates awarded. But we know that our education system does not provide the same kind of literacy for all. Although some children overcome many limitations in their desire to learn, no national curriculum will iron out the inequalities inherent in where children go to school. What counts as literacy, and how children learn to read are at the heart of the differences in our society. Those who read well, in educational terms, are granted leave to continue to read, to study, to become prestige literates. Some are able to continue into the learned professions; others, no less skilled, leave school early. Recognition of a person's high-status literacy is a social and not necessarily an intellectual distinction.

Skilled and efficient readers make reading work for them

31

because they discover what it is good for. Some have entrepreneurial purposes served by reading. They know how to read plans, maps, figures, to interpret texts about medicine and engineering as well as curing the sick and building bridges. Others have a strong inclination to please themselves by reading poetry or novels. All successful readers discover that to read well is to be confident that they can. What then should we know about modern reading so that we can learn to use it for our own distinctive purposes and at the same time fulfil the obligations to society that literacy lays upon us?

First, we should know that the expectation that everyone should learn to read is a comparatively new idea, not more than two centuries old. The legislation which first enforced universal literacy in England came in 1871, quite late compared with other countries, although, by that time, many people had found ways of being taught. Before this time, the only country that had as nearly total adult literacy as can be expected was Sweden where, from the seventeenth century, the law of the Lutheran Church and the state required that all adults who wanted to get married had to read aloud to the local minister to prove that they could read God's law directly.

The spread of popular literacy increased more quickly in Europe after the French Revolution, and so did efforts to prevent the production of inflammatory reading matter about democratic ideas. But, as more and more people began to teach themselves to read, and as the organization of the economics of new industrialization needed efficient scribes, schools seemed to offer a means of achieving both mass literacy and social order. After 1871, schools taught reading and disciplined the pupils. Schools also defined what counted as literacy in terms of what the pupils had to read and the words they learned to copy. Reading in the buildings provided by School Boards did not include the same texts as those read by young gentlemen in the traditional 'Public' schools where education was associated with social privilege. Even now, the idea that a literate population is more creative than threatening has not fully permeated popular education.

Powerful literates are those who read a lot, and know their way around the world of print. The habit is established fairly early, but it can be acquired in response to understanding what reading makes possible. Children learning to read sometimes 'take off' because they discover not only the pleasure of being skilful but also the approbation of their elders. Literate adults make their reading work for them. They use books as tools, as sources of information and means of checking. They choose with confidence what they want or need to read. By scanning pages of newspapers they rapidly sort out the football results from reviews of new CD discs. They read different texts at different speeds, knowing when a sweeping glance will do and when the words need careful inspection, interrogation, contradiction. Their familiarity and confidence in ranging over a wide variety of printed matter comes with having intentions and purposes in the world which they know can be supported and furthered by the ideas that others like them have already recorded in books and articles.

All expert readers understand, practically, consciously, how reading works. They have given themselves private lessons for years by confronting texts of increasing complexity, knowing that, no matter how difficult the reading seems to be, the written word will yield its meaning to the reader. It is not simply intelligence, special schools or even social class that make efficient readers, although these things undoubtedly help. It is knowing what reading is like, including what it feels like, and what it makes possible.

Some of the things that expert readers take for granted are worth considering. When we think of 'a reader' we may have a romantic vision of someone sitting alone, reading a book, silently, with enough leisure to read at length without interruption, the kind of reading busy people say they wish they had more time to do. The fact is, readers read wherever and whenever they can, often together. But nowadays reading is a matter of distinct choosing; it is easier not to do it, to find excuses for not making the effort, because our lives are more publicly social than those of our great-grand-parents. On the other hand, there is, at present, a distinct hunger for education which urges people to read. If the number of books sold is any guide to the number that are actually read, then as a society we must be more literate than at any time in the past.

As we read silently, we are not just leaving the sound out of the words. We are turning the monologue of the written text into a dialogue in which we are both the teller and the told. We reduce the distance between ourselves and the writer, a distance over time and space. Good readers rely on their understanding that the nature of language itself lets them anticipate what is coming; they expect to know and under-stand how the text 'goes'.

Somewhere, however, in the reader's understanding of what they are reading there is a *tonality*, a voice which is not theirs. Actors and others whose concern is to make writing audible spend much time thinking how the words are to be said in order to present the characters they are to play. The most subtle appearance of tonality in texts is irony, when authors count on their readers knowing that the sense of what they write is different from the meaning of the words. This is a complicated reading lesson which, like others, the texts can teach. Where once we believed that these aspects of reading were learned after much experience, we now know that children discover them early, chiefly as the result of the many different voices they hear in the contexts of film and television, and in the great variety of books provided for them to read.

Reading silently and still getting the idea of a voice in the page is not a modern accomplishment, although some commentators still want to claim it as such. Nor is reading aloud a sign of immaturity. It was an accepted thing to do when there were few texts and few readers; to have read to yourself in medieval times would have been a kind of greed. Even before that the Greeks knew about silent reading; Aristophanes refers to it in his play, *The Frogs*. There is nothing intellectually superior about silent reading; it is a cultural not an intellectual matter. But, on the whole, skilled readers read silently because they can go faster. They turn their reading quickly into a kind of thinking. Certainly, reading *feels* like thinking when we try to discover what we do when we read.

Behind the visible words of every written text there lurks the writer's *con*text, his or her life in the world and in the mind, in actions and in language. The words of the text are laden with the meanings of their time and place, augmented by the writer's reading as well as by the assumptions of the culture. To the reading of any text the reader similarly brings her or his context, and his or her language with different assumptions and other reading experiences. The conflux of reader and writer seems to make the giving and receiving of a simple, incontrovertible message impossible. Yet we know that, more often than not, readers and writers do reach an understanding. Far away as we are from John Bunyan, and although we cannot interpret *The Pilgrim's Progress* in the same way as his contemporary readers, we still share enough in our lives and in our common language to make sense of the text. If this were not the case, how could we read anything older than ourselves? However, where there has to be no doubt, no debate about meaning, as on busy roads or in situations of danger, we do not trust words. Instead we put up warning signs to command obedience. 'Stop' is internationally understood without a need for any alphabet.

Obvious as all this may seem, it is a warning against assuming that reading has remained the same since the invention of writing. Part of our difficulty in helping children to learn to read stems from a belief that the same texts always mean the same, and have to be read in the same way by each new reader. In fact, the opposite is the case. We have to learn to read not just words, texts, or even a variety of discourses, but the contexts and conventions of how these discourses work. A child with a beginner's book discovers that this is the learning book, different from the one she reads in bed at home, and reading is both the same, and not the same, when she does it in each place. No text or book 'stands by itself', much as it seems to do so. It needs a reader to bring it alive, just as a musical score is silent until someone plays it, despite the sounds it made in the head of the composer.

The contexts and conventions of texts become familiar with repetition. We recognize a fairy-tale by 'Once upon a time' and know what will follow. In much of what we read we expect to know 'how it goes'. The most straightforward reading is of a *known* text, one we have read before or had read to us. When the Bible was the reading book for thousands, readers knew what the words 'said' before they looked at the print. Children who know nursery rhymes by heart have very little trouble in teaching themselves to read from a book when they realise that they already know the words on the page. They learn to say what they see when they know they see what they say.

But the test of modern literacy is to be able to read *new* texts, those writings that we see for the first time and of which we must make immediate sense. Like universal literacy, this is a fairly recent development. Thus, to read aloud at sight, and to convey the sense of what we read, is an astonishing performance, yet we expect seven-year-olds to be able to do it after only two years in school.

So we see that reading, for all that it appears to be what readers have always done, changes, becomes different, in every generation. As language changes, as societies change, so what counts as literacy also changes. Both language and literacy are in constant evolution. Some people are dis-inclined to admit this and so cling to the myth of a past literacy that was better. When there were fewer books and a smaller proportion of literates in the population, reading seemed to be the same for all. Now that there are more readers than at any time in the past, more books to choose from and new literacies, we must accept that differences amongst readers and amongst texts are normal. There is no going back to a single text, a single way of reading, a single way of defining 'good' readers.

We expect children to learn to read the language they speak, but this too is less straightforward than it seems. Most people in the world are bilingual; those who speak only

English are the exception. When bilingual children learn to read their parents expect them to become literate in what they, the parents, recognize as the more socially *powerful* language. Thus, Indian children in England are to read in English, North Africans in France are to read in French, Catalans in Spanish because, in each case, their best interests seem to be related to these languages. This is not necessarily so. The evidence is that, in learning to read, children learn best in what they feel is their *stronger* language: the one in which they are most at home.

Compare the situation of modern bilingual children with the traditional case of boys learning Latin. As far as we know, no one in Europe *spoke* Latin as a mother tongue after A.D. 700. But as Latin continued to be the bureaucratic language of Europe for many centuries after that, to learn it was to attain a prestige literacy. So Latin has continued to be taught as a written language in many schools, in England and elsewhere, because there are those who insist that the strenuous reading and translation of an *unchanging* language are the best introduction to literacy. The claim now seems exaggerated, especially to those who suffered rather than enjoyed their lessons.

The era of our modern literacy began with the printing press. Scholars argue about whether printing brought about changes that were directly the result of more books being read by more people, or whether printing itself was the result of other changes already taking place. Certainly the upheavals of the Reformation, with which the spread of printed books is always linked, began before reading was common. Francis Bacon, who saw what the later effects of the spread of printing might be, said that printing was one of the three inventions that changed the world. (The others were the mariner's compass and gunpowder.) Any new technology which changes the tools or the presentational forms of what is written to be read reawakens the argument about whether literacy brings about or is changed by social innovations. Now we discuss whether television and computers will make reading books a redundant occupation. It is possible to argue in reply that new methods of producing book texts, especially those with illustrations, encourage both reading and readership.

What is certain is that we now extend the idea of 'being literate' to other areas of our lives which have no direct connection with reading and writing the language we speak. 'Numerate' has been evolved to mean 'knowing how numbers work'. 'Television literacy', so-called, is linked to being able to 'read' television; that is, to know how the 'text' of a programme is put together. Alongside traditional text literacies—prose, poetry or plays on a printed page—there are different meaning systems in our world which we are expected to recognize and interpret, such as acronyms, bundles of initials taken from a group of words: B.B.C., N.S.P.C.C., T.G.W.U. and the like. Logos are signs that indicate a domain of interest: a school's crest on writing paper, a confederation of sportsmen, television companies and their programmes, banks. These, and all the latest devices such as X-rays, scanners, radar, computer systems and diagrams are the result of changes in literacy technology which, in their time, change what we think literacy is good for. Only one certainty remains: reading now has to mean more than it ever did, and more people now must see reading as something different from what they learned to do in their first years in school or else their children's literacies will simply bamboozle them.

What Reading Makes Possible

Reading is the process of turning written language into meaning. When we read we expect to discover what it is the writer wants us to know.

The obvious advantages of reading seem to be practical ones: reading a letter is perhaps the most usual, or a newspaper or a notice. Although I use my ability to read almost unconsciously, as if it were an extension of my eyes and my ears, I appreciate it when I look for the times of Sunday buses in an unfamiliar town, for telephone numbers, words in a dictionary and whatever is stored as a record of something I need to know. Asked why they think children should learn to read, most adults say it helps them to learn. Certainly teachers count on it to do just that.

The instrumental and organizational uses of reading are not confined nowadays to books, so what reading now makes possible is bound up, as we have seen, with signs, pictures, screens, diagrams and flashing lights. We have learned these new literacies because the habit of turning symbols into meaning is so deeply embedded in our culture that we don't need to learn to read more than once. We do, however, discover that there is more than one way to do it.

To be able to read, and to be a reader are not exactly the same. The ability to read for practical ends, important as it is, differs from the reading which readers enjoy, the kind that makes them addicted to reading. This reading is sometimes disparagingly, but in fact wisely, called *recreational*. Readers know they are re-created by what they read; not simply because they learn new facts or ideas, but, more particularly, by discovering how written texts *make worlds*, realities, other than those they live in. Experienced readers know how life extends into literature and reading itself is part of the experience of the text as they read it. Think of it thus: the only way to experience a novel as a novel is to read it, or to hear it read. Reading is what we have to do in order to know what novels are. In the process of reading a novel, where am I? At home, sitting in a chair, or in bed. But not really. I feel I am where the action is, where the sufferings are, of the people or events that the writer has made me care about, in nineteenth-century Russia, in a house in Suffolk or on the high seas, or in a quite different other world. I am on holiday from myself, yet when I finish I know myself better. This explanation does not really match the experience, and I never make it clear to those for whom it is an alien idea. But other readers recognize it.

Readers re-create experience, extend it, think about it, resist it even, as a distinctive form of desire. They know that certain kinds of realities are created by means of the interaction of language and imagination. When I read a poem in the Underground train, staring above the heads of my fellow passengers, as I go to work at 8.05 a.m., I am simply somewhere else. Try it, now; here is Shirley Geok-Lin Lim:

> *Last night I dreamt in Chinese.*
> *Eating Yankee shredded wheat*
> *I said it in English*
> *To a friend who answered*
> *In monosyllables;*
> *All of which I understood.*
>
> *The dream shrank to its fiction.*
> *I had understood its end*
> *Many years ago. The sallow child*
> *Ate rice from its ricebowl*
> *And hides still in the cupboard*
> *With the china and tea-leaves.*[4]

I learn to make meanings, to analyse meanings. I can do all of this at my own pace, re-reading, skipping, turning to the end, pausing for thought when I like. I can go in deep, as it were, when my interests are most engaged. Certain authors seem to be my friends, for all that they have been dead for centuries. Reading makes me excited about ideas as much as about events and people. Sometimes I grasp only part of what I know the writer has made quite plain. At other times I feel I could have made it clearer for the writer. This isn't arrogance; most dialogues work in this way. I expect reading to be an adventure, with the possibility of surprises. Reading can be both a kind of day-dreaming and very hard work.

Skilled readers practise reading says James Britton, as doctors practise medicine.[5] We all become good at it in our own way, for our own purposes. Sometimes readers are made timid by others (the judges of literary prizes, perhaps) who are always sure of the worth of what they read. Other readers feel that they ought to like a best seller although it may be something well advertised rather than well written. The reward of reading practice is to know one's own mind in the matter, whatever the nature of the text.

I used to believe that reading was a solitary activity and literacy a cloistered virtue praised at school. Probably I liked, as I still care for, the peace of reading on my own. Now I know reading as a fully social activity, shared with my family, students, children in school and those who have read more than I ever shall. In engaging with others' reading I discover more of what is in the text; I add their meanings to mine. Together we explore what written language, in all its many forms, is like, from the carnival of children's books to the disturbing arguments about *The Satanic Verses*.

The great secrets of reading lie in narrative *fiction*. We shall discuss later why stories are so important. Here we simply note that fiction teaches us many important reading lessons because, as Jonathan Culler says, it 'can hold together within a single space a variety of languages, levels of focus, points of view, which would be contradictory in other kinds of discourse organized towards a particular empirical end.'[6] All of this is in the reading of a good modern detective novel. Readers discuss the meaning *and* the force of a text. It is a strong defence against being victimized by the reductive power of so-called functional literacy, the half-baked kind that most people know is less than their entitlement.

Practised readers know how to choose books for different occasions, different moods, different places. They stop if the torment of *Wuthering Heights*, or *Beloved* becomes too great, but they will go back to them again. They are avid for new reading experiences, reading over their neighbour's shoulder in a crowd, or the proverbial cornflakes packet.

When we have experienced the fullness of reading as reading, then we can put it to work for other purposes: to order information, to distinguish the rhetoric of different subject matters, to use it as a tool for investigation, and as a means of finding out how we want to be able to write. Reading extends our understanding of language, its nuances and subtleties, the play that goes on in writing between what is said and what is meant.

Being literate comes from knowing what reading is good for, from engaging in it so that we enlarge our understanding

41

not only of books and texts, what they are about and how they are written, but also of ourselves. But none of this, not the power, enjoyment, understanding nor the pursuit of knowledge that reading makes possible is available to those whose early experience of reading has been joyless, unplayful, lacking the pleasure of entering into stories or the reward of sustained effort.

Thinking

Most of what we know and think about lies deep in our practised skills and habits: making tea, for instance. From time to time however we find ourselves *considering* what we usually take for granted, as when I stop to ask myself who actually picked the leaves off the tea bush. When something unexpected happens, or our plans go astray, we reflect on our actions and on our thoughts. 'Whatever made me do that? What was I thinking about?' Then we seem to be attending to a kind of inner speech, the dialogue we have with ourselves in our heads.

Reading and writing contribute to some aspects of these kinds of thinking: going back over things, wondering why they are as they are, planning, revising, revisiting. Even when what we are reading is a story of events that could never happen to us, we treat the plot as a series of possibilities. We say we *imagine* what is happening. When we write a letter to explain a set of complicated circumstances we are having a kind of imaginary talk with the reader, surmising the reactions to what we set down. Almost as soon as we learned to read and write we became used to the dialogue of the imagination that always accompanies these activities.

When literacy was less common than it is now, it seemed that those who could read and write had access to the special kinds of knowledge that resided in books. We still speak of 'retrieving' information from print, assuming that the writer put it there for that purpose. We 'look up' dictionaries, encyclopaedias, train timetables, and what we understand as the result makes a difference to what we do or think. Literacy seems useful not only for catching trains, but also for helping us to understand what we understand. We feel that, as a result of reading and writing, we can tap into ways of knowing that have been accumulated over the centuries by other readers and writers. Do our literate habits change the way we think? The instinctive reaction to this query is to say yes, without being too sure why we believe this.

Even now, with universal schooling, those who read and write for a living or those whose work demands continuous contact with print are credited with intellectual skills that seem different from the more common kind of intelligence. The thinking part of reading and writing is difficult to describe because it is invisible. The process is elusive even when we chase it in our own thoughts. We talk about it in relation to *ideas* which are, at the same time, common and rare. Having a 'good' idea is a fairly usual way of solving a problem. Having a new idea as the result of reading or writing can change one's whole life. Certain ideas, written and read, have influenced the course of history, not always for the better. When people are anxious about the influence of books they ban or burn them in case they have the power to change people's thinking.

Thoughtful literates sometimes insist that important thinking, the kind that makes a difference, is *logical*. This means that the thought processes follow certain paths, helping the thinker to solve puzzles according to certain rules, as in mathematics and science. Logical thinking is generally associated with the control over the natural world that has so distinctively characterized the civilization we know and inherit. So literacy seems to offer the prospect of becoming logical to those who master reading and writing. The 'illiterate', by failing to read and write, are thus considered illogical. In addition, logical thinking is characterized as objective, generalizable, abstract. That is, this kind of thinking seeks out conditions of truth that hold in all foreseeable circumstances and sets the patterns for discussions where 'what follows' can be deduced 'correctly'.

Logical thinking is seen as powerful and often incontrovertible. The association of scientific thinking with literacy gives literates access to both powerful texts and special privileges. Scientific and economic literates then undertake to tell others how the world works and what counts as important.

Powerful as it is, logical thinking in the scientific mode is only one kind of thought. Scholars, scientists and other literates are not constantly rational. They make mistakes as do others in the running of their financial affairs and their private lives. In all societies, and in all individuals, there is logical and non-logical thinking. But the dominance of science in our culture encourages the notion that rational thought has to be learned by means of a long apprenticeship in reading and writing in school, library and laboratory. However, when we consider composers and painters, concert pianists, scene designers, architects and a host of other experts who make a difference to our understanding, we know that they too think long and hard about what they are up to in modes that demand other logics, other literacies.

Children begin to think as soon as they are aware of other people and the world around them. They engage in thinking before they can speak, as any parent knows who has picked up the toy repeatedly thrown on the floor. Children's awareness changes when they learn to talk. They know 'how people do things'. Later, reading and writing add to the complexity of what they come to know. Psychologists and others are constantly on the look-out for concrete evidence that children's thinking is becoming more generalized, more like adult 'abstract' thought in ways that language makes possible in the hope that, once they know how children's thinking develops, they can help it to develop even more effectively.

We have to admit, to insist, even, that there is no incontrovertible evidence that children learn to think logically as a direct consequence of learning to read and write. What they do learn is to behave like learners, especially in school, where they are expected to use reading and writing, and other symbolic forms like mathematics, as ways of interpreting the meaning of events and experiences. Children do this when they discover reading and writing as *complete performances*: a whole story, a poem, a picture book. When they see events framed in pictures, or writing as something to be contemplated as a coherently organized whole, then they can wonder about 'what happened' or 'what will happen next': that is, the nature of actions and consequences. Listen to the conversation of a four-year-old and an adult when they have read together *Where the Wild Things Are* and the nature of children's *speculative* thought becomes quite clear.

Reading a story is, for a child as for an adult, a way of discussing what *might* happen; to ask *what if*, in the open dialogue of speech, or the concealed dialogue of imagination. Reading and writing create a mental space for thinking, the space that children inhabit early in their play. From studies of how children's language develops we learn that individual boys and girls follow different patterns in speech and in thought as they learn to make sense of the world and to reflect on their lives. There is no straight line to abstract thinking. Language and thought meet and change each other at the bumpy intersections of events. There are, however, schooled ways of regulating thinking, *conventions* for writing about sciences or poetry, for example, that children have to learn. By learning to write and read like a poet or a scientist, pupils in school learn the conventions of poetry and the discourses of the sciences which control what counts as thinking in these roles. They join the group of those whose literacy they learn, so their thinking becomes a social as well as an individual intellectual activity. Young thinkers look for apprenticeships with those whose words and thoughts interest them, footballers as well as photographers, actresses as well as accountants.

Researchers are constantly trying to sort out the intricate relations of language and thought so as to discover what difference literacy makes to thinking. A.R. Luria, a famous Russian psychologist, went to a remote Siberian province to compare the thinking process of those who had never been to school with those who had had some instruction in reading and writing. He found that the non-literates answered his logical puzzles by drawing on the ways of thinking that were common to their community. When Luria said: 'All the bears in A (a place) are white. Z (a person) met a bear. What colour was it?' His non-literate companion said: 'I don't know. I've never been to A and I've only seen brown bears.' That is, the companion concentrated on the *topic* of the question when Luria wanted him to look at the *form*. Others who had been to school responded differently. They had learned that the answer comes not from attending to the bears, or to their personal experience, but to the way in which the first two statements are related; that is, to the form of the language.[7]

The assumption is that writing makes possible the inspection of the relation of one statement, or proposition, to another, because the reader can see the sentences and thus work out the nature of the formal aspects of the link between 'all' and 'one'. But there is no evidence that this reasoning doesn't happen in speech. We say things like 'All the shops shut at noon. If you don't get there before then, your letters won't go today.' Certainly the extended time for thought that the permanence of a text makes possible lets a reader or a writer ask herself 'supposing the opposite were the case?' Then, a mental re-run of the described situation and a closer inspection of the form of the propositions sort out the pattern of ideas. But this doesn't deny or lessen what the thinker knows to be the case in common sense. Nor does it prevent her from imagining a totally different bear story.

As they come to know about stories, pictures and books, young children discover that there are words for things in the world and for things that go on, as we say, 'in their heads'. There are also words about language itself: 'word' is one such. From early reading I discovered many words, many forms of language I never heard in talk and I knew that these represented different *places* for using them. I don't think my parents ever said 'murmur', although 'whisper' was in fairly common use. I met 'murmured' in stories and had to guess from the context that it told the reader that the speaker

46

uttered something softly. I learned to scan ahead for such clues when I was likely to be asked to read aloud in class.

In the same way, words like *decide, hope, think, fear, guess, wonder, imagine, believe, worry, blame* and a host of others, many of which children use correctly before they can explain what they mean, refer to mental operations, thinking and feeling, and not, like *run, jump, play* and *see* to visible ways of behaving. Children learn how to promise by saying 'I promise' long before they can reflect on the necessary conditions of promising in general. But when a promise is broken, they know that the consequences are likely to be sad. Their experience of fairy-tales has already made this clear.

Not only when we are children but throughout our lives literacy extends the range of convenience of words we know and gives us more words than we would hear in talk. It also helps us to think about something by giving us the words to do it with and a wider range of examples, in stories especially, of how people behave as the result of deliberate reflection. As we collect words for thinking from the books we read, so we understand our own thinking better.

The kind of thinking that literacy seems best for is thinking about language itself. But even before they can read, all children have some *metalinguistic* awareness because language is also a plaything. 'I'll huff and I'll puff and I'll blow your house down' is a dramatic enactment of the feeling of the words in the mouth as well as a threat in a particularly good story. We shall come back to this when we discuss early reading. Here I mention it because some researchers say that children need to be taught this kind of attention to and awareness of words if they are to discover that reading and writing are language activities. I believe that children discover for themselves the power of language play when they try to sort out sense from what their culture calls nonsense. They know quite early on that to say 'pigs fly' is as comic as watching someone fall downstairs. It simply isn't what should normally happen. As soon as they tell jokes, and that means long before they understand them, young learners are aware of the mismatch of words and sense.

47

The best complement writing offers to thinking is to make visible how thinking changes the world and how the world changes thinking. Earlier I mentioned Socrates' objections to writing and said that because Plato wrote down what he said we could think about what both of them were thinking about. So literacy makes available the history not only of peoples and societies but also of ideas, and the cultural changes that affect them. Literacy has also given us different frameworks and discourses for entertaining guesses and possibilities and for being curious. We can sort out alternatives more schematically in writing so that comparisons and contrasts are more immediately grasped. In reading and writing, as we differentiate what is actually meant from what is said, we feel we are *watching* our own thinking because we learn to order it.

The relation of language and thought is a fascinating subject, not least because it makes clear that language is socially learned. That's what common sense tells us. It can also be *schooled* for a variety of logical uses. Thanks to Vygotsky we understand that language and thought have different roots, but when they come together, both thought and language change. As soon as they listen to a story or help to make a shopping list by writing words children discover that they can have meaningful intentions for reading and writing which help them to sort out not only words but ideas and to go beyond common sense to a state of useful learning.

To read is to think about meaning; to write is to make thinking visible as language. To do both is to learn to be both the teller and the told in the dialogue of the imagination. When we discuss stories we shall discover more about what seems to happen.

CHAPTER 2

Differences

Every day of our lives, as we read newspapers and magazines, make lists and write letters, check our money or the TV programmes, we see our literacy at work. Or rather, we don't, unless we encounter something unusual, because we take it so much for granted. Being able to read and write seems a common accomplishment. But although literacy is at the heart of our social cohesion, the way society works, it is also a strong factor in individual and social differences. There are boundaries of literacy that are hard to define. Yet, in a sense that is generally understood, literacy, like language itself, is a map of any society. It separates people, differentiates them. Not everyone has the same range of literate expertise or confidence. This creates other differences of which we are, uneasily, aware.

When, as now, the nature of literacy and what we do with it changes, we become even more conscious that not everyone is familiar with its new forms. The introduction of decimal coinage was ignored by the sellers of vegetables in my local market for nearly two years. A home where parents and children familiarly make use of a video recorder, a computer or a word processor is bound to be a different place to do school homework—especially if the school expects wild-life programmes to be customary family viewing—from one where those electronic marvels are longed-for luxuries. When literacy is defined in terms of new technologies or techniques, such as 'desk top publishing' for ordinary office papers, then the popular conception of what it is to be literate shifts. My literacy is different from that of my

49

children: I still write drafts in pencil rather than on a screen.

All parents want their children's literacy to be more efficient than their own. Their anxiety expresses itself in concern about the early stages of learning to read in school. But there has never been a common experience for all children learning to read and write, nor any agreed standard of performance. What parents see are differences in children's school success, and the fact that all the money spent on public education still leaves many pupils in Britain unable to read and write satisfactorily when they leave school for work. Literacy may seem to be commonly expected of all people, but clearly the nature and uses of each person's literacy are very different.

The education of today's parents has been different from that of any previous generation. It has been longer. Television, rather than reading, has shaped their view of the world and their ways of understanding events. Most of them look forward to a degree of social mobility and choice of life style which they expect to earn. Consequently they want to be reassured that their children will learn to read and write successfully as soon as possible, that they will pass in school tests and examinations. For most parents literacy is an *entitlement* which schools are expected to 'deliver' so that children may prosper.

There are some parents, however, who are less confident in their dealings with social institutions. They are usually less able to choose their life style and are consequently more aware of the differences between home and school. They too are concerned for their children's prospects, so they are worried in case the teachers should treat their children differently because of their social class or speech or family history. The children have no lack of ability to learn to read and write, but their experience of literacy at home is often different. They may not send birthday cards, but they are probably experienced readers of labels and price tickets. Suppose, then, that the child of middle-class parents gains the same score on the reading test as a child whose parents are travelling people (traditionally called gypsies). The chances are that, despite the equal scores, the teacher will interpret the literacy and the later chances of the second group less favourably.

When adults compare their lives with those of others, they often relate the differences they see, of class, money, dwellings, possessions and expectations to 'making the grade'. So they want their children to achieve, or in some cases to continue, the socially defined literacy that seems to be related to material success. In fact, neither school nor a set of learning procedures can guarantee increased competence for everyone. In a society which is clearly riven with historical inequalities literacy is interwoven with different sets of social practices, different roles for people to play. To be literate nowadays is to be aware of differences, to know how they are constituted, both historically and socially, and to be determined to surmount the barriers and boundaries which they produce.

We are all more aware of differences than we are good at explaining them. Consider, for a moment, the great annual Literacy Event of our culture: the habit of sending greetings cards at Christmas or New Year. We send these written messages to people we talk to nearly every day as well as to those we haven't written to for a year. A huge industry has grown up around this exchange of formally or informally expressed goodwill. Directors in boardrooms and children in classrooms adopt the rituals of wishing. The writing act has overtones of obligation; the making of lists of names is a delicately poised social event. The institution of the Christmas card is not an old one, but it has deep roots in historical rituals associated with the seasons. As a single act of literacy it manifests maximum diversity and difference.

And yet, if we are looking for something *basic* in the socially imposed literacy of our time, perhaps the addressing of envelopes and the writing of a message followed by a signature will do. The differences in this accepted practice exemplify those of most literary events, common or individual, in all our lives.

Being in the Know

The sending of greetings, at any time, shows how we are constantly trying to balance several kinds of awareness about literacy. In our complex technological world what counts as being literate still means being able to write our name, but it also includes a complicated network of social understandings about the way people act in the world. Being literate includes the degree to which we are, or want to be, 'in the know' about what is regarded as important. In the common sphere of our cultural and social life, certain kinds of knowing make a great deal of difference to people's lives. So, literacy becomes a means of *access*, a way of getting to know what counts. Information, then, is 'the difference that makes a difference'. If this were not the case, then, as Kenneth Levine says: 'The inability to read would be on a par with tone deafness, while an ability to write fluently would be as inconsequential as whistling in tune'.[1]

Recent changes in social behaviour make this clear. When I was a student I had a small bank account in a huge, marble-floored and pillared bank. My ignorance of banking made the cashier, who, after all, was giving me only what was mine, seem like a fiduciary of high status. I signed a cheque with the utmost humility. I had never even heard of an overdraft. At that same time a mortgage was something I knew about from Victorian novels; it brought sorrow and downfall to worthy families. Now housekeeping and house-buying involve these transactions, and the papers that accompany them, as everyday events. Again, where once the Stock Exchange was almost a secret society whose arcane workings were known by brokers and their clerks, now share-holding and the literacy that accompanies it are much more general. Yet as more people engage in these financial enterprises, others are further excluded from them. Consider this, choosing *not* to buy shares implies understanding how the money system works and what it stands for, something quite different, in terms of literacy, from not knowing what a share, in this sense, is.

Financial literacy serves this argument as an example of literacies that make a difference to people's lives and increase the differences between them. The dependence of most societies on literate communications is shown most clearly when lives are at risk. For example, the warning about smoking that appears on cigarette packets and in advertisements has about it a certain distinctive *written-ness*. The very form and order of the words are meant to offset the lure of the cigarettes themselves and the seduction of the clever advertisement. But 'Middle tar, as defined by H.M. Government: Warning: smoking can cause fatal diseases' isn't what we say to our friends when we try to persuade them not to smoke.

A more dramatic example was the need to bring about a steady rise in public knowledge about the nature and consequences of AIDS.[2] Every British household received an official pamphlet in which the significant details were spelt out and preventive measures made clear. At the same time, programmes on radio and television, articles in journals, involving the professional exchanges of experts, popular discussions and the resources of advertising were organized to bring about distinctive changes in common understandings and in social behaviour. At the height of this operation everyone encountered a variety of statements in different media, all with the same message. To remain ignorant needed more effort than to be informed.

It all happened very quickly. Whatever the effects of the campaign on individuals, there is now no going back to the time when AIDS was a medical secret. Health educators now call for clearer, more specific written information to be given to those most at risk, especially the young. The specialized training of nurses and doctors has to include the nature of public awareness. This is the kind of difference that modern forms of writing, reading, seeing, talking and listening are able to make possible. To be literate is to be, socially, in the know.

The trouble with official written documents is that they have to say the same thing to everyone. The writer seems far away from the reader. That is why most people prefer information and news to be made available on television. Then the expression on the face and in the voice of the teller is part of the message. The football results are always in a different tone from information about hurricanes or bombings. But we all know that written language still has a higher official status than the spoken word. If we need confirmation of contracts, we upgrade information or agreements in the formal sentences that seem to impose greater obligations. Libel is treated more seriously than slander. The poll tax, much discussed by politicians in Question Time, reaches those who are obliged to pay it as a series of formal declarations and requests in writing. The removal of this legislation makes necessary an expensive change in written laws and statutes.

To be fully in the know as literates we have to understand not only what the writing says, but also what it implies, and how the written-ness carries its own particular kind of authority. A dog licence would differ from a notice about dogs on pavements. Written language sets apart, differentiates, those who know the difference it makes from those who don't. It separates those who are really in the know from those who have only 'heard it said'.

Being in Control

However different the beginnings, the schools and the expectations of parents, most children learn to read and write. The most noticeable distinctions come later, in what we all do with the skills we acquire; how they affect our understandings. One of the distinguishing features of habitual readers and writers is their curiosity about language. They enjoy it. They use it with feeling and flair when they talk, tell jokes, invent word games and do crossword puzzles. They are, in a sense, in control of language, as a skilled player manages a football, a versatile violinist interprets a score or a racing driver handles a car.

The part of the new National Curriculum that deals with

literacy states that learning *about* language is essential because children need to know about different kinds of language forms and their functions. (In the old days this was called 'learning grammar', or writing 'correct' English.) At its most generous, this requirement suggests that all children are entitled to learn how language works so that they may make better use of it. But it can also mean that compulsory learning about language puts a strong brake on children's creative use of it. Then the language controls them.

Most children discover the power of language long before they go to school. As it becomes part of their serious play they find that they can use words to control other people. A child who repeatedly says 'No' to lovingly prepared food has tyrannical power. But when children discover words or word-like sounds as playthings they begin to please themselves with what they say and do. Even an early game like 'Peep-bo', where the world disappears and appears again, seems to work by the power of the word. In the same playful way children discover in words the boundaries of sense and nonsense. The little girl who says 'My daddy is an old lady' and falls about laughing, has learned that it is possible to say correctly what is *not* the case. From nursery rhymes they discover play-words, 'hey diddle diddle', and make up others. By directing their attention to the words themselves, children thus extend their control of language. As they play on the boundaries of sense and nonsense they know that, to a significant extent, they are in charge.

As they talk with children, adults help them to become sensitive to different language contexts. 'Please' and 'thank you' are learned in events of asking and receiving; 'hello' and goodbye' are beginnings and endings. In addition, parents whose literacy has made them aware of how language *orders* experience, make comparisons, showing likeness and difference in both the world and in speech. They *name* differences. 'Here is big Teddy. He must look after little Teddy.' While there is no evidence that what is said in this form is directly learned by the children, the rituals and repetitions convey the surplus meaning of 'this is what we say when we put the teddies together to see the differences between them.'

Children become 'context sensitive' to what language can make happen; that is, to its *performative* use. They discover that talking is also action. 'Don't say "perhaps" say "today"'' was the instruction a little girl gave her babysitter about sweets. 'We don't want some, we want lots,' said some greedy visitors, who got what they insisted on, so impressed was I by their awareness. As children come to control language so they control the actions of others, wheedling favours from adults, boring or enraging their friends. Other children experience control *by* language; they are told what to do, what *not* to ask. There are noticeable differences between children who are used to verbal teasing and to playing jokes with words and others for whom the stricter obligation of speaking when they are spoken to still holds. Both groups will learn proficient literacy, but there is evidence that the difference between those who control words and those who are controlled by them is governed by early experience, usually of giving orders or receiving them.

The significant difference between controlling language and being controlled by it is a kind of social confidence, our ability to say straight out what we mean. In this context, television is a great help; it shows ordinary people that others like them can ask sound and sensible questions and that politicians can give less than coherent answers. I'm inclined to believe that we are all better at speaking up for ourselves than our grandparents were. At the same time many written texts and the reading skills to make sense of them have become the provinces of small highly literate groups who are not concerned to share what they know. Beyond the spoken word they are in control of technologies, computers and other networks of language. They devise in-group languages which deliberately mystify outsiders.

Recent incidents show what is meant by being in control. The pro-democracy risings in China as well as those in Eastern Europe were linked by the information exchange made possible by fax machines. Thus, even when governments suppress the news, it can come in from outside. A different kind of knowing comes from language itself. We now have dictionaries which can be renewed, almost every year if necessary, so those in the know are interested in *concordances* which list every word in every text, with the immediate context and account of the meaning. But to be in the know and in control of everything that counts as current understanding, and *what to do with it*, will still never be the same for all.

Some people believe that being literate is 'knowing the facts'. My experience reacts against this because I am persuaded that, as human beings, we shall always interpret what we know in the sensitive context of our own human experience, and we shall undoubtedly teach our children to do the same.

Culture and Class

When young children are learning to speak their mother tongue they are also discovering what their elders want them to know about the world. They become members of a family, a network of relations, a neighbourhood. Until they can make their own choices, they behave as others do. All the repeated activities and events, including ways of asking and explaining and the words that describe these operations, guide children, day by day, into the social life, the culture, of the group they belong to. The accumulated experience that counts as culture comes to us, in its most durable form, as language.

In my childhood I called the garment I wore next to my skin a 'semmit'. My children knew it as a 'vest'. As we name things, so we enter our history and do so again as we learn to read and write. As they approach literacy, children's implicit understandings of what language is and does, that is, the social context of their early learning, becomes an integral part of their reading and writing. What they see people doing with pens, paper and books is what they expect to learn. So, when we look at how children become literate in our British culture we are bound to find that their entry into literacy, as into life, is set about with subtle and sometimes disturbing differences. We have already said that access to powerful literacy is differentiated in historical terms of class, and money.

Although there are many different forms of modern literacy, two social markers survive from the last century to differentiate the quality of literacy that counts most. These are speech, and books. The literate are assumed to be 'well spoken' and the literacy of the learned is, in our culture, bookish. In our twentieth-century educational system bookish literacy is still the mainstream. So parents who want this kind of literacy for their children will teach them to read and write early. They will also try to send them to schools where this early competence and confidence are maintained and continued.

As yet, most schools as institutions make some acknowledgement but little use of children's pre-school experience of print outside books. Instinctively, teachers favour children who have been read to and who will clearly make their way to literacy success, because, in the school's terms, they already know what reading and writing are about. These are often social rather than professional judgements. Likewise, teachers often ignore, or fail to recognize, a whole range of competences which other children have acquired from different cultural contexts. The strongest contacts that some children have with print, what they have taught themselves to decipher in the streets, for example, or what has been read to them in languages other than English, are often treated as irrelevant to the knowledge about literacy they are expected to acquire in school. The child who helps in the family store at weekends, whose mother tongue is not English, has specialized competences not immediately recognized.

Despite all that is now known and published about language in public documents like the National Curriculum, most people still find it difficult to believe that all varieties of English, Cockney as well as Caribbean,

Devonian or Scots, are equally valid ways of talking. Dialect speech does not *interfere* with becoming literate. There are shifts, slow but positive, in this understanding, but Standard English, the written form of our language, is nevertheless the language of school, and has a correspondingly strong association with being literate.

Bilingual children, those who speak more than one language, and bidialectical children, that is, most of the rest of our population, challenge us to acknowledge the linguistic resources they bring to learning to be literate in English. In one of London's wealthiest boroughs, Kensington, bilinguals are 30% of all the children in school. Their language abilities and cultural diversity contribute distinctive resources and particular manners to our society. The catalyst effect of the many cultures and many languages of the children who are now at home in our society is changing our traditional literacy out of all recognition. The teaching of history and geography, and the texts to be read in English lessons, cannot be the same in the next decade as they were in the last.

Some children now in school are the responsible literates in English for the older members of their families. They take the initiatives, not only in shopping but also in the necessary encounters with officials. They interpret the culture of school to their parents. Children who have had this kind of responsibility are specially sensitive to social contexts. They learn early to take control of their literacy for purposes which affect their community as well as themselves. They experience and recognize bilingualism as a different, more complex cultural experience than simply learning English.

English is now a world language, the commonest second language in developing countries. Monolinguals, who read and write only in English, are virtually only half as literate as the rest of the world. Differences like this have never impinged on our lives as they do now. When in 1992 and thereafter our European links will have greater statutory force, how shall we regard ourselves if we simply assume that we have no need to speak or read another language?

Behind our awareness of ethnic diversity in our culture are other, deeper modes of differentiation which emerge as racism, and questions of prejudice touch the teaching of literacy at every stage. We have still to make coherent distinctions between 'equality of opportunity' and 'equal opportunities' in literacy as in everything else.

The deepest social forces at work in the differentiation of literacy are those related to class. We know this. It is both a fact and a feeling. We also find it difficult to express what this means in terms of being literate. When I take an early morning train to a university town outside London I travel with numbers of school children. Their social behaviour and speech are indistinguishable. They spend most of the journey talking about the previous evening's main TV programmes. They help each other with their homework. But I know that those in uniform will go to institutions where their sameness is authorized, their approach to reading and writing is shared by the school and the parents. Their focus is on *results*. The children in ordinary clothes go to a 'mixed comprehensive'. If their parents choose to send them there they may well appreciate the diversity of social experience the school offers. As guardians of their children's progress they watch over written homework and augment what they see as necessary learning when examinations draw near. Those who have no choice where their children go to school hope that the school will do its best for them although they expect no favours. The children, however, often see school as a way into a wider world.

This is a simplistic description of what we never really confront in our divided society. We want to give every child 'a chance', but don't want to acknowledge the fact of difference philosophically, historically or even practically. At our most simplistic we see differences in class literacies in terms of school uniforms, homework and examinations. Mercifully, new literacies, television and computers, have found a way of breaking some traditional social boundaries.

Gender

Once we are alert to the social differences that correspond to literacy differences we cannot ignore the implications of gender. The traditional mythology, a kind of folk-distinction, that girls are better readers than boys because reading is a sedentary occupation more suited to quiet females than to rumbustious males is hard to shift. It is also nonsense. When our patchy understanding of *how* boys and girls read texts written by women and men comes to be extended by a study of their responses wider than the answers to examination questions, we shall profit from our appreciation of the differences.

Meanwhile, we begin by acknowledging that there are historical differences in the ways boys and girls learn to read and write. Since the seventeenth century the literacy of boys has been defined by school. In the grand style, it meant learning to read and write in Latin. The learned professions, including practical ones, like 'natural philosophy' which we now call physics, were set in the context of traditional classical learning. It is interesting to note, however, that the education of boys has its own ambivalences. Engineers still have to shake off the popular assumption that they are better at practical processes than intellectual ones. Nevertheless, medicine, most of the sciences, mathematics and architecture are pursuits still generally perceived as male. To enter these professions girls still have to prove themselves as being 'strong'.

We know that social perceptions of gender have changed and are still changing. When we write, we can no longer expect 'he' to include 'she'. Early reading books that continue the myths of gender stereotyping are criticized now for social ignorance. (Sometimes the writer's efforts to cope with this problem are clumsy and over-anxious. My grandson's book about tractors has a picture of a woman in the cab and the ambiguous caption: 'Women drive tractors as well as men'.) It is no longer possible to produce books for children where the main character is a boy on the grounds that girls will read boys' books but boys ignore stories with heroines.[3]

The roots of literacy as well as *literary* differences between boys and girls are deeper than these superficial details. I believe we need to know more about the double articulation that gender gives to literacy: women writing about men, men writing about women are only a part of it. The unquestioned power of male writing has been undermined by a bifocal subtlety as women critics rediscover earlier women writers who turned the particularities of local, familial experience into ways of 'reading' society. To be literate in this domain is to know that there is more than one way to read *Huckleberry Finn*.

When we put differences of gender alongside those of language, culture and class it becomes obvious that instead of trying to ignore differences or to smooth them out we have to see that difference itself is at the heart of our enquiry into what it is to be literate. It has to be seen as a challenge to acknowledge as important and relevant all the different moves which children make towards becoming literate. Those whose families are not bookish will not be appeased by attempts to 'compensate' for this. Others whose culture and language are different from the mainstream writing they encounter in school want these differences to count in what they choose to read. Girls whose mothers' lives have already been shaped by *literary* awareness of gender differences will expect to be the heroines of their own stories. The languages children speak and the cultures they represent, the books they read and the insights they derive from their culture, are all important different modes of being literate. To accept the challenge these things present is to see not problems, but new resources for the literacies of our time and those of the next generation.

Texts

What difference does a book make to our view of reading? Do

texts do us good, make our reading better? Does reading improve as the result of literary encounters? Which books are good for our reading? Some of these questions presuppose that there is a definable relation between literacy and literature. If so, what is it?

As I have already suggested, we no longer claim that 'to have read' a group of selected texts is the singular mark of a literate person. And yet, 'bookishness' still distinguishes some people from others, and the distinction seems to be conferred by literary reading. We may have given up the traditional idea of being 'well read', but we recognize that those who shape public opinion, civil servants, journalists and broadcasters, include in their commentaries a view of the world which owes as much to books as it does to first-hand experience.

The new National Curriculum lays great stress on pupils in school reading a 'wide range' of 'different kinds of writing'. But the writers of the official document gave up the idea of producing a list of authors whose works would be useful when they discovered that what they offered as examples could be turned into a list of prescribed books. Those who favour a 'cultural heritage' view of school reading will select texts which they believe will 'lead children to an appreciation of those works of literature that have been regarded as amongst the finest in the language'. Others whose view of children's reading matter 'emphasizes the role of English in helping children towards a critical understanding of the world and cultural environment in which they live' will choose different texts. These views are not mutually exclusive. The problem is to ensure that children will be able to take advantage, at different stages, of what different texts offer them.[4]

Three things now make access to texts easier than at any time in the past: universal literacy, cheap popular printing, and widespread distribution. Bookshops are now more popular places. Libraries have lost much of their exclusive stuffiness. Books are, comparatively, cheap. There is no doubt about the role that literature, however defined, plays in the reading done by children, at all ages and stages. What children willingly read, the books they choose, define literacy, and literature, for them. Their growth in literacy depends on their freedom to choose, to value, to exploit and to reject different texts, different kinds of literature in response to their own purposes and intentions.

In the early stages, adults choose books for children. They do this remembering their own early experiences, or prompted by what is popular, promoted or available. They are guided in their choices by their own ideologies and values, by what their friends suggest or what they think the school approves of. But, sooner than their parents often realize, children become choosers on their own account. They have preferences which we do well to respect, even if we do not always care for what they choose.

Important texts are those that are important to their readers. We are now returning to the view that literature is what the literate person regards as worth reading. This brings to a head our understanding of literacy as a freedom rather than an obligation.

With this understanding comes an awareness of different ways of reading the same texts. Different media offer different readings. Stories become plays: *Lark Rise to Candleford* packed the National Theatre for months. Children's picture books become operas: *Where the Wild Things Are, Higgledy, Piggledy, Pop.* New productions of *Peter Pan* and *Hansel and Gretel*, with distinctive social analyses, are for older children and adults. Television transformed C.S. Lewis's *Narnia* tales, in all their period stuffiness, into a nationally shared text. Of course there is a quantity of ephemera to contrast with more carefully wrought prose, but most trivial writing quickly disappears, and young readers soon discover what they are prepared to re-read. This is their first definitive step in the development of critical awareness, though we still know very little about the difference it makes in reading development.

Again, the differences in texts, the variety and abundance of them, are to be welcomed, used and understood as different ways of relating significant language to felt experience. What *makes* this difference, certainly at the start, is the readers' discovery that texts, words on a page, have different *voices*. Children learn this nowadays from television and transfer it to reading. But before they do that, they hear, every day, stories being told.

Oral story-telling is in the process of being widely revived in cultures where literacy is centuries old. One of the claims we have already made for the benefits of literacy is that it overcomes the limitations of human memory. Writing remains. But in human remembering the past stays alive, so story-telling not only supplies children with memories they cannot yet have, it also gives them 'virtual' memory, the idea of remembering what they have heard others tell. Behind this revival are whole libraries of books about narrative, its power and importance, not least in the moves which the young make to tell stories of their own. Story-telling lies at the back of all literacy, powerful in its effect and distinguished by its cultural differences, as we shall see.

Universal literacy has made clear that, as they have read the stories written by others, more and more people have realized that they have stories of their own worth the telling. The prevalence of written biography in our day is only one indication of our consuming curiosity about other people's lives. Telling is faster than writing, more immediate, vigorous and attention-claiming. So the revival of an old oral tradition now goes hand in hand with the new literacies of radio and television.

No writer nowadays can command the attention of every reader, however successful the publicity campaign. No reader can read everything that is written. Different texts make different claims on our attention. Writers produce different texts for different media as well as for different readers. Consequently, we have to decide how to balance the power of the writer with the power of the reader as part of teaching literacy in school.

Learning and Teaching

If literacy is more than traditional ways of reading and writing, if the manufacture of word processors and the analysis of what counts as social knowledge are in their different ways related to modern literacy, how is literacy to be taught and learned?

It would be strange indeed if all that linguists, anthropologists, social scientists, psychologists and literary critics have uncovered about the nature of language in society were to make no difference to our teaching, to children's learning and to the texts we read together. Yet, in spite of all we know about children's growth in language, there is a strong resistance to changes in the practices associated with reading and writing in school. The belief that 'in the old days' standards were higher because the 'basics' were universally taught, resists even the clearest evidence that children *learn* to read by reading and to write by writing.

Teachers rarely change their approach to helping children learn as a direct result of being told what it would be good for them to do. A more particularized concern for the progress of individual children is an important sign of their willingness to do something different. If they find themselves wondering why Samantha or Imran doesn't make the text *mean*; why Harold will read only about cars; why Jean, Jella and Jo never, but never, pick up a writing tool voluntarily, then they will actively consider a change of teaching strategy or a different kind of text. In other cases, teachers respond to ideas that involve them in taking risks, ideas that suggest 'Suppose we did . . .'. Confident practitioners and beginners, both, look for different ways of teaching when they believe that children have somehow failed to grasp what reading is all about. In the end teachers know that their own particular, continuous, minute observation of children will tell them what 'works' with each child. They look for the means of reinforcing the effectiveness of what pupils show as their strengths.

After promoting and prolonging this discussion of differences and emphasizing their importance it is unrealistic to suggest that all children, everywhere, will learn to be literate in the same way. The opposite is the case. The teacher's definition of literacy is worked out in the social context of her or his own classroom in terms of the differences of the children who contribute to their common life and shared experiences. Children teach each other; they also teach their teachers. When they know they can read and write they believe they have taught themselves.

Literacy, now, means living with differences, in school, in the world, within societies and cultures. Awareness of the importance of differences, and their relations to how children learn, is part of the common understandings of most parents with children at school. To discover how children become confident and discriminating readers is a task for teachers, parents and children working as partners. Together they can turn the resources available to literates in the world to promoting reading and writing in school. If trust between the children's care-givers and the professional educators increases, this new kind of partnership will make a substantial difference to the literacy of all children in a changing world full of powerful literates who are not always inclined to do them good.

Not all parents, however, are ready to take on this broad view of literacy, or to tolerate the differences we have examined as important resources for children's learning to read. They want their children to pick their way securely through the current explosion of information, through what they see as 'disinformation' and textual rubbish, to the safety of clever essay-writing in expository prose, with correct spelling and grammar. They want only good books for their children, a quick sure start to reading and steady, monitored progress towards the high literacy of the professionals.

We have to make it plain, therefore, that there is no real confrontational difference between those two sets of aspirations. The difficult thing for all parents to grasp is that, once the young discover from their elders that they are *entitled* not just to learn to read and write but also to be 'in the know' as the result of becoming literate, they will take control of their literacy for their own ends. They will still need good models, but should also avoid slavish imitation. For the children whose parents have had, in the past, less of the knowledge and power that literacy makes possible, the demand for this kind of entitlement is greater. It is also different. They want literacy not as a privilege granted by others but as something they are *bound* to have. Those who have always known what literacy is worth may be surprised to learn that there are different views of what literacy is for. Both traditional and modern literates have to live with difference.

CHAPTER 3
Beginnings

Do you remember how you learned to read and write? Try to. Most people I ask, especially the confirmed literates I work with, say they can't, or only vaguely. Some of them see a particular virtue in this failure of recollection, as if their early learning were the root of their later success. Perhaps that accounts for the prevalent idea that most good readers and writers learn to do these things easily. Mercifully, this is no more than rumour. We are all learning to read and write all the time. When there is something different to read, something unexpected to write, we see the limits of our literacy.

Many experts who study literacy in depth are reticent about their own early learning experiences. Paulo Freire is an exception. His lifetime of championing the rights of people in developing countries to their own distinctive literacies is grounded in his reflections on his own beginnings. 'Recapturing distant childhood as far back as I can trust my memory, trying to understand my *act* of reading the particular world in which I moved was absolutely significant for me. Surrendering myself to this effort I re-created and re-lived in the text I was writing the experiences I lived at a time when I did not yet read words.'[1]

Freire's phrase 'reading the world' reminds us that this is what all the early learning of children is about. They construct the world by sorting it out in mental imagery and language, and representing it to themselves by naming, and then remembering. When we first held a book, the sensory contact—the feel of the pages and the binding, the colours of the illustrations, the smell of the print—was probably more powerful than our awareness of the significance of the story. The rhythms and the tone of the reading voice may have been more prominent than the words. Initial literacy is rooted in memories of people, places, books or, perhaps, in the absence of these. When children begin to read they cannot tell others how they do it because they don't know. But they sense that, somehow, there is a kind of dialogue going on with a voice on the page. Learning to write seems to be easier to understand; it comes later and is visible. As they watch others doing it, children see words appearing. Yet the puzzles remain: how to make the pen move, and how to know which words to write. Watch the efforts of a three-year-old. See the concentration on the tip of a crayon and wonder, again, how it all happens.

Traces of these early sequences remain in all of us. If you have strong feelings about what you want your children to be able to do when they become literate, these may have their origins in what happened to you at that stage. My literacy autobiography began to surface as I was teaching very clever schoolgirls how to answer examination questions about Shakespeare, Jane Austen and Yeats. The texts were the same for us all, yet we often disagreed about the meaning of a chapter, a line, a word. Then came the problem: whose meaning counted in the exam? And again, how did any of us come to know and understand the difference between what words mean and what they say? When an author writes 'That's a fine thing to do' for a story character to 'say', how does the reader know whether this is an ironical statement or not? Until this time I thought I just knew. Then it seemed important to find out *how* I knew. Doubts set in. How could I be sure that my interpretation of what my class and I read together was the one the examiners wanted? How did the examiners read the set texts?

With something of a shock I realized I thought reading was like breathing, something everyone did to live. I had never met anyone who couldn't read or write. Once contemplated, the absence of literacy in anyone's life seemed intolerable, but surely not difficult to remedy. It also made my literature lessons with these intelligent sixth-form girls seem a form of dilettantism. I thought that if I could teach someone who had never learned to read or write then I might discover how we learned to interpret writing and print. So I entered the lives of adults who lived under the shadow of illiteracy, determined to discover how they could learn to read. As my students and I struggled together to bring to life the words on the front page of a newspaper, or to regulate the wandering hands that fumbled with unfamiliar ball-point pens, my early learning came back, but not quite as I had expected.

No matter how hard I tried, I could not reproduce in these inexperienced, stigmatized men and women, the *confidence* of my own early literacy. Where I had never even entertained the idea that I could *not* learn to read, they were over-whelmed by their failure. After a hard day's work they came to lessons not expecting to achieve much, yet scarcely daring to step beyond their poor opinion of themselves or to risk another disappointment. They resented their non-literate state, which they saw as offering evidence to the world that they were stupid, when clearly, they were quite the reverse. As they began to trust me I discovered that their learning was shot through with pride and anger; pride that they were more worldly-wise than their sheltered teacher, anger that I had been luckier in my early schooldays when they had been ignored, left out, passed over. Not even when I encouraged them to choose something to read, to pick up a book, or even to discard it, could I make them feel like readers. Worst of all, what I took to be pleasure in writing they acknowledged only as the kind of unsatisfactory effort they already endured in the kind of jobs that near-illiterates find.

My mistake was to try to offer them my kind of literacy, to encourage them to *be* literate, when they had no expectation of this as a state of being they could lay claim to. Only when I made reading and writing *work* for them, as a tool, as a means to an end, did I understand where they, and I, could begin. It was too late for the idyll of reading pleasantly by a fire, at bedtime, or under the tree in the garden. Instead, charts, diagrams, recipes, letters, forms, DIY instructions encouraged 'getting down' to reading and writing. Only when a father asked if he could learn to read stories to his children did I hope to inject into our lessons the sense of delight that I found so desperately lacking in their lives as readers and writers. But, for all the fun we had with fine picture books, comics and puzzles—his choosing as well as mine—this late-learning adult still could not admit that this was reading for real. He wanted to hurry his sons along to history and geography books, to the learning he had missed.

Working with older beginners taught me the lessons I had learned without being aware of them: that as we find different uses and purposes for literacy so our literate skills both increase and diversify. My favoured pupils on their way to university knew how writers use language to tell, to persuade, to explain, and to create poetry. The serious adult learners had a fixed or limited series of contexts in which they believed reading and writing would prove useful or appropriate. To interact with a writer was an alien idea; to argue with one, an impossibility; to laugh with one, a sign of frivolity. Sometimes I felt they believed I didn't take literacy seriously enough.

My new beginning in literacy grew out of my increasing understanding that there is no single literacy, no definable set of common activities that produces the literateness of individuals. Instead, there are series and sets of literate practices which individuals choose to engage in. Yet whatever our beginnings, when we know what literacy is and is good for, we should all be confident enough to increase and diversify the scope of our literacy when we want to, or have to. My adult pupils could all read a cigarette packet, but they had no idea that this counted as being able to read, or that finding the racing results in the *Daily Mirror* was a literate accomplishment. With help, most of them became efficient readers and careful writers of what they saw as relevant to their adult lives. But many gave up before they discovered writing as a powerful way to argue, and reading as the means of encountering ideas they did not need to adopt but only to consider. Very rarely did they find a book exciting, or experience a feeling of power as part of what they wrote.

Clearly there are aspects of being literate that stay with us as adults because they are part of the felt life of our childhood. We learn early how to make the effort of reading and writing pleasurable and successful. In doing so we come to know how to stick at a task in order to complete it, to discover ways with words other than our own, to be a reader of the writings of others and to expect others to be the readers of what we write. A good apprenticeship in literacy needs more than the 'mechanics' of the skill; it also has to engender a particular kind of confidence in knowing that readers and writers offer meanings to each other.

What Emerges as Literacy?

Most children discover the beginnings of their literacy in their family, their first powerful learning environment. Literacy is *familiar*. Even where there seem to be few books and not much writing paper, the question 'What does that say?' is provoked by magazines, television and T-shirts. Early literacy is visible in children's understanding that signs and writing are systems of symbols that mean something.

Children become involved in literate activities on the family occasions when reading and writing are part of a complete event, such as making a shopping list, reading a book, singing a hymn in church or writing a message with a picture on a Mother's Day card. In hundreds of different ways, reading and writing are linked to noticing, talking and thinking about what happens on television, as when the commercial repeats the name of the car or the cake. Literacy becomes familiar not as a medium, separately, but as ways of creating and understanding written messages.

Adults take care to draw their children's attention to situations and contexts where signs and symbols are clear. The little green man in the traffic light indicates when it is safe to cross. 'Man' says the baby in the push-chair. Mothers and fathers point out and explain different formats of writing. A picture postcard means someone is on holiday. The name carved on a bar of soap is a presentation of letters that can be traced and felt. To turn the pages of a book is to learn how it works, to listen to the story is to hear what it says. By pointing to pictures in newspapers or lifting the flaps in the picture book *Where's Spot?* children learn that symbol systems are part of meaningful events. For nearly twenty years now researchers have scrutinized the forms of written language that enter the lives of young children before they go to school. They describe literacy as *emerging* from the social background of children's lives, from their language, and their observations of literate adults. This definition of *'emergent'* literacy enabled the researchers to look at a much wider range of activities for evidence of children's learning.[2]

Again, this meant looking differently at what we have always known, that children read words on wrappers, bags of potato crisps and cornflakes boxes. This ordinary evidence, described as reading 'environmental print', is part of the changing cultural process of learning to be literate. So children's recognition of commercial presentations of familiar commodities—chocolate, hamburgers, cereals—now counts as significant in emergent literacy. Researchers also point to the influence of advertising material in the lives of those whose literacy has hitherto been underestimated, like ethnic minorities in cities and the rural poor. In fact, all of us adapt our reading habits to the ever-widening scope of graphic designs around us.

Parents differ in what they think and do about the first stages of their children's reading and writing. Before the first school year most families include children in what ethnographers call the 'literacy events' of the home. Children in day care or nursery schools are introduced to picture books and drawing. In reception classes or places where early literacy is encouraged, boys and girls find literacy materials: paper and pencils, books and paints to use in their play. Those who play at trains make tickets and timetables. Where there is a toy telephone there may also be a pad for messages. At this stage, literacy is one of many kinds of learning.

As school looms, parents become aware of the gap between the informal learning of early childhood and what lies ahead. So naming objects, reciting a name and address, recognizing letters or even chanting the alphabet, holding a pencil 'properly', all become more deliberate parts of the activity. Where once the adult and child read stories, now they look at print. The number of the questions to the adult increases, and the answers are often repeated in a more exact form. Where the child was once encouraged to make a shopping list in her own way (by drawing a can of beans or a banana), now she is helped to write the words 'correctly'. Gradually children are encouraged to look at reading and writing as distinctive things to do.

So there are paradoxes in our new understanding of the beginnings of literacy. We are encouraged to see all children as making sense of the writing they see around them, and of the literacy practices in their lives. But we also know that, when they go to school, children find that the familiar literacy of ambient print is only part of what they have to learn to understand. The school context of literacy is print in books. So, although parents are encouraged to recognize what their children do to promote their own learning, they are also urged, by television programmes and magazine articles, to read to their children the complete texts of stories in books. Often the result is that the relaxed informality of early encounters with written language is gradually overlaid by the seriousness of recognizing words and the process of 'getting them right'.

We know that adult expectations concerning children come to affect, and even to determine, the way children think about themselves. So avoidance of the possibility of early failure—not keeping up with the class is its most usual form—may be part of the impulse behind what parents try to accomplish in their children's literacy before they go to school. But the jolly picture frieze with letters pinned round the bedroom wall can so easily become a nightly test of alphabetic order. Making letters with dough may be transformed into the effortful work of writing a name with a pencil. Children try hard at what they want to learn, especially if there is cheerful encouragement of their efforts. But they so easily catch an adult's anxiety if they seem to be slow or fumbling. At this stage they cannot have an adult's view of literacy, not even of how they will learn. So encouragement and emphasis on their success are much more helpful than indifference or visible disappointment.

Children approach literacy practices as they do all other new experiences which have a 'firstness' that most adults have long forgotten. The exploratory power of children's interests and their ability to take risks help them to cope with whatever comes their way. A baby learning to walk will stumble, fall and get up at once, because the pleasure of mastery overrides hurt. If children's first experiences of writing and reading are shot through with pleasure and success, then that feeling remains as part of the event and the learning process. If they are anxious about performing in order to fulfil the expectations of others, then their first school steps are often fraught with uncertainty, not about doing these things, but about doing them well enough.

What Barbara Tizard calls 'passages of intellectual search' are always part of children's probing of words and events 'of the mind'. They really do want to know what letters and words are, and what people do when they read and write. Our problem is to know what, and how, to tell them. A four-year-old and I had a very complicated discussion when I said she couldn't borrow my pen because I needed it to write letters. She told me that I could write letters with a pencil. I meant letters to send; she meant the letters of the alphabet. Again, I've often tried to explain to children that books are made by writers when what we are looking at is a picture book which the children know is drawn or painted, not *written*. As adults we know the whole literacy scene very well. We do not always recognize, or tolerate, the piecemeal way by which children enter it. We assume that their brilliant competence in talk, their amazing under-standing of different ways with words (they know quite early what book language is like), will lock into what we want them to learn as quickly as we explain it.

What I'm leading up to is this. Neither the discovery of the importance of emergent literacy, the literacy events of the family and the culture, nor the imitative practices that parents help their children to engage in before they go to school, can ensure that they will become wholly and finally literate. Learners have to discover, in their own ways, what reading and writing are good for, what is in these things for them. They have to want to read with *desire*, and to write with *intent* beyond that of pleasing adults. We know this from the cases of children, from all kinds of families, who taught themselves. The only danger I know in early reading is that the surrounding adults may insist too much that the child must achieve their kinds of literacy in the way that they, for all that they cannot remember how it happened, believe they learned.

Given time and encouragement most children who learn to talk learn to read and write. Too much emphasis on the 'mechanics' of letter and word recognition dries up the sources of desire which stem from the most characteristic activity of childhood, play. The foundations of literacy, of understanding what reading and writing are *seriously* good for, lie in children's playful explorations of these as cultural behaviour.

The Privileges of Play

When parents hear that reading to children or showing them how to write the letters of the alphabet are helpful things to do before school, they willingly undertake these activities. Books and writing seem to be the real beginnings of literacy. They demand effort, like work. So, after school begins, parents hope that lessons they have given their children will be continued in the formal lessons of school. When their children come home and announce that in reading time they 'just played', parents are often uneasy. This behaviour seems too random to be a good beginning in literacy.

The fact is, play is hard work in any area of learning. Before they go to school children persistently make great leaps in all their development by playing. In childhood the chief function of play is to sensitize children to the way people round about them behave, to let them practise being human. The consistent element in play is desire, wanting and achieving. Desire is deeper than anything we superficially mean by pleasure. Children take play very seriously; they work at it, because they long to accomplish what they see others are good at.

We still call 'play' many activities that can only be mastered by disciplined effort according to *rules*. We speak of playing a game or a musical instrument; yet these need strenuous practice. When we play we turn our desire into meaningful activity by demanding of ourselves concentration and effort. We take as our models those who are good at what we want to be able to do. All art, music, sports and active recreations, as both performance and enjoyment, are strictly disciplined and joyously excessive. They are play at its best, creative, deep, civilized. What children and adults do in play is never random nor aimless. Their desire is to engage in what they long to be good at because they enjoy it.

So if children discover in reading and writing not only the cultural habits of their society but also the desire for the meaningful and rewarding effort that they associate with play, they will take the trouble to learn the rules. Mercifully, they usually have learned the important ones, the rules of language, before they begin. Children who do not enjoy reading are usually those who have never discovered what makes it a source of desire, something they can be good at if they try, and if they continue. That's when learning to read and write is like learning to ride a bicycle. In both cases you have to believe you will succeed in order to do enough, and to learn sometimes by falling off or by making mistakes.

Perhaps what unsettles adults about the notion that reading is successfully learned if it becomes a desire in play, is the association that play has with fantasy, the imaginary, the illusory. Many books for young children seem to foster this link; the characters are animals, the events are im-probable. Some parents tolerate the make-believe of play and play in books until their children learn to read. Then they expect the age of reason to begin. Then reading and writing are for learning.

For all its apparent imaginative excess, children's play is always firmly related to their growing understanding. They invent situations, characters, actions, when what they desire is beyond their immediate capabilities. Whatever they lack in stature, skill or strength they turn into an imaginary situation. Then what they *can* do is adapted to bring about what they want. They cannot fly, but they spread their arms, make whirring sounds and rush about being aeroplanes. They scold their toys, as mothers and fathers. As giants and monsters, they dominate their friends and frighten their pets, cast spells as witches, to accomplish in imagination what they cannot, really, bring about. Thus they discover power and ways of turning the tables on those who dominate them. In doing so they create rules for a game, and then act according to the rules. Thereby they give up the arbitrary nature of their longings.

Early reading and writing are learned in the contexts of games with rules. Taking telephone messages, making notices, reading a story to the dolls, and whatever else they know of literacy in life become rules in play. These are called 'ways of taking from the culture'. Young children who go to the library also play at 'going to the library'. The rich, meaningful quality of symbolic play is, generally, that it is *for real*. Literacy begins not only in being read to, where the adult is in charge, but also as symbolic play for real.

Language Play

The most important play for real is play with language. It begins very early, sometimes unnoticed as anything more than babbling, calling out or the repetition of certain noises. In children's prolonging of sound-making we soon see the

human instinct for games, especially when they talk to
themselves just before they settle to sleep. Then they turn
words into playthings.

> *Ba-bee, ba – bee*
> *Nice girl, nice girl, nice boy*
> *Ba-bee, want a drink*
> *want a teddy*
> *want a lolly.*

The serious business of learning to speak so as to join in
conversation is inseparable from the playing with language
that generates poems and stories. When children's early
words come out, singly or in phrases, they are never wholly
instrumental. A whispered 'Please' is a kind of wishing
magic that produces chocolate. 'No' has all the determining
force of every negative or denial. Early language shows so
clearly how feeling and learning are locked into each other.
Rage brings out words of terror ('won't!') which often shock
the speaker. Periods of calm produce poem-like phrases, 'Go
to sleep, now'.

In the last twenty years, children's language development
has been at the centre of research in many disciplines—
linguistics, psychology, sociology. Ways of encouraging
children's speech, notably in the case of those with special
difficulties, have been diversified and increasingly successful. Perhaps we have still given too little attention to
children's imaginings, how they pretend, take on rules and
try out different speech styles. But if we listen for even a little
time, we hear them using different tones, different 'registers'
as they pretend to be different people. By the time they
discover words in a book, children have had some play
experience of 'doing the voices' of different characters, so
they are ready to tune the page.

Here is another example. A child is playing at arguing and
discovers something of how it works. The transcript comes
from Barbara Tizard's and Martin Hughes' book: *Young
Children Learning*. The child and her mother are discussing

some old jam tarts which the child has discovered in the rubbish bin.

> Mother: *You can chuck jam tarts away if they're old jam tarts.*
> Child: *Yeah, but if they're not, you don't.*
> Mother: *No, but if they are, you do.*
> Child: *Yeah, but if they are not, you don't. If they are old, you do.*
> Mother: *No, if they are, you do*
> Child: *If they're not old, you do.*
> Mother: *If they are old, you do.*
> Child: *If they're not old, you don't.*
> Mother: *For the final and third time you do.*[3]

The child is trying to see why, and how, the other person views the situation differently. This is a continuation of her earlier learning when she discovered that her 'I' is a 'you' to her conversational partner. She is also chanting, as in the recitation of a poem, discovering that words can be treated as things to be handled.

We have known for a long time that children soon come to understand enough of the rules of social interaction to adapt their utterances to suit the situation in which they find themselves. Appropriate speech includes not being rude to Grandfather, or not asking questions on some delicate family matter in the presence of strangers. We are always delighted and amused by the words children transfer to new contexts: 'That's a wrinkled old car'. Behind these two aspects of children's language are an implicit understanding of the social rules of language, and a way of stretching their available words to cover feelings as well as observations. Here's a child watching a spider creeping up the side of a bath: 'I'll fizzle it, and I'll whoosh it away. Not to come tingly.'

In language play children discover the special ways by which the rules of language can be combined in order to bring about what they want. In the sophisticated games they play with their friends, children submit to the rules. A friends says, 'It's night now', so stairs have to be climbed even if none exist, doors are shut, beds are slept in, even if the sun is shining. In this game, the rules are the rules of living. But, almost suddenly, the rules of language can be extended, so that to say, 'Open the door' makes it possible to say, 'Open the light' instead of 'Switch the light on'. When children use a stick to gallop round the garden or the play park, they separate the meaning of 'stick' from the stick itself and supplant it with 'horse' and act according to the meaning of horse. Long before they go to school children know that they can speak of their legs and the legs of the table without believing the two things are the same. Play produces *metaphor*.

In play children discover that it is possible to separate what is said from what is meant and still make sense. By adopting other roles, they can try out other forms of speech. Understanding both words and the world becomes, for children, more and more complex and yet still manageable. They acquire, in both proverbs and clichés, little pockets of folk wisdom. 'He hasn't a leg to stand on.' (He has, of course.) 'They couldn't organize a tea party in a baker's.' 'He's a fly-by-night.' 'You'd think she owned the Crown Jewels.' Even when they don't fully understand what is meant, children know that it is more than is conveyed by the words alone.

When they know that language, like behaviour, follows agreed rules, children begin to explore the rules and, of course, to break them. They want to discover the boundary of sense and nonsense, what is meaningful and what is not. They find you can say, 'I am dead' when this is clearly not the case. Then they exploit nonsense purely for effect, as in:

> *Three children skating on the ice*
> *Upon a summer's day*

or when they say they hear with their nose and smell with their eyes. Splitting apart the agents or ideas that go together is at the heart of riddles. As they learn to play with language children come to objectify it. Their play is *metalinguistic*.

Kornei Chukovsky, the Russian poet who, in 1925,

insisted in the teeth of political opposition that the construction of reality depended upon the understanding of nonsense, called children linguistic geniuses and tireless explorers. He showed how, in their early years, they not only learn to talk, but also to inspect words and to play with them. 'Why are you dying to have a cup of tea? Will you die if you drink it?' 'Hotsy totsy hullabaloo, Hootsy tootsy that makes two.'[4] The *metalinguistic awareness* that the experts say is the mark of the good early reader and the risk-taking of young writers is born in speech games, the nonsense rhyme, the topsy-turvys of re-inventing the familiar, and all the lore and private subversions that children make up with words.

> *Happy birthday to you*
> *Squashed tomatoes and stew.*

As soon as children discover that certain things are deliberately *not* said, they explore the scatological with linguistic daring. They discover excess, especially in meanings, that Chukovsky calls 'intellectual effrontery'. 'When the water runs away, who is it chasing?' To be able to say 'The sky's falling', and survive, is a discovery about language and the way of the world. In discourse that denies itself: 'I won't tell you what I'm going to say', 'Sit down, but you have to stand up first', the nature of paradox emerges as a word game. So jokes follow quickly, riddles become a powerful way of attracting the attention of others, proverbs carry the tradition of certainty.

As they become aware of language rules and how they operate, children use 'anti-language' to break up the hierarchies of common sense, so as to re-define for themselves what *counts* as common sense. In the carnival of their word play they are discovering two sets of ordering: of the world, and of their language. In doing so they learn how to signal 'This is play', so that their utterances are not to be taken literally. They know when they are talking nonsense. The comic verse of the nursery rhymes, the folk-tales and the singing games are at the heart of the matter. Not only are they memorable as speech, they also form the bedrock of all play, the alternative world. Jack and Jill, Old Mother Hubbard, Simple Simon, Polly, who put the kettle on, the three men of Gotham are all there, ready to pop into stories, play-acting and a million children's books, generation after generation.

> *Mrs Red went to bed with a turban on her head*
> *Mrs White had a fright in the middle of the night*
> *Saw a ghost eating toast half-way up a lamp post*
> *Mrs Brown went to town with her knickers hanging down*
> *Mrs Green saw the scene and put it in a magazine.*

If they have played with language in any of these ways, children are not strangers to narrative fiction. They understand stories which contain a world where the rules of everyday life are the rules of the narrative and people behave as expected. But fiction can also subvert these rules, in ways that imagination, and language, make possible.[5]

Let us now apply these understandings to the whole range of language in which children's lives are immersed: television drama, personal stories, new pop lyrics, proverbs, talk and arguments, and slang. Then it is clear that play with words, which generates metalinguistic awareness, is not the privilege of only those families who are used to self-conscious literacy. Segments of a wide range of discourses appear in the play talk of most children. But literate adult observers may notice only those that are like their own. Children are as likely to create alternative worlds from the detachable pieces of life in a TV serial, like *Eastenders*, which their parents are watching, as from the expensive nursery rhyme book which no one has yet read to them.

The question is whether children's language play counts as a *literate competence* when the children begin, formally, to learn to read and write. The evidence suggests that children who have a repertoire of oral songs and verses begin to learn to read by discovering that they can tell themselves how to *see* what they say. The phonology or sound system of our written language is richly exploited in oral language play. This experience is undoubtedly helpful in early reading of all kinds of texts, especially in English where the written representation of the sounds of the language is sometimes confusing for beginners.

It is in the realm of play that children also discover how to manoeuvre themselves into writing. They adopt writing roles before they expect their marks on paper to be read by others. If they make lists and write messages when they play at house, and an adult responds to their intentions by seriously reading aloud what seems to be written down, then children are more concerned to learn the rituals of the writing system, to learn the rules. Observers of early writing are persuaded that children intend to make meaning from their earliest squiggles, and that their first attempts at writing are more logical and intentional than they were formerly perceived as being.

If we look at children's symbolic play in greater detail we discover that it includes gestures, role play, singing, drawing, dancing and rhythmic percussions. In the adult world there are ways of writing these down which we call *notations*. So the beginnings of writing may be related to other things besides language; music, for instance. Because the move from speech to writing seems, for those who have mastered it, the most direct notational shift, other forms of representation may go unnoticed.

Two recent examples of children's play offer powerful evidence of different kinds of early literacy. As they involve recent technologies they are, virtually, new literacies. In a remarkable account called 'Maps of Play', Myra Barrs tells how a five-year-old boy, Ben, on holiday with a group of adults, played, for most of each day, a private fantasy game based on events from the television series, *Masters of the Universe*. His characters were represented in the game by three doll figures. As he made the dolls fly through space Ben provided the commentary, dialogue and background music of the actions in a barely audible voice. The episodes were warlike combats, or imitations of the television versions of old legends. Listeners could appreciate the intensity of Ben's concentration, identify the weapons and the fights, hear the words that were extensions of his ordinary vocabulary, but, for the most part, this was a continuous, repetitive private world, created and peopled by Ben's imagination, a series of adventures played out, for days, as solitary *enactment*.

A turning point came when Ben invited a young adult to share his game, by offering him a small diagram, or map, on a scrap of paper. Here is Myra Barrs' account of what followed: 'The map was then used as the basis of an imaginary adventure game in which Michael (the adult) was the main participant, an actor in a drama directed by Ben. The shape of the map was basically that of an inverted triangle, and the 'start' position was in the top left-hand corner of the triangle where Ben had drawn a 'Michael' figure, a little man with a prominent laser gun. This was the first game and was a very simple prototype in which both Ben and Michael developed a means of communication and, so to speak, of notation.'[6]

After this initial event, seven or eight games were played in three hours; the maps became more complex and a formalized system of notation emerged to indicate 'jumping, swinging, shooting and general zapping'. Ben had learned that he could draw not only letters and digits, but also, *action*.

Myra Barrs includes much more of this deep play in her perceptive account. Its relevance here is to show that the beginnings of literate activities are not always as straightforward as our view of children's learning.

This becomes even more apparent in a second example. As part of an experiment to discover how young children differ from traditionally literate adults in their first encounter with micro-computers and word processors, Suzanne and Ron Scollon describe the activities of their four-year-old son Tommy. Their distinction is simple and compelling. The adult's approach is linear, literal. One typing mistake results in frustration. The child's approach is global and recycling; if something doesn't work, it is of small consequence; he begins again or does something else and comes back later.

The Scollons suggest that it is children's habituation to games that shows why they are more *interactive* in their use of

the computer. Many parents would agree; their first introduction to computers has often been their children's
addiction to computer games. There are clearly two ways of
playing them: by working through the game rules or
inventing new ones. The most imaginative and inventive
games are devised by the children themselves.

Having watched his parents use a word processor,
Tommy discovered how to create and store text files and
print them out. Although the contents of his file were
'nonsense' texts, he could recognize his message when he
called it up. The Scollons say: 'Although Tommy does not
read or write any form of connected text, he already has an
interesting level of competence in manipulating a discourse
frame, the operating system of a fully professional word
processor.' Tommy can also enter musical notations on a
score displayed on a screen and play them back. He can
change and edit them, and hear them in playback on a stereo
system. So he knows two different kinds of notation conventions. Tommy's parents say: 'What he composes may be
musical garbage at this time, but we believe that his interest
in learning to operate this editing system shows an involvement with the computer at the level of operating systems of
discourse frames rather than at the level of simple visual
messages.' The Scollons' main point is that children as
young as Tommy gain control of the general operating
system of a computer, as distinct from the computer
languages in which the programs run, more quickly than
adults usually do.

Tommy, at four, has mastered computer procedures; he
can take the right steps to make a file accessible. He can type
catalog to get the list of programs, then type *Run Trilogy* to get
his game going. One day, when he saw a book with the title
Trilogy he knew the word, and made the leap 'from a
procedure to accomplish something in the works to a
conceptualizing of a relationship between a symbol and an
idea': the leap a child makes when 'the penny drops' about
reading. Watching Tommy working with the computer has
suggested to the Scollons that we are now getting much

clearer insights into the ways children begin to understand the nature of symbolic representational systems.[7]

The great virtues of children's play, virtues even beyond its usefulness in introducing the young to a wide range of symbolic systems are two fold. First, in play, children, no less than adults, experience a release from the apparent inexorability of the here-and-now. They enter alternative worlds in what D.W. Winnicott calls the 'third area' where they try out what they are to learn and experiment with the rules.[8] Then, in play, children 'walk tall'; their limitations are not confining, their imagination lets them invent possibilities. The beginnings of the power of literacy lurk in the privileges of play where the reality of the everyday life world is *reframed* as it is in a book, a game, a computer. As a result communications are loosened, dialogues are extended. Our interactions with ourselves and others avoid becoming 'an endless interchange of stylized messages, a game with rigid rules, unrelieved by chance or humour'. The words are Bateson's, reproduced here because they seem to emphasize what children learn in play, especially play in the wider domains of literacy.

Being Read To: Making Marks

Adults with long reading histories have some recollections, however faint or inaccurate, of being read to as something companionable and pleasant. Whenever I want to call up what early reading *felt* like, I have only to re-read or recite parts of *A Child's Garden of Verses* to bring back the long, dark, firelit winters and the howling cold of the Scottish east coast that R.L. Stevenson also knew. I have no idea when I learned the two-verse poem that begins:

> *Whenever the moon and stars are set,*
> *Whenever the wind is high,*
> *All night long in the dark and wet,*
> *A man goes riding by.*
> *Late in the night when the fires are out,*
> *Why does he gallop and gallop about?*

but I still hear those words in my grandfather's voice coming from nearby.

Stevenson played a significant role in my being literate. For most of my childhood I knew he was a poet, a writer, something one could *be*, instead of a shopkeeper, a kirk minister, a dentist or a fisherman. I believed he was my grandfather's special friend; certainly their paths could have crossed. A book about lighthouses written by Stevenson's father is also part of my memory. The friendship, possibly illusory, seemed to stretch to me when I was read to, sung to, recited to, told the lore and history of that Calvinistic culture. It is bound up with sea sounds, lamplighters, being in bed with chest colds, the sound of fog horns and the thunderous verses of Sunday Bible reading. I report all this simply to emphasize again that children's literacy environment is not something apart from their everyday life, but is constructed from the ways in which they and their elders interact with each other as feeling and thinking begins.

Stevenson said that 'Fiction is to grown men as play is to the child'. Some commentators believe this meant that he disparaged his own writing for children as something juvenile. I believe it shows he took children seriously. The problem now is to distinguish the truth and structure of feeling that lines like his hold for some people from the nostalgia that can be too constant a part of reading reminiscences. But for me Stevenson was a firm starting place; everything I read that he wrote upheld what I came to know reading was good for.

Although the cosy pictures of reading round the fire have little or no reality in our contemporary life, researchers, educators and people in general agree that reading to children helps them to become literate. We feel this to be the case more than we actually know how it is so. Studies of parents reading to children are scarcer by far than the popular books that now urge them to do it. We seem to be content that everyone knows what 'reading to a child' consists of, although the nature of the activity is only in the first stages of description.

At best we have assumed that it is the *amount* of reading that counts, that picture books are the beginning of things, and that the parent reads and the child listens. In fact, these notions are not borne out by the available evidence, which shows how children, before they are nearly four, talk constantly about the story, the words and the pictures, as they are being read to. Their part in the 'being read to' emerges as a very active partnership indeed. The 'book' may be a pamphlet or a magazine whose contents are beyond their immediate grasp, yet their questions are genuine enquiries: 'Do the flowers grow in the packet?' was one response to a seed catalogue.

If families are children's first reading environment,then early reading and writing have to be characterized in family terms. We see this clearly from the accounts which some parents have scrupulously kept of their children's entry into literacy. Hugh and Maureen Crago, for example, recorded most of the interactions and commentaries on the picture books and stories which they read with their daughter for four years after her first birthday. It is an unparalleled and detailed account of the child of bookish parents moving from being a listener to a re-teller, and then to a narrator of her own tales. Dorothy Butler's moving study of her invalid grandchild's growth into life understanding as the result of being read to is perhaps the most remarkable of all. But, however convincing the evidence and the details of these and similar reports, it is not necessarily true that children *have* to be read to if they are to become successful readers, or that 'being read to' means a book at bedtime.

There is, in fact, no obligation, necessity or compulsion for children to be read to at bedtime, especially if that is when the adults are at their busiest. Reading events demand that both parties, children and adults, should enjoy them. Beyond this, there are no rules. There are also many ways of reading to children, and no absolute guarantee of the exact effects of the reading on children's later uses of literacy. As many observers now remark, reading to children isn't the one unbroken filament that binds them into literacy. Having said that, I am sure there are still many reasons for believing that when adults induct their children into literacy in this way, the young persist more actively in their attempts to read for themselves. The interactions with a reading adult give some idea of what the reading enterprise is all about, and how a book works. The comfortable closeness remains in the child's memory long after the book and the other details of the activity have been forgotten.

The act of reading to children is a shared, imaginative process that involves the inseparable factors of language, thought and feeling. In her close analysis of a mother and child reading together, Henrietta Dombey shows how the reading pair are attending, in different ways, to the author's words and *negotiating* their meaning by referring to events and objects in their own remembered experience. More particularly, the child initiates the exploration of the meanings of the text and offers a version of it. This shows her making sense of both the words she hears coming from the page and what she remembers from another context. Taking someone a present happens in life as well as in *Red Riding Hood*. The adult explains the unfamiliar part of a story (what the upper part of a mill is like when the Little Red Hen takes her corn there to be ground into flour) by referring to the familiar attic in their home. These moves bring the reality of everyday life to the fantasy of the story, and the events of the story into the realm of ordinary experience (in this case, climbing up into the mill in the same way as one goes up the ladder to the attic).[9]

Also, as dialogue between the parent and the child goes on throughout the adult's skilled reading of the text, the child sees how the words on the page guide this meaning-making. In particular, she learns the sequences of events as a kind of tune that seems to come from the page. Gradually, from repeated readings, and from encounters with other books by the same author, the listening child discovers that the words have the *feeling* of the author about them. Just as they anticipate their favourite TV programmes when they hear the opening music, children come to distinguish the distinctive tones and tunes of illustrators and storytellers. They also detect differences, and expect different pictures, different ways of telling, from different books, until they discover that stories, like play, are a kind of game with rules which the author invents and subsequently invites the readers to play and to share.

When they are read to, especially where the text has been carefully composed to take account of their inexperience and to *exploit* it, these episodes in children's early literacy differ from all other language interactions in childhood. The language of a book text is quite distinct from that of speech and conversation. Only when they are read to do children hear unbroken discourse at length. The sentences follow one another, stop, start, swoop on or introduce new voices in dialogue. The cohesion of the pattern generates the coherence of the meanings, so the young listener learns how to distinguish characters and actions, as well as to recognize consequences, to discover sequences of repeated events and to engage with moral dilemmas. A story as short as 'The Wolf and the Seven Little Kids' displays not only the rules of story-telling but also the discourse patterns of a culture.

I emphasize all of this because, while much attention is rightly paid to the contents of the story in the many books which encourage adults to read to children, the nature of the text—how the story is told—is often taken for granted, as if it were neutral substance, reading *matter*. But those who take writing for children seriously are careful to make the reading itself a particular kind of experience. They indicate in the opening lines how the game of the story is to be played:

'Rosie the hen went for a walk . . .'

and, later, surprise the reader with the unexpected.[10]

Besides learning how stories go, and all the different ways they can be told, children who are read to discuss stories with adults. They begin to clarify the categories of their thinking. For example, a recurrent puzzle is the notion of an older brother or sister. Younger children are absorbed by the idea that someone in their family has been in the world when they weren't even there, so they worry away at the problem, trying to understand if they will ever catch up with someone older. Perceptive writers hear both the thinking and the feeling tone of childhood dilemmas, and understand how to present them in concrete instances. *Titch* by Pat Hutchins is a good example.

In addition, being read to reassures children by letting their fears be named; the dark can be less threatening when spoken of aloud. They learn to anticipate Christmas and other festivals and to recall their earlier occurrences. The past and the future are more concretely set in order. The explanation of possible, as well as actual, worlds, those that differ in their organization, and their inhabitants, from the nearby world of first-hand experience, also allows young readers to begin to examine the emotions and intentions of the characters and thereby to extend their understanding of their own. This is the beginning of reading as '*deep* play', the confrontation with the inner self, as well as 'play for real'.[11]

Gradually, children begin to discover that they can possess the contents of books as something like memory. After the adult's reading ends, they hear echoes of the text as they recall the story. They feel their way into the meanings and enlarge their associations as they remember what happened and repeat the choice phrases as spells or incantations. ('. . . and it was still hot'). They also discover that whoever read to them has given them the complete text — a poem, a story, or simply a riddle — as a total experience they can return to on their own. They can even remake the story in their head, so that Goldilocks and the three bears can become friends, or Cinderella may send the prince packing because she would rather stay at home.

All of these are the well-attested experiences of the bookish. They are not, however, confined to any one privileged group. Teachers now know that the conditions for reading of this kind are reproducible in nursery schools and play groups. Nor is there any limit to the number and kinds of books which generate imaginative reading by adults who choose to share them with children. But, as I have explained already, there are other ways into literacy, some of which need less adult attention or a different kind of partnership. We assume all too readily that adults teach children to read, or at least that they are dominant figures in the learning of early literacy. As children begin to sort out the writing system, the adults have to help but not to interfere. The balance is a delicate one.

As with reading, the early stages of children's learning to write have their roots in play. When they begin to imitate adult writing actions children find they can make pictures and help others to understand what their drawings represent. Gradually they discover that they can draw not only objects, but words, speech, so they make long strings of what they believe looks like writing, and are often prepared to 'read' these.

This understanding—that one can draw language—wasn't part of my early induction into writing. I was encouraged to draw, but no one helped me in my early attempts to represent what I saw, and I knew my strange shapes were not what a ship or a mountain was really like. I had no idea that I could make visible the words in my head, although I saw people writing every day. For me, learning to write was an apprenticeship in copying. After my struggles with my slate, I worked hard to reproduce on double-lined paper a fine printed script. There followed carefully executed 'joined-up' longhand, which I practised with the assiduity of a latter-day scribe. My strict obligations were, I believed, to be exact, tidy, careful, with 'd's and 't's a different height from 'l's and 'h's. Threatened by the possibility of spelling errors and the misdemeanour of ink blots I taught myself to be controlled, expert enough to win prizes and praise without ever discovering that the clamorous voice, the story-telling dialogue in my head, could find its powerful way on to a page to be shared by others. So the remarkable things that are now evident about early writing have no counterpart in my past except in the skilled handling of tools. What I now know about children's beginnings in composition I have learned from gifted teachers, whose skill in promoting the many ways in which children make meaning are beyond praise.

Left to themselves, children initiate their own writing by setting themselves to find out how the system works. They can do this successfully even before they can read, in something of the same way as Tommy Scollon mastered the system of his computer. Glenda Bissex, whose account of her son's progress is now a classic, shows how Paul invented a system of sound-letter relations, 'based on using letters to represent their letter names (as in DH for *day*), or abstracting sounds from letter names (as "duh" from the letter *d* or "ch" from *h*) and on categorizations of sound in terms of place of articulation . . . At five he wrote *TADE* for *Teddy*, his dog. When he changed the spelling to *TEDE* he pointed the change out to his father', and in other examples showed how he was aware of his own learning, and able 'to note differences between his own and the conventional spelling systems and was able to explain why he was incorrect'.

The note that five-year-old Paul Bissex was allowed to leave on his door, *Gnys at wrk* (Genius at work), challenges the belief of some parents that children should learn to spell as soon as possible. Caring adults who are traditional literates, together with those who blame their literacy inadequacies on their early learning, are made very uneasy by the idea that children don't have to be competent scribes before they take in how real writing works. They want their children to show that they have submitted to the discipline of acquiring the necessary linguistic understanding of the relations between orthographic symbols, phonemes and morphemes, that is, letters, sounds and fragments of meaning, as well as the principles underlying the system, as a *way of remembering*.

The alternative possibility is that children like Paul Bissex discover and teach themselves the writing system as a means of *sharing* what they want to communicate. They do not, as some traditionalists have suggested, reinvent the wheel or evade 'remembering' the 'correct form of words' if these are handed out to them. Instead, they move from what they understand as a possible system to a principled grasp of the conventions, and in so doing discover the rules for the conventions that make them less dependent on the hazards of memory. That is, they become better spellers because then, anyone will be able to read what they write.

To bring this about they persist, reflect, learn, correct, order and refine their *thinking* as well as their spelling. Here is the challenge in Glenda Bissex's own terms: 'When we speak of children's development in writing, we mean development towards those forms selected and refined by our culture. Often we do not appreciate the forms used in other times and places, that children independently explore but must un-learn as part of their schooling. We tend to see our writing system as a given, and children developing towards it. Yet if we step away to gain a broader perspective in time, we see the writing system itself developing: we see that the child's literacy learning is cut from the same cloth as mankind's written language development.'[12]

In her account of Paul's writing from its earliest begin-nings, Glenda Bissex shows that children attempt to represent the sounds they make in speech and that their attempts are not random but have an internal coherence. Gradually they begin to compare what they write with what they see both around them and in books. They learn that writing is not speech written down, but a different kind of language. Literacy learning, like language learning, is not merely imitative but rule-governed and *creative*. In the case of writing, composing counts for more than copying.

The complexity of the descriptions of early literate understandings arises from the fact that language can be symbolically represented. It is always more straightforward to do things with language than to explain the processes. These glimpses of Ben, Tommy and Paul at work are not instructions as to how children should be helped or taught before they go to school. Nothing is to be attributed in this context to the fact that they are all boys. The examples are, however, a firm indication (and there are others) that children's schooled literacy has a prehistory, a period when children actively try to discover the nature of literate behaviours. The beginnings of writing are located in the shift from drawing things to drawing actions and then to writing words which can be read by anyone who understands how the writing system works.

Beginnings – Again

There is no one beginning, no single system of entry into literacy. So what, learned early, makes a difference to later literacy development; what helps, or what hinders, when children go to school? Will teachers provide enough ways of learning, enough opportunities and encouragement for the differences to count?

Some contrasts are worth thinking about. Although the first stages of being literate are located in the family they are also part of the network that relates each family to a community, to society in general, and therefore to its history. Children who go regularly to church or to Sunday school hear kinds of language that are absent from their lives outside home during the rest of the week. Those whose family traditions involve them in encounters with non-English texts and a different alphabet—Greeks, Arabs and Jews, for example—expect their traditions and their texts to be prized even outside their circle. Two questions arise. Is our children's literacy emphasized as a way of confirming their belonging to the literate tradition of their family and its culture of childhood, or is it to be extended to make possible a more encompassing understanding of other traditions? Then, are not schools bound to take account of different literacy traditions and also to exploit and extend them on behalf of the children who are involved?

We know that different beginnings make a difference to children's expectations of what literacy is and is for. So there can be no simple, single, straightforward account of early literacy which ignores all the possible contexts, styles and cross-cultural patterns of oral and written language. We have to live with differences. As more and more explicit details emerge from studies of what different groups of people *do* with their literacy, we have to widen our understanding of what counts. We should even try to imagine a set of powerful literacy practices in which an early entry into reading books might count for less than a stringent sequence of accountancy techniques.

In this chapter I have examined certain patterns in children's informal, pre-school literacy learning which are traditional to our culture, patterns of behaviour related to play, and reading to children which, still, seem to make a difference to children's later experience of literacy in school. The evidence is strong that when writing and reading are correlated with children's intentions manifested in play, young learners will extend their play strategies to encompass the task of learning to make language mean, in both its spoken and its written forms.

Adults who read to children both model for them the process of reading and offer them a set of different contexts for their shared conversations, thus extending the experiences that they share. Children in their everyday interactions with adults discover that it is possible to talk about what happens in books, and also to apply their everyday understanding of the world to interpreting what they read. Thus, attitudes and beliefs, the shaping forces of children's thinking and consequently of their contributions to society as they grow up in it, begin by being associated with the interpretations that others put on these. Long before our children know about guilt as an influential drive in their development, they know it as a feeling. *Where the Wild Things Are* is then more than a story; it is a place to locate the feeling, to explore it, and, in a more accurate sense, to re-visit it, to name it.

So in their early days most children develop what some have called an *orientation* to literacy; a set of expectations of what reading and writing can be like: the pleasure of a story, a way of playing with language, a notational device for drawing action instead of words. These expectations can be significantly different and still promote successful reading and writing. Indeed, it is the range of these expectations that should please us most, since they give rise to the considerations of *alternatives*, which constitute a powerful mode of being literate.

Some children, however, are less successful than others in discovering a track through the waste of written material that overwhelms us. Generally they haven't been helped to take in hand for themselves the game of making written language mean, so they have difficulty in deciding how to 'frame' the enterprise of learning to read. For them the alternative is to become writers, powerful message makers.

Our traditional initiation to literacy seems to reside in being read to and reading texts. But we know that, for the different literacies of our day, this will never be enough. What we cannot yet fully determine, however, is what we should expect of children if they are to enter this range of potential literacies, wider than at any stage in the past. The evidence of Tommy Scollon and Myra Barrs' Ben suggests that we need to be more aware of children's potential skill with notational systems in addition to those that are, like writing, based on words. Think of the number of young musicians who read scores, artists and designers for whom signs and different semiotic systems are more meaningful, of the different demands of crafts and technologies, from civil engineering to eye surgery. Our world now uses, expects, literacies beyond any beginnings yet mentioned. Television and computers are still only on the margins of what has to be made operational just to keep our society going. Therefore our continuing choice of literacies based on books and written texts may need at least some revaluation in these new and extending contexts if only to see if they are still as important as we have traditionally believed them to be.

CHAPTER 4

Why Are Stories Special?

Sorting Out the World

At the supermarket where I buy my groceries there are children's books on shelf racks at the checkout. Most of the shelves are low enough for little people to pick up the books to look at, even to sit and read, oblivious of the trolleys that sweep around them. The books have coloured drawings of everyday objects, with single words or short sentences underneath. They are about naming things: trucks, cars, colours; about counting balloons, sweets, flowers; or about the letters of the alphabet, in different shapes and sizes. The books represent one way of becoming literate. They are perceived as a staple related to everyday life, like bread or fish fingers.

From my spying point in an adjacent queue I watch the seated children turning the pages and see the waiting adults as they put the books back on the shelves or into the shopping trolley. If there's an argument about which book to buy, the adults have the last word. After a thirty-second glance they choose a colouring book, one about numbers, or about telling the time, or a title such as *Colours*, *Opposites*, *Fruits* or *Babies*. In the context of the supermarket, literacy is factual and economic, directed not by children's desires, but, like food, by adult assessment of need, use or value.

In our role as parents and in our recognition of the way things are, none of us can stop anticipating the day when our children leave home to go to school. So we are impelled to look at the early stages of schooled literacy that these little books seem to represent. We hear from neighbours, friends, the news media and those who offer advice about children's development that the success of their education depends on their learning to read and write early. We are urged to teach them the letters of the alphabet, to recognize common words at sight, to name colours, to count to ten, and to converse sensibly and clearly with their elders. So here is the supermarket fitting the products to the consumers. Just as cookery books on the adjacent shelves give dietary advice and recipes, so books for children not yet in school offer a kind of literacy assurance by combining pictures and words on a page.

Although the marketing is new, the idea is quite old. In 1659 there appeared in English a picture book called *Orbis Pictus*—the world in pictures. Written by the Moravian educator, John Amos Comenius, and illustrated with woodcuts, it was famous all over the Protestant world of its author. Although Comenius' life was dogged by tragedy, persecution and the bitter consequences of the Thirty Years' War in Europe, this gentle teacher persisted in believing that education could change the condition of humankind. His picture book was to enhance children's understanding of the world by acting as a kind of encyclopaedia—enlarging their experience by showing and naming a range of activities, objects, crafts and ways of learning. It offered 'original images' (that is, pictures); 'precepts', the verbal interpretations of them; and 'imitations', the child's active response to the images on the page. Comenius showed his readers a bath, linen clothes, a school, all with their constituent parts and utensils which were named in lists of words alongside the pictures. The operations and tools of the carpenter and the blacksmith were similarly displayed, and the readers were invited to pore over scenes which depicted the virtues of Humanity, Justice and Liberality and to learn such words as *prudence, fortitude, consanguinity*. As in every later picture book through the ages, including those in the supermarket, the pictures showed recognizable aspects of the world children knew, as well as those which lay beyond or outside their everyday experience of looking and listening.[1]

This way of naming the world may seem a fairly naive realism. The fact is, however, that children 'read' pictures very early. By the age of six months they can look at a family photograph and recognize their parents. We don't really know what they see, but they certainly respond to imitations of things they have never encountered. A young reader who has a book about trucks soon begins to distinguish bull-dozers, lorries, goods vans and trailers by using the word for each even before seeing any of them on the road. A child I know, who heard her father say that heavy goods vehicles made mincemeat of everything else on the motorway, pointed to just such a one in a picture and said 'mince-meater'. The effective function of the little caption books is not only to teach children to recognize pictures, but also to sort out the world in their heads, a process which is as imaginative as it is actual.

This universal habit of naming things goes on without books. Children hear their parents referring to coins as money; socks, shirts and shoes are recognized as clothes, the different items in the supermarket trolley come together as shopping; spoons and forks can be cutlery even if the knives are absent. The apparently spontaneous way by which children seem to know that language helps us organize our lives comes from looking, listening and saying. It doesn't *need* books. But to see the words is to begin to understand what writing can verify: that the objects are knowable by being named; that to read is to learn to name the world beyond what is local and present. The next step is to discover what the story is: the move from words to sentences.

Now let us suppose that the patient adult who has helped a three-year-old to turn the pages of *Trucks* more than twenty times is suddenly bored by the repetition of single words and decides to introduce a dramatic incident in which the milk tanker and the furniture van are racing each other up the motorway. Their drivers now have names, homes to go to, children to bring presents for. There are actions, events, consequences because, in the imagination of the teller and the listener, there are people who do things. It is very difficult, impossible almost, to turn the pages of even the most factual-seeming picture book for children without telling a story.

The rest of this chapter argues a special case for the relation of stories and storytelling to literacy, and the claim I am making is this. As with naming, we rely on stories to sort out the world. Like naming, storytelling is a universal habit, a part of our common humanity. As far as we know, all cultures have forms of narrative. Stories are part of our conversation, our recollections, our plans, our hopes, our fears. Young and old, we all tell stories as soon as we begin to explain or describe events and actions, feelings and motives. Everywhere stories spring up to confront us. On our way to the supermarket we pass a sign: 'Accident: can you help?', with a date, a time and a telephone number. 'What does it say?' asks our four-year-old. The story begins.

From the stories we hear as children we inherit the ways in which we talk about how we feel, the values which we hold to be important, and what we regard as the truth. We discover in stories ways of saying and telling that let us know who we are. So, before they even attempt the first stages of literacy, children have heard and told many stories which are more than *just* stories. If we are to understand the relation of storytelling to literacy, we must see the value and nature of narrative as a means by which human beings, everywhere, represent and structure their world. We not only thrive on stories; we also survive by telling and retelling them, as history, discovery and invention.

When we read stories to children, we may regard the activity as the pleasurable, indulgent, *play* side of the operations that help them to understand the nature of written text. Imagination, making up, fiction, are tolerated as a form of relaxation or recreation, for adults read novels and magazines in this way. We accept *real* literacy to be related to work, to making things happen, to the non-fictive, to information, to business.

In fact, we cannot sustain this separation. The narrative habit isn't confined to fiction but is embedded in every kind of discourse. Think of a sermon without a serious anecdote, a vote-seeking politician who sticks to statistics, a salesman who tells you about the motor of the food processor without mentioning the food. We can explore the nature of literacy in much greater depth by looking at the part narrative plays in the early stages. But before that, we have to understand, again, that the narrative habit is much older than writing, and that it is not in books that today's children first learn how stories go.

We see children entering the *universe* of narrative discourse when they begin—very early nowadays—to watch television. Television is the modern child's *Orbis Pictus*: it brings pictures of the entire world into almost every home. It stimulates children's curiosity about every possible event, creature and object that can be presented as *moving* images, while, as the same time, naming what is happening to them. The butterfly emerges from the chrysalis, while David Attenborough maps the words of his story on to the images. 'The great cells of the caterpillar's body die and the dormant cell clusters suddenly begin to divide rapidly, nourishing themselves on the soup of the disintegrating caterpillar body. The insect is, in effect, eating itself.'[2] These may not be the words of the science text book, but the same story lies behind both tellings, the story of the living world. Even the youngest viewers catch the dramatic significance of this story as it unfolds. Here is what Barbara Tizard recorded of another conversation between a four-year-old and her mother.

Helen was watching a television programme when she saw something of interest.

Child: *What's that, Mummy?*
Mother: *It's a chrysalis. After they've been caterpillars when it's time for them to start being butterflies, they make a sort of shell for themselves and stay inside it for a while. They change into butterflies. That one's just come out of his chrysalis.*

Children and adults can link a television programme about a butterfly, conceived as rational explanation of a visibly miraculous-seeming event, with the imaginative recreation of the same event in *The Very Hungry Caterpillar*. Here, in these pages through which the caterpillar quite clearly eats its way (there are holes to prove it) is the same story in another telling. Stories are not about what is the case or what is improbable fiction. They encompass both rational explanations and imagined possibilities until such time as the need arises to *write* these things differently for different purposes. Hence the special place of narrative in the growth of literacy, not only in the young. If we are to understand this, we must begin by giving up the idea that we, as adults, tell stories to children and the truth to ourselves. Story-telling, as a habit, is both universal and lifelong.

Episodes

We learn to tell stories in early childhood from those who first tell them to us. Stories are part of our first conversation; they create our first memories. The habit of storytelling pervades our explanations, hopes, fears, dreams, plans and every recollection, whether we notice it or not. Nursery rhymes are short narratives; the songs that rock children to sleep are often stories about the future: the cradle will fall, Baby Bunting will have a rabbit skin, Daddy will buy a mocking bird. Each incident of every day is a possible tale for us to tell to others so as to satisfy our deep need to understand the nature of events and our part in them.

The rules for telling stories and the kinds of stories we tell are handed down in the history of our language. From folk-tales we learn the accumulated wisdom of those whose survival depends on outwitting the powerful. Our belief that fair dealing is to be preferred to treachery comes from tales of princes and princesses where rank is the stamp of virtue. *King Lear* began as the simple tale of a girl who loved her father as much as meat needs salt. We learn stories as proverbs, anecdotes, sermons, fables, and the words they come in fit the shape of the telling we expect to hear. My grandmother's stories always had two of the old Scottish rhetorical traditions. She began by announcing the family lineage of her characters: 'You remember Mrs Macrae of Burnside? Well, her niece by marriage, a Miss Crowthorne who lives in Largo, was in the baker's when the minister, Mr MacCallum from Auchterarder, came in.' Her tale completed—it was usually an account of the downfall of the proud or the outwitting of the self-satisfied—she would end with a triumphant epigram: 'and that put his gas on a peep.'

This habit of introducing a tale and rounding it off shows how we take segments from the ongoing flow of events and turn them into *episodes*. That is how we recognize narratives which are, at the same time, announcements, commentaries, illustrations. Children learn how to do this from the innumerable examples they hear during a day. As they learn to speak they are invited to join in the creation of such episodes. 'Let's tell Daddy,' says the careful English mother, 'what we did on our way back from the shops. Where did we go after we bought the bread?' 'Church,' says the two-year-old. 'Yes. We came back through the churchyard and we picked?' . . . the voice rises in query . . . 'Daisies.' The answer is prompt and confident. 'And we couldn't get the buggy through the wicket gate, so you held the daisies and I lifted it right over the top.' In sequences of this sort the child and her mother shape the episode to which they return at a later time, 'Do you remember when we picked daisies in the churchyard?'

The ways in which we tell stories and encourage our children to tell them have distinct local characteristics, like my grandmother's Scottish rituals. Some adults emphasize truth-telling from their children. 'Making it up' is frowned upon. For them, fiction is 'telling stories' of the lying kind. Others encourage fictions, fantasies, wit, word play, and the outrageous excesses of the tall tale. The challenge and jousting of Caribbean rapping can be heard in the narratives of young Black children in London. The slow, careful unwinding of a family saga is more likely to come from the long memories of northern storytellers.

The modes and manners that children acquire from storytelling before they learn to read and write are important in their becoming literate. The texts of their first books are shaped as episodes. Written stories differ significantly from oral ones, yet, the conventions of beginnings and endings are there in both as 'once upon a time' and 'happily ever after'. In the literature of every literate culture there are long underground trickles of an oral past, including those which carry the ancient ways of structuring a sequence of events. The first reading lesson is to discover the voice of the storyteller behind the words on the page. For a time, a more experienced reader supplies it; later, the learner takes it over for herself.

Because of television, children and adults alike now hear and see many more and different kinds of storytelling. Television is a new public space for storytellers, whether they are talking directly to their audience, reading the news, or using actors and all the other devices of dramatic narrative to involve the viewers. Behind the selection of material for nearly every programme is a producer's idea of what makes a good story. As listeners and watchers, we are regularly engaged in a particular kind of narrative activity.

In contrast, being read to, that early literate habit, begins for children as a storytelling with a book. In this setting the story can be heard more than once. The timing, the pace of the reading, the lingering on certain parts of the tale are all a matter of readerly regulations. The words on the page stay the same, yet each re-reading is different. The sequence of episodes must remain intact, however, and the formal repetitions have something of the older oral storytelling, where the Billy Goats Gruff go trip-trap, trip-trap over the bridge, the Three Little Pigs are threatened with 'I'll huff and I'll puff', and Max makes his journey to the Wild Things and back. By means of new television episodes and the old spellbinding formulae the young make important moves in the expectation of what reading, and, later, writing, might be like.

Making Worlds

As we have seen, when children play they invent situations

so as to bring about what they want to happen. If we watch the play scenes they derive from real-life situations, from television or from books, we see them creating imaginary worlds. Then they use what they know of the real world to organize the episodes that they invent.

Stories, like language itself, are ordered by conventions. Storytelling is a kind of game with rules. Some of the rules relate to the way the story is told; other rules govern the kinds of things that are allowed to happen, depending on whether the story is to be 'made up' in imagination or related to the events of everyday life and our understanding of the laws of nature. In play, children sort out what *is* the case in the world from what *might* happen in a story. Exactly how they do this we are not sure; we call it imagination. But we know that they understand, very early, that while Jemima Puddleduck wears a bonnet and has conversations with a fox, this happens only in the world Beatrix Potter has arranged for her to live in.

In their story play children can be themselves in a real world or in an imaginary world. Or they can be imaginary people in that world, or imaginary people in the real world. When, for instance, they play at being their parents, they scold their children even if in real life they are never seriously rebuked. For an afternoon, they may become members of a robber gang, but at tea-time, still dressed in combat gear, they eat ordinary biscuits. When they play at being children, they create rules of child-like behaviour and make themselves obey them. Without any previous negotiation with their play partners they use the speech of story-children or story-parents and act in character. ('I've told you to clear up and go to bed.') This multi-consciousness, the switching of roles and language would be more surprising if it were less ordinary. The worlds of children's play are like the worlds we recognize in novels. Both are created by the power of our fictive imagining.

Being a character in a story is a dominant feature of children's play in our culture. Children fictionalize themselves as they play, and they create the world where the fiction allows them to explore both the world they know and the one they 'make up'. The world of images is as real as any other, rule-governed, and yet wholly at the disposal of the one who makes it. I think there is a definite connection between this imaginative world-making and what we call being 'lost in a book'. It is an understanding that habitual readers and writers recognize, but one which eludes all those for whom reading and writing are more intermittent activities.

When I explain this to myself I return, again and again, to a game I watched as it was played over a period of three months by two little girls, one four, the other three. Their enactments occurred on a staircase and in a space where they could be observed and heard. The game was called 'going to the cimtry'. In the first episode the children dressed up as an adult and a child. Wearing their best hats, dresses and shoes, and with picnic baskets, handbags and extra doll children, they went on three buses. Finally, after subsequent episodes of ticket collecting, road crossing and sometimes a struggle with an umbrella they arrived at the cemetery to pay a visit to the dead brother of the older child. In real life this episode occurred for her every Sunday, so this game was a recapitulation and exploration of the puzzling fact that, although she knew her brother from photographs and recollective talk by her parents, and also went to visit him, she never actually saw him. He was therefore a character in the world of story.

The younger child enacted the story-play version of a little child. At first she followed the narrative lead of the older one by obeying instructions and behaving like a toddler, a period she knew she had outgrown. Yet she also became the flower seller and the bus conductor: adult roles she understood. For the older child, the narrative was dominated by her need to locate her brother; where was he? For the other, it was a form of growth in the ordering of experience by following the rules of conversation and of story-telling. The girls created their alternative world as they sat on the staircase—the top deck of the bus—by means of social talk with adult overtones. 'We must hurry. He wouldn't like us to be late.' The story world was richly detailed from what they knew of journeys, visits, everyday events. By this imaginative, metaphorical storying means the children were trying to understand loss, separation, being, death, the mysteries which adults explain so little.

The outing was always a success. If we consider it as a text with characters and dialogue it is a short novel created from a series of episodes. The children set off; they came back. As they linked the going and the returning, both of them made a world for the satisfying encounter with the complicated events and feelings that lay in the middle.

Reading to Children

When they played together, the girls in the foregoing incident were already moving into early literate behaviour. Their conversation was full of echoes of stories they had listened to. Their almost daily recapitulation of the incidents and events of 'going to the cimtry' brought together characters from fiction and their own recent experiences. 'Can we bring with us the tiger who came to tea?' 'No,' it says, 'No dogs allowed'.' So they taught each other to take words from books and stories, just as they practised going on a picnic, for these are things that people do.

Reading to children before they go to school is now widely and, I think, wisely recommended. But, straightforward as it seems, the practice is by no means self-explanatory, except perhaps to those who like reading stories to children and who convey their pleasure to their listeners. Others, for whom neither reading nor stories holds much attraction, can easily be made to feel guilty, quite unnecessarily, if they think their children's literacy prospects are at risk because they do not read to them at bedtime. What, then, is the relation of being literate to being read to, and why, in this context, are stories important?

The first point is obvious. Reading to children introduces them to the language of books which is, quite simply, different from speech and conversation. When I read a story which began 'There was once an old house. In it lived a man, a woman and their four children' I was stopped at that point by the question 'What's "in it"?' so I recast the phrase to 'in the house' and all was well. Barbara Tizard reports a similar conversation between four-year-old Rose and her mother who are reading about puffins.

> Mother: *Spotter puffins are the ones who go out and find out where all the fish are to be had.*
> Child: *What do fish be had.*

Dr Tizard says that the mother interpreted the child's question as asking where the puffins went, and explained this to her. But Rose's question may well have been prompted by the unexpected from 'to be had'. At this early stage in their language learning, children are still alert to differences that adults have stopped noticing.[3]

Before they go to school, a read story is the longest monologue of connected language that children hear. They discover text and discourse in the sustained, cumulative building up of related episodes: how one thing follows and is related to another. The rhythms and structures of written sentences, the patterning of events, the conventions of story beginnings and endings are all significant features of written language which they learn without instruction. By being read to, children grow in their understanding of the symbolic uses of this language and of its *constitutive* nature, how it makes worlds.

In a very short time children produce written forms in their speech. 'There was no trace nor sign of it,' said a distressed little girl who lost her ball in the park. We know that children's vocabulary expands very rapidly at this age, and if we listen carefully, we hear the words that originate in stories. By hearing stories read aloud children discover what, for a time at least, seem to be the rules of the reading game. For example, the end of a story transforms the beginning. Part of the satisfaction of *Where the Wild Things Are* comes when the rowdy, disobedient Max returns home from his adventure with the Wild Things to find his supper in his own bedroom, 'and it was still hot'. As they listen children are examining social behaviour and also discovering that their emotions can be located and named. They know how Max feels. So, when they become characters in their own stories, they begin by tracing their way along a narrative path that is already partly familiar.

The most striking evidence we have of this comes from the stories children tell, if we let them go on long enough. (Our inclination, sadly, is to cut them short.) By introducing characters from familiar stories into their own narratives, they seem to pull in with them the traces of where they come from, a plot sequence, book phrases and transformations of the original story. Carol Fox, whose work has greatly enriched our understanding of children's narrative competences, recorded, in one year, eighty-six story monologues from her five-year-old son, Josh. As he retold the stories which had clearly made a deep impression, *Hansel and Gretel* and *The Wizard of Oz*, his mother identified the sources of other incidents in his narration. Some of these were everyday events, others were a kind of reinvestment of folk-tales, nursery rhymes and family sagas. Even more remarkable is this young teller's range of ways of telling, the rhetorical contact he makes with his imagined audience:

> *and he . . . say . . . as you know . . . do you know what they had? What a dream . . . they heard* big bumps *coming along and they looked out of the window—and what did they see? A big fat tall heavy giant . . .* [4]

Maureen and Hugh Crago also kept detailed records of what happened to the stories they read to their daughter. Her spontaneous retellings showed a repeated pattern of risk and resolution: 'shut doors are opened, bad things give way to good ones'.[5] As they hear stories, children discover how to fictionalize themselves, to create episodes of what might be, to try out possibilities in other worlds, and to give their feelings a place to be, a local habitation and a name. 'The creation of an imaginary situation is not a fortuitous fact in a child's life,' say Vygotsky, 'but is rather the first manifestation of the child's emancipation from situational constraints.'

So the importance of reading stories aloud to children is not solely nor simply to give them a rich experience of book language before they go to school. That will certainly happen. But the stories themselves provide the listeners with an increasing imaginative repertoire of ways of coming to terms with their emotions, which, unlike all other aspects of their being, are full-sized from the day of their birth.

As they tell and re-tell stories, children are coping with complicated problems, of space and time, being and non-being, rules of behaviour and interactions with adults. They use stories as *metaphors* to bring together in a meaningful relationship what they still need to discover and explore. Here, again, is Josh, in his long story about God and St Peter, sorting out the puzzle of who gets into heaven. Dracula, whom God had earlier despatched to his grave, reappears with all his teeth 'done by a special dentist underground who was magic'. The episode continues as Josh narrates:

> *Then the head came back on. Dracula was magic just like any other person. St Peter said to God, 'There's no way to get this evil man.'*
>
> *'Well, the only thing we can do is really try hard to chop him up in little tiny bits.'*
>
> *'But he might come alive again,'*
>
> *'We'll never get him. We'll just have to take care of him – Dracula?'*
>
> *'What?'*
>
> *'You want to be on our side?'*
>
> *'Yes, I'll be pleased to.'*
>
> *'Right then. He's our friend,' said God to St Peter.*

Josh knows how to 'do the voices'. He also understands how, in dialogue, a character advances the plot. He can keep the attention of his listeners by pointed climaxes and resolutions. More particularly, as he links narrative style and techniques with the development of story characters, he resolves the problem of how to turn a monster into an ally, that is, how to deal with threatening, un-named fears. All of these skills he will exhibit again when he comes to read and write. But they are more than aspects of literacy; they are *literary* competences. Josh has discovered how fiction holds together a variety of languages and different points of view in a way that no other discourse quite does. He doesn't know he can, but, like the other children in Dr Fox's study and many, many more, he learned how to do it by being read to.

Adults who read to children act as a model of literate reading behaviour. They also let the child listener enter it, usually by finding a link with everyday events they share. Children ask questions about the story and answer those asked by adults. Gradually the listeners take over some of the telling; they say the words in unison with the teller. This, and their ability to sit still for an extended period, to talk about characters and events, are all recognized as signs of literate progress in the early years.

Although I know that not all children have, or need to have, stories read to them at bedtime, I believe that occasions of relaxed talk, such as story-reading provides, are good for them. Conversational exchanges about books and stories are more finely tuned, more discursive than shorter bursts of talk about actualities. Stories extend into the discussion of 'what if' and 'perhaps', and encourage recollection that is the beginning of going forward. 'You remember, we went to Granny's and she gave us green ice-cream? Well, we're going to have . . .'

In our society we have tended to see this story-reading and discussion as the privilege of only some children. Television has changed that. Many different story-tellers, from all over the world, engage with young children in what feels like face-to-face spellbinding. They have brought back, extended and celebrated storytelling as a distinctive performance, and in so doing have narrowed the gap between spoken and written language. Stories are acts of communication and children want to know how to play that game by the rules. They discover by listening and then joining in both telling and reading. All they need is the company of enthusiastic readers and tellers: older children, nursery-school keepers, grandparents, librarians as well as parents, storytellers all.

To make stories unfold to children as living events is the special care of authors and artists whose medium is the illustrated picture book. Nowadays they are part of early literacy, world-wide.

Texts – and Pictures

Not all children have stories read to them, but most expect to see pictures every day as part of their double-order environment. Our interior walls are lined with illustrations, and television offers everyone alternative ways of seeing the world. Visual images dominate children's early learning, their emotions and their understanding, long before they know that our buying and selling society invests heavily in our restless eyes and our memory for pictures. Children's growth in literacy is tightly bound up with how they learn to look and what they expect to see.

Paradoxically, adults believe that beginning readers need help with texts as words but assume that they will understand pictures without instruction. It is generally felt that where pictures and words appear together, the function of the pictures is to support the readers' approach to the text, to enhance and deepen their understanding of it. This is indeed the case, but, in terms of modern literacy, by no means the whole of it. Picture books nowadays are a distinctive kind of production, one in which the history of text illustration meets the semiotic sophistication of graphic design and the modern intricacies of narrative discourse. Illustrated stories now owe as much to the worlds of film and advertising as to the history of literature.

The relation of pictures to stories and the nature of the readers' interactions with both are an important aspect of literacy too little regarded and even less understood. Picture books are not only for children. Every magazine, from *Radio Times* to *Time Out*, every coffee-table art production or exhibition catalogue proclaims the visual nature of literacy for all. Whatever is created specially for children assumes a whole panoply of adult involvement where the young reader is, in part, the excuse. In the context of our present concern about learning to read, we expect adults to read illustrated narratives *with* children as part of their entry into literacy. What is scarcely acknowledged is that adults thereby become members of the readership of the writer and the artist.

Telling a story in words and pictures is a way of ordering and re-ordering the world in a culture that takes visual images and narrative for granted. Children learn to turn pictures into stories and to read the author's words; adults are surprised that neither stories nor the world are quite what they expect. To read Raymond Briggs' *Mother Goose Treasury* with a child is to rediscover the gutsy, irreverent, carnivalesque tradition to which these rhymes belong. His *Father Christmas* is not a story of the idealized present-giver, but of a harassed working man who creates the magic of Christmas out of his responsibilities. *Fungus the Bogeyman* topsy-turvies the sanitized order of things to show the social nature of what disgusts us. In *Gentleman Jim* and *When the Wind Blows* Briggs also exploits the possibilities of comic-strip books for serious social comment, a motive universally acknowledged in mainland Europe but very little appreciated in Britain. To learn to read comics is to enter a particular form of literate behaviour that extends from childhood to political cartoons and beyond. Picture books are not simply privileged reading for or with children. They make reading for all a distinctive kind of imaginative looking. Without the pictures, the text is decontextualized, and without the text, the pictures are only part of the full texture, the counterpoint of the artist's meaning.

For beginning readers, contact with a storyteller by means

of pictures is, however, particularly powerful. The effect of illustrations on children's early understanding of stories can be quite long-lasting, because striking pictures, those that remain in the memory, work, as ancient illustrators knew well, as icons. My copy of Arthur Mee's *Children's Bible* published in 1926 had a reproduction of Reynolds' painting of the infant Samuel, kneeling, his hands clasped in prayer, his eyes clear and expectant, as he awaited the divine summons. I turned that page quickly, always with a thrill of not-quite fear. The prospect of being called in the night, and my trepidation at being expected to reply in the words of the text, stayed with me as a complex reading experience which I could not have explained at the time, but which I still recognize.

Children treat pictures in books with a kind of searching wonder. As they look, they have a particular need to pause, to seek things out. Artists understand this; they do it too. So they give the young readers a perspective, a place from which to look. Children who are encouraged to linger, to explore and to say what they see, teach the adults, who are inclined to rush on with the story, more than their glance grasps about the world of the artist and the writer. So, together, readers, artists and writers create the world of literate seeing.

I discovered this again when I listened to Josh retelling and re-creating his many versions of *Hansel and Gretel*. He had obviously looked carefully at Anthony Browne's 1983 illustrations of what is a very powerful story for preschoolers. In the opening pictures of the children at home with their parents, Anthony Browne includes three mirrors: one above the living-room mantelpiece, a second on a dressing table and the third on a wardrobe. Each reflects the room space where the artist expects the reader to 'be'. If the readers were really in the room, they would be looking at their mirror image; they would see themselves. Jane Doonan, who brought this to my notice, says, 'In the book it is what we do *not* see that reminds us that the space we occupy is the inner consciousness and not in the world of physical reality. We are inside the emotional event, not the woodcutter's cottage.'[6] I am inclined to say young readers discover how the mirror works by being, in imagination, alongside the characters in whose activities they explore their own need for both safety and adventure.

By illustrating in contemporary fashion a story which adults think they remember, Anthony Browne offers his young readers the excitement of their *felt* recognition of the plight of the children in the story. Adults have a different kind of confrontation with the pictures; they recognize Hansel and Gretel as children at risk. Browne also shows how the fixed icon of a page is quite different from the visual movement of television. Readers can take their own time to organize the meaning of the story by finding repeated motifs (the bars on the birdcage, the bedstead, the windows of the witch's cottage; the recurrent black triangle). In each successive work, *Bear Hunt, Gorilla, Knock Knock, Look What I've Got* and others, Browne uses his pictorial skills to draw the readers into his story so that they ask: who says that; who sees that? The result is, by the time they are ready to read *Alice in Wonderland*, he has taught his readers to *see*, in his illustrations, the surreal quality of Carroll's text.

For all that they seem to make reading easy by making it pleasurable, artist-illustrators and picture storytellers put young literates to work. They count on children's understanding of how a simple story goes, so that the readers can fictionalize themselves, especially where there are pictures and no words. Then they can extend their visual imagination in ways that later reading will demand. Jan Ormerod's *Moonlight* and *Sunshine* have family characters to guide the readers' recognition of familiar events, but the moods created by the artists' colouring of light and darkness are more important than what happens. Children experience the pleasure of reading before the tyranny of word recognition takes over. No book has been more successful than Raymond Briggs' *The Snowman* in capturing the imagination of its very young readers. Its translation to television and video recording, where it acquires music and movement, changes the still depth of the original. Yet the vitality of children's seeing is visible in the responses they make to both versions. Even two-year-olds who are too young to put the whole story together are active in their pursuit of the familiar image of the Snowman on socks, balloons, sweaters and even on birthday cakes.

Artists who work principally in the domain of children's picture books cross the boundaries of all modern media. Shirley Hughes' *Up and Up* is like a silent film. Her readers *see* flight as the result of her cunning adjustment of the readers' perspective, as subtle as any camera trickery. Shirley Hughes is adamant that children need to be encouraged to look as well as to see if they are not to become passive about images. In *Chips and Jessie*, a book for eight-year-olds, she mixes the conventions of the comic strip with a straight bookish text to show what pictures can do that text cannot. In the prose, the story comes out in the traditional linear sequence. In the pictures, events occurring at the same time—the scuttering of a hamster behind the kitchen pipes and the children's conversation about a spooky film—are presented simultaneously. Text and pictures together create the dramatic multiconsciousness that lies at the heart of Shakespearean comedy or a Marx Brothers film.

Author-artists teach young readers the myriad conventions of storytelling and make them memorable. They also show that stories can be changed. None do it better than John Burningham. In *Come Away from the Water, Shirley* the reader discovers two kinds of storytelling running together: the naturalistic narrative of a family day at the seaside and the imaginative fantasy of the child character's encounter with pirates, a story grown out of other stories. The lesson for the reader is that what seems ordinary in a story is just as much a convention of the telling as what appears as fantasy.

In a more recent Burningham book, *Where's Julius?*, the pictures take their revenge on the text. Mr and Mrs Troutbeck and their son Julius eat three meals a day. When each meal has been cooked and is ready for serving, a parent asks: 'Where's Julius?' The reply indicates what the artist then shows. Julius is building a house out of old curtains, chairs and the broom; digging a hole to get to the other side of the world; riding a camel up a pyramid; cooling hippos, watching the sunrise, throwing snowballs at Russian wolves and shooting rapids in South America, each picture more amazing than the one before. The narrative trick is: the story cannot be *retold* apart from an attempt to describe the pictures. When the readers are asked to say 'what happens?' they try to remember the sequence and details of the meals. The artist's double-page spread of colour, the events of Julius's imagination, are beyond words.

Children's illustrated books have a long history, but they have never before proliferated, as narrative fictions, as they do now. Stories in picture books have more disparate, mixed, more widely dispersed audiences than ever before. The books themselves are part of the debate about how reading should be taught. They also provoke contradictory kinds of criticism and appreciation, social as well as literary. They are a new kind of international currency since their short texts are easily translated. Within this apparently specialized domain, as the publishers and distributors decide what parents will buy for their children, we catch sight of what literacy looks like, especially to those who have a vested commercial interest in it.

For this enterprise publishers, distributors and parents have created the myth of 'what children like', by which they judge what children are to have. The fact is, children have to discover what stories in books *are like* before they know if they like them. In the early days of their literacy, when they are being read to, reading is an invitation to take part in storytelling activities where looking, listening, seeing and certain kinds of secrets go along with the inner speech of their thinking. The Ahlbergs, Janet and Allan, show how this works. In *The Baby's Catalogue* five families, together with the accessories of babyhood, are shown in pictures of breakfasts, dinners, teas, books and bedtimes. All the families have these events in common, yet they are all different. One family is Black. Every picture shows both sameness and difference, simultaneously. The suggestion is that all children can find themselves in the book by recognizing what they already know about the world. At the same time they discover what they have in common with others, despite the differences. We are beginning, or perhaps are a little further on in, the process of realizing that our multicultural society must find itself reflected in books for children.

The obligation that rests with all who make, produce and distribute children's books is not simply to ensure that all children are represented in them. It goes beyond the appearance of one Black child in a picture. The anthropomorphism of animals is quite usual in our culture. It is neither traditional nor comic in others. When we speak of children's books as a mirror of childhood, we have now to ask, 'whose childhood?'

Early story books introduce their young readers to the history of literature, or to selected parts of it. Maurice Sendak once said: 'It was Randolph Caldecott who really did put me where I wanted to be. Caldecott is an illustrator, he is a choreographer, he is a stage manager, he is a decorator, he's a theatre person; he's superb, simply.' Sendak, in producing books which children can read, also gives them a cultural memory. He isn't the only artist who does this, but the visionary quality of Sendak's work shows just how deeply the world of the picture story is embedded in childhood. Like William Blake he knows that reading a picture book is an experience where there can be no separation of means and ends; the reading *is* the experience. Sendak, again like Blake, helps children to see and to name the unseen, the fantastic, the Wild Things of their imagination. It is difficult now to believe that *Where the Wild Things Are* caused such a fluttering in the dovecots of the child psychologists when it first appeared. I simply remember how much my three-year-old laughed at the picture that reminded him of his grandmother. There was, of course, more to it than that.

Illustrated stories enhance the readers' vision; their seeing stretches to meet the artists' exploitation of their being good at looking. The story is an image; the images a story. I am

eternally grateful to Pat Hutchins for *Rosie's Walk* which has
taught hundreds of children that stories include what the
reader knows and what the text needn't say. Where, in the
words that set out the instructions to judges of the Emil
Award, 'text and illustration are of excellence and so
presented that each enhances yet balances the other',
children learn important lessons in literacy which are related
to the plenitude of literature. Picture story books make
possible the acquisition of literary cross-cultural conventions of narrative. Varieties of discourses and rhetorics,
as well as important ways of knowing and understanding,
come with the most universal of human practices, articu-
lating problems of the world as stories.

Not Only Stories

Stories are special because we spend much of our time telling
them and listening to them. Most of the books we 'get lost in'
are stories. Most adults can acknowledge the change of
consciousness that comes with reading a novel. We also
know that the different kinds of stories that adults prefer and
children learn to read are shaped by our social and cultural
values. I have never much enjoyed horror comics, but I
know that for some readers they represent the same kind of
'what if . . .' as Gothic novels which rank as literature.

Psychologists tell us that the 'alternative' worlds we create
in our imaginations, the stories we read or tell ourselves, are
necessary for our mental health. R.L. Gregory says that 'it is
living by fiction which makes the higher organisms special'.[7]
One glance at the lists in Sunday papers of the ways we
entertain ourselves confirms his view that 'society is created
by, and in turn creates, the fictions by which everyone of us
lives'. Nevertheless, we know that the idea that we construct
reality out of the stories we tell makes some people uneasy.

We understand children's need for stories to name the
unnameable in their lives, where giants are their full-sized
terrors, and characters like Hansel and Gretel and the Wild

Things stand for the complex, irreducible paradox of loving and hating at the same time. But there are other functions for storytelling about which we know much less. Argument, for example, dissent, disputation, the fierce language battles that we call quarrelling, are often attempts to construe events differently, to tell an alternative story about the way things happened.

How many times have we heard 'You did', 'I didn't', as a kind of slanging match? Before they know about the nature of chance or hazard, children expect what is *fair* to be controlled or brought to pass. They want to change another person's view of events, quickly. To argue successfully without physical violence, children learn to anticipate the point of view of their opponent, to see how he or she presents a situation. If a parent says, 'You can't go out, it's raining' the child counters this with 'Coat and wellingtons'. The parent's tale is that rain makes wet; the child's version is that this can be prevented. In fiercer debates with older children, some young ones are encouraged to stand up for themselves in ways that override forms of politeness. To make their view prevail, they are to be fiercer characters in their own story. Argument is often narrative before it is logic.

In some well authenticated accounts of children's development in literacy, especially the part that relates to their learning to read in school, there are strong statements about the need to read stories to children. I have mentioned this already, and suggested that the reading of continuous narrative prose offers children a language experience that is special, different from all others. But if we insist that literacy *depends* on children having stories read to them, then we may ignore forms of adult-child and child-child interactions that are importantly linked to learning to have one's say in the world on which, later, critical literacy depends.

CHAPTER 5
Schooled Literacy

We all believe we know about school because, with very few exceptions, we have all been there. Apart from birth and death it is our one common experience, although our memories of what happened are entirely singular. We look back on our education as *schooling*, convinced that it shaped our lives or, at least, made some difference to what came afterwards. School was where our elders taught us what they expected us to learn in the context of the literacy of that time and place. They also tested our potential for literate behaviour, passed judgements on our prospects, and arbitrated our opportunities. Our schooled literacy was shaped in a *class*, a word we also use for other groups, and separations, and differences.

In school, literacy is primarily associated with learning to read and write. This includes engaging with books and the different ways by which information is collected and stored. School changes life experiences—knowing that smoke goes upward, or that lightning heralds thunder—into the ordered language of school lessons and subjects. Children become pupils, apprentices to different ways of speaking and writing. They learn to frame their understandings by reflecting, classifying and formulating. To do this they trade their personal knowledge with their teachers by means of ordinary talk and listening so that it becomes a different way of learning. Reading and writing take them to libraries, the archives of what others have recorded, so that they discover different kinds of language, different experiences. Pupils discover how an early important enlightenment, that words *mean* something, later becomes a wider, more general understanding: what is said is not always what is meant.

Dickens immortalized the difference between schooled knowing and personal knowledge in his schoolmaster, Mr Gradgrind, who asked a school class, 'What is a horse?' Ignoring the experience of Cissie Jupe ('girl number twenty'), the horse trainer's daughter, he insisted on the definition:

> *Quadruped. Gramnivorous. Forty teeth, namely twenty-four grinders, four eye teeth, and twelve incisors. Sheds coat in the spring; in marshy countries, sheds hoofs, too. Hoofs hard, but requiring to be shod with iron. Age known by marks in mouth.*

The chapter in *Hard Times* in which Dickens depicts the interactions of pupils and Victorian schoolmasters is called 'Murdering the Innocents'.

Although those days are long gone, children still discover school learning as control and discipline. Asked to tell the class their 'news', even the youngest children know that this is a different kind of rhetoric from casual conversation: a prelude, in fact, to the more formal act of writing. However relaxed a classroom may now appear, teachers rely on language rituals to order the children's learning, and most parents are reassured by formal school behaviour.

In primary schools, reading and writing emerge in activities across the whole curriculum. In secondary schools, distinctive rhetorics, ways of writing, are associated with subjects: physics, biology, history. Literacy is embedded in the language of timetable activities and in the implicit rules for the exchange of information, questions and answers, as well as within the acts of reading and writing. Gradually, pupils adapt their classroom behaviours to accommodate the prevailing view of 'what counts as being able to *do* this subject?' This includes the process of learning how others have done it before them. They learn the rules of the process of *discourse*, the texts, reading and writing in the context of what they are expected to understand.

When we look back on our own schooldays, or watch children growing through their school experiences, we may well ask what part school lessons played in our being literate. The reading and writing exercises, questions and answers, worksheets, notes, textbooks, libraries, the bookishness of growing up, or our escape from it, all of these become blurred in memory as the years pass. How long after leaving school do we still remember what was said about our homework? Do we still base some of our judgements on something we significantly learned as relatively inexperienced readers? What did our schooled literacy add up to that we should see it, later, as important? Parents and teachers need to confront their own experience of childhood learning to see how literacy has changed.

I remember, clearly, the inevitability of examinations in June; the annual judgements. From the age of ten until twenty-three, my summers began in torment and ended in apprehension. The weight of books covered in pale blue paper from my uncle's drawing board (or brown paper from old parcels), packed hurriedly every morning into my solid leather satchel bumped against my legs as I ran for the bus. Once settled, I'd take out whatever had to be learned 'by heart': Latin or French verses, a geometry theorem, or, with luck, a poem. The bookishness of school both pleased and scared me. Although lessons centred my interests and enlarged my world, there was always the need to perform, to show in writing that learning has been accomplished. But I doubt if I ever thought about being literate as part of it all.

Literacy is not a school subject; it does not appear on any timetable as a lesson. Yet it links writing and learning with growth, development, and, more particularly, with imagination. We believe that children have to go to school in order to learn to read and write so that they may write and read to learn. But, plainly, that isn't the whole story. Little of the world's literate behaviour has, until recently, been part of schooled literacy. The essays and worksheets that children are required to write are rarely seen outside school. The books they read in subject areas: history, geography and science, are out of date in a decade. The reading and writing that pupils do in school are shaped by the purposes of schooling. Whatever counts as school learning has its own distinctive literacy that children are expected to learn as part of the 'subject'. When television replaces textbooks, even in a single science or geography lesson, schooled literacy changes.

All children have to adapt their behaviour to the conventions of a school class. For some, this is not a fundamental difference. The books are those they read at home. The teachers speak the same language as they do. For others, school is a different world, a different language. When the teacher asks, 'Was it raining when you came to school?' no one is absolutely sure at first whether the question is the beginning of a conversation, or the first move into a class topic on 'water'.

To become literate in terms of school, children have to learn the school's conventions for speaking (how you ask to go to the lavatory), for reading ('this is how we hold our books'), and for writing (the difference between 'rough' and 'neat'). In the reception class, pupils take time to discover that when Miss talks about reading, she means both what happens in the morning when, singly, the children read to her, *and* in the afternoon, when they sit on the mat and she reads a story to everyone. Gradually, as their confidence and discriminations increase, pupils learn to relate the topics of lessons to ways of writing and reading about them. Graph paper appears in mathematics and geography, or when the class keeps a record of rainfall in the playground. Reading and writing seem most ordinary in English lessons. But even then, letter writing has an unusual formality, and reading a story takes a long time because there are a great many questions to be answered.

Successful school literates are those who satisfy their teachers and become confident in so doing. They discover that books come in all shapes and sizes, to be flicked over, pored over, ignored, snatched, re-read as seems best at the time. Familiarity with *all kinds of discourses*, the languages of subjects, is the mark of school success. But behind it lies days and years of approval, of learning how to do what is required. The confidence that they know what reading and writing are *for* is what schooled literates carry into the world outside school.

In learning to read some children learn other lessons. There are certain standards of performance that regulate success or failure. This is a totally new experience, lifelong in its effects. There is no failure in childhood before school. So if they begin to tell themselves 'perhaps I won't be able to do this', children's views of reading change. Books are no longer fun; unfamiliar words bring unknown threats. The amount of reading practice needed for confident fluency is no longer pleasurable, and the stumbling uncertainties increase. Teachers begin to speak to them differently.

The education authorities who pay the teachers, decide the curriculum and monitor children's learning on a national scale, link schooled literacy with measurements of efficiency and appraisal: tests, assessments, examinations. The current words are: *targets, levels of attainment, account-ability*. In terms of education, literacy is the *result* of schooling. Therein lies its public significance.

We all know about the importance of school examination results. When we first visit our children's school we ask questions about how reading and writing are taught. Does this school get good grades? When are the children expected to read on their own? What can we do to help? When our children go to school for the first time our eyes are on the day they will leave. So when the reception class teacher shows us the playground and the arrangements for lunch, we want to see the books for reading and mathematics and to talk about homework, because our heads are full of apprehensions about the final judgement. How can we be indifferent to what teachers demand of children? How can we avoid being sized up by teachers as 'good' or 'indifferent' parents? So we watch over the intellectual progress of our young just as we care for their health because we know that the world's valuation of them comes with schooled literacy.

Teachers also worry about results. Their professional

reputations are bound up with them. Whatever happens, they are held responsible by parents and the authorities for their pupils' success or failure. So as more importance is laid on official measurements of children's progress and attainments, the more difficult it becomes for teachers to risk new ways of teaching or using new kinds of materials. Also, they are always beset by the obligation to balance the needs of individual children against the learning of the class as a group. Will that child's difficulty prove to be more than temporary? Does she need an extra lesson now? Is it worth trying out that new idea for writing in pairs that the advisor talked about, or will the parents complain to the governors that the bright children are being held back? In addition to their traditional obligations teachers are now to keep detailed records of pupils' performances and comment on them. Will their judgements be taken seriously? There is no single, simple relation between teaching and learning. Yet, in terms of results, most people persist in believing there must be.

Quite early in their careers pupils discover that approval is linked to marks and reports. The final judgements of schooled literacy, examination results, are written on important thick paper. These control where pupils, quite literally, *go* after school; to be workers, or to continue as students in universities, polytechnics, or training schemes. In the ranked hierarchy of our society literacy assumes a relation with power and money. But we never really ask how the literacy of an engineer is related to that of a poet, or how well those who market books have to be able to read them. The social results of schooling are part of a complex social system for evaluating and rewarding knowledge, yet we pay teachers very little.

We do even less to make continuing literacy a prospect or a real possibility for our young. From time to time as I bundled my way to secondary school I caught glimpses of what the life of the mind could be like. How did people know what events implied? How did they think about thinking? What did my parents and teachers mean when they talked about 'going on' in school? The consequences of literacy were never very clear to me before my last school years, except that most of my contemporaries became typists. I was employed for a month during a wartime summer in a government office as a clerk, copying the names and addresses of real workers from one completely stamped card to the front of a new one. My mind wandered so much that I made many mistakes and was considered inefficient. I knew that, after school, work of this kind was to be avoided.

Children learn to read and write as they are helped to learn. Schooled literacy carries with it an obligation to perform various literate tasks. But if this is all that results, then perhaps we need to look again at what we believe reading and writing are for, when we now present to the young the virtues and values of education in their clearly different world.

A Necessary Partnership

Today's parents and teachers are distinguished by the fact that they have been at school longer than any previous generation. They are also aware that they need each other; parents because they know that what counts as knowledge is defined by the school curriculum, teachers because they know that what children learn in school is only part of what children need to know. The necessary partnership of parents and teachers is defined by the lives of children and the social conception of childhood.

Their interests come together in the teaching of reading. Where once teachers guarded their expertise as a series of professional pedagogic secrets, now they are aware that if they are to make the most of what children have learned about reading before school, they must share with parents, both those who are well aware of schooled literacy and those who need to understand it, what happens in classrooms. In their turn, parents are more concerned about literacy in the early stages of their children's schooling than at any other time. They believe rightly, that success in reading in the primary school is the necessary foundation for all later school learning. If children quickly feel that they are successful readers in school, they believe they will be successful learners while they stay there.

Increasingly, over the last decade, books, magazine articles, TV programmes, educators and health specialists have offered advice to parents about the part they should play in their children's move to school and the support they should offer thereafter. As a result, a policy of 'openness' in education now seems normal. The legislation for governing schools includes the rights of parents to know how their young are being taught to read, write and to do mathematics. A more liberal exchange of details of life in school and life at home is becoming part of the ordinary processes of education.

There can be difficulties and misunderstandings. Although parents don't expect schools to be the same as in their recollections of their own school days, they want to see what they recognize as *results*; the kind of progress their children are making, and how they compare with others in the class seems, in the case of reading, to be demonstrable. So if there is no common class reading text and no test score for each child, parents are often disappointed with teachers. If teachers know that the means of instruction they use are innovative—reading a variety of books instead of a reading 'scheme', for example—they are sometimes reluctant to discuss what they do want with parents in case they arouse suspicion or hostility. Children sense disagreements between teachers and parents, even when they don't understand the cause. They also learn that they can disappoint both their parents and their teachers if they do not perform in ways expected of them. If the two sets of obligations conflict or confuse, the children are soon out of their depth.

Despite improved communications between home and school, each side may still expect too much of the other. Teachers complain about a lack of parental understanding of the difficulties of dealing with a class of thirty children and say that many parents overestimate their children's capabilities. Black parents point to racist stereotyping in the texts used for the teaching of reading. Working-class parents claim that not enough is expected of their children, and that in reading especially they should be 'stretched'. Mythologies about the differences between boys' and girls' reading competences confuse the scene even further. For different reasons, many people in all sections of the community feel that the education system is failing a large number of children in the teaching of reading and writing. The new laws that stamp the partnership of home and school as official are to be welcomed, but they will not, simply by appearing on the statute book, make much difference. A wider, more critical enfranchisement of all who are involved in education is still necessary.

What, exactly, do parents want in a partnership with their children's schools? Briefly, information, especially about what happens, and a chance to offer observations without seeming either aggressive or stupid. They want to know how reading and writing are taught, which books are read, what kinds of records are kept, and how progress is maintained. They also want to know how to help their children at home, and to understand some of the special terms that teachers now use: 'shared' or 'paired' reading, 'levels of attainment' and the other mysteries of new methods; 'real' books, for example. They also want to put their point of view without seeming to harass their children's teachers.

Teachers know that parents are most susceptible to the views of education that appear in the press or on television. They know that success is never news, but failure makes the headlines. If they could have more acknowledgement of their expertise from those who have benefited from it, if parents would sometimes say, loudly, that their children were being well taught, teachers would feel less harassed by ill-informed public opinion about education. When parents complain to the press about the way their children are being taught to read before discussing it with the school, teachers feel especially vulnerable. As we have said, the involvement of parents in their children's literacy is at its most intense at the early stages. A wise headmistress once explained it thus:

'When children begin school, to their parents reading is the whole school world and everything threatening in it.' Teachers know this. Many of them are also parents, so they understand the social and emotional pressures. They are also aware that their skill in introducing young readers to school reading can have a most profound effect. Many teachers want to discuss literacy with parents because they understand the concerns they share. They also want to offer advice where asked, to explain how reading is taught in class, and why the direct comparison of one child's performance with that of another is not always helpful in the first few settling-in months of school learning.

Partnership between parents and teachers, vital in the early stages of literacy, continues to be important as children's competences increase and their interests widen. Once children seem to be launched, that is, as their increasing skills match the school tasks that are presented to them, parents forget their earlier anxieties. Now they worry about which subjects the teachers think their children are 'good at'. They observe their children's enthusiasm for some homework tasks, their boredom with others. Some children escape from writing exercises as often as they can, others write reams. Where there is no sign of a product, a history essay, a geography fieldwork topic, completed mathematics exercises, parents again begin to worry. They know that success, what counts, is written evidence of learning: the command of mathematical symbols, map reading, science equations and English essays about literature. However remarkable teenagers' prowess on the playing field may be, their marks in the English examination will probably count for more in determining their future.

Too little is known exactly about how the beginnings of reading and writing are developmentally related to later learning. The evidence of how children become effectively literate could be collected from the records that will now have to be kept of their moves through school. My hunch is that this would be only half of the story. School learning emphasizes one kind of literacy, the schooled kind. But as this is still the kind that seems to be important, parents and teachers must welcome the opportunities offered by the new National Curriculum for more continuous discussions about what counts as progress.

An Historic Change: the National Curriculum

Literacy is always in the making. Each generation produces its own educational changes, its moves towards Utopia. Better schools are always just around the corner of the latest reading crisis or of the next government report. The optimism of advance in, say, modern writing technology—computers, thousands of coloured pens and print shops—or in the newest scheme for teaching reading is continuously set against evidence of school failure or the shortage of teachers.

The recent transformation of mass education in England and Wales from a localized to a centralized system, as set out in the Education Reform Act of 1988, will be more far-reaching in its effects than most earlier legislation on teaching and learning in school. This Act not only changes how schools are financed and governed; it also introduces a new National Curriculum, a set of ordinances about what *all* children are to be taught. A new school literacy has, formally, arrived.

A common curriculum for all schools is not a new idea. It has its roots in the nineteenth-century conviction that literacy taught in the formal conditions of school would make the poor more amenable to the necessary conditions of factories. Throughout this century, literacy has been directly related, in political terms, to the economics of production. (Assembly lines and piece work have much in common with certain kinds of reading lessons.) The Education Reform Act is more specific than some earlier legislation about what has to be taught in school as, in simple terms of amount, more of what counts as knowledge is now available in forms of public record. The puzzle is, what are we to tell all children that they are to learn? The problem is, how can they learn it and discover in the learning that the crucial lesson is to ask *their* questions about it? The ultimate test of schooled literacy is not being able to read and write. It is what we, or more possibly, our children, *do* with these abilities, these skills, these competences.

The new National Curriculum has three *core* subjects: English, mathematics and science. In addition there are *foundation* subjects; a modern foreign language, technology (including design), history, geography, music and art, and a *basic* subject, religious education, which all pupils must study. In all subjects there are *attainment targets*, objectives set out for pupils to reach. The targets are further divided into ten *levels of attainment*. At each *key stage*, ages 7, 11, and 14, and the end of compulsory education, pupils' competences are to be tested in two ways: nationally by *standard attainment tasks* and locally by *teachers' own assessments*. Each school will have its own development plan within the National Curriculum as a whole. Never before in our educational history has there been such a detailed plan for schooling literacy and learning.

As a school subject, English carries two kinds of responsibility: first, as the *standard* language to be learned by all pupils; then, as the medium for children's schooled learning of speaking, listening, writing and reading. So we can say that, after September 1989, to be literate in England and Wales is to fulfil the requirements of the attainment targets set out for Standard English. Both parents and teachers now have a common point of reference in law about *what* is to be learned. The *how* is, of course, left to the teachers to decide. They will also be held accountable to both officials and to parents for children's progress.

There is no doubt that this is an historic change. Never before has literacy in England been so closely schooled, so emphatically linked to the *delivery* of results. As I write, the planning and the implementation of the orders that form the passing of the Act have just begun: the moves are still to be made that will take the theory of the Act into the practice of schools, but undoubtedly, the political will seems to be there to enforce this legislation. Sadly, many good teachers who feel that the burden of its implementation is too great, have left the profession. The general principles of the Act to promote 'the moral, cultural, mental and physical development of children' so that they are prepared 'for the opportunities, responsibilities and experiences of adult life' will need the best kind of partnership between home and school that we can devise. Here are changes indeed. Whatever we feel about them they will become the reality of schooled literacy for children for many years to come. Although it is too soon to conjecture what will actually take place in classrooms, every parent must know what is proposed.[1]

Entitlement

The National Curriculum is announced as the *entitlement* of every pupil in maintained schools. (The independent schools can, as usual, do what they like. To keep their rolls full, however, they will have to get results comparable with those demanded of pupils in the public sector.) So, we are bound to ask what counts as every pupil's entitlement in literacy? As the word recurs in the official documents without exact definition, it is worth examination.

At the heart of all schooling in Britain are the inequalities that are implicit in everything we have said about being literate. We know that some pupils emerge from school with the authorized version of literacy, while others, who have attained the same national standard in examination results, have also been forced to meet the demands of school as an alien place, where their language and their culture have, in many subtle ways, been regarded as inferior. Thus, any discussion of schooled literacy as the *equal* entitlement of all is compromised from the start. Just as there is no common culture, there is no common attainable entitlement to literacy for all children, only the same recurrent uncertainty about how they get enough of the right kind to make a difference.

Entitlement is a deeply paradoxical idea. The word tucks ambiguity into every sentence that contains it. When it means giving someone the right to something, we wonder who confers the right, because this implies a kind of permission. So, can children have the fullest possible literacy that we want for them, or only what they prove they are worth? If literacy isn't an inalienable right but conditional on performance at 7, 11 and 14, who will say who the literate are? Who will judge the judges?

As a society we fudge public understanding of entitlement, as the word itself lets us do. We are made uneasy by the dilemma it raises for us. We ask questions such as: is a boy or girl at school in East London entitled to the literacy of an Eton scholar, given that the same abilities are proven in each? We know that it is not the gatekeeping effects of examinations that stand in the way of most children's progress to higher education. It is the stratified nature of a social life which our education system perpetuates. Powerful literacies remain in the hands of those who have social class as well as skills in common. In Britain, specialized literacies are available to very few compared with the numbers of other industrialized nations. This is what the National Curriculum is presented as seeking to cure. But, again, it is clear that, under the new arrangements, control of literacy is more visible than arrangements for its increase. Acknowledgement of entitlement is not a straightforward declaration of common rights but a continuation of differences.

To be serious about entitlement is to believe that every literate citizen has acknowledged worth in society. Just as all children come to school expecting to learn to read, so all pupils should see their literate accomplishments as extending beyond their days in school. Once they know that they in their turn will contribute to what counts as literacy, pupils are interested in its possibilities, its extensions, and progressions in a wider field of intellectual endeavour. At school they need experience of how this can come about.

I wonder, therefore, if we are to give our young literacy as a genuine entitlement, whether we may first have to dignify reading and writing as *labour*, work, a continuous learning process that is more than bookishness. My son-in-law is an engineer, an inventor, as was my father. I know very little of this literacy. Yet I cannot see an oil platform in the North Sea, mobbed by helicopters and waves, nor a Channel ferry with its freight of cars and passengers, nor can I fly in an aeroplane six miles above the earth without thinking of the precision of design and welding, mathematics and science, all the abstractions and crafts which are current important literacies. For me, they will remain a mystery, except perhaps as metaphors to describe the world we live with. But for the generation now in school, understanding of them is crucial for survival. The young have to learn the literacies that sustain them. So, when we visit schools for our children, look at their early reading books and ask about computers, we have to think of results as related to particular kinds of entitlement to engage with *future* literacies, as well as with the scribal and archival literacies of the past.

English in School

Nothing about English as a language, or as a symbol for other aspects of national identity, is unproblematic at this time. At the heart of all educational enterprises and worries is an awareness that English in school can become for some of those who speak it as their mother tongue, as well as for those who learn it as a second language, a source of failure. Not surprisingly, therefore, in preparation for bringing all schools into line by means of the National Curriculum, the Secretary of State for Education began by seeking to define what teachers and their pupils should know about English. Two groups of experts were summoned to do this bidding. A Committee of Inquiry (the Kingman Committee) proposed a *model* of English that would form the base of teacher training and of children's knowledge of the language of school. A working group on English in the curriculum (the Cox Committee) set the targets and levels of attainment as well as programmes of study for pupils from age 5 to 16. The implementation of both the model of English and the

programmes of study is left to the teachers: they become
responsible for the results.

The common point of reference and emphasis for both
committees was the nature, forms and functions of Standard
English; it is part of the pupils' entitlement. They are to learn it,
and 'if necessary' to be taught it. No wonder most parents and
teachers are worried. Whose English counts as 'Standard'?

According to the Cox Report, Standard English is a
dialect which has 'historical, geographical and social
origins', although with variations it now has 'world-wide
use'. (Cox leans firmly on the idea of English as a world
language, perhaps to avoid the more blatant ethnocentrism
of Kingman.) 'Dialect', says Cox, 'refers to grammar and
vocabulary but not to accent.' (That is, you can speak
Standard English with a Cockney as well as a Chelsea
accent.) 'It is not to be confused with "good" English.
Speakers of Standard English can use English just as badly
as anyone else . . . It is, however, a social dialect, that is the
native [my italics] language of certain social groups.' In ways
like these, officials who write reports wriggle round the
differences and distinctions of social class so as not to say
that the powerful users of Standard English are those whose
'native' language is the important one. Parents of working-
class and bilingual children know this only too well.

Like 'entitlement', *standard* is a word that hovers between
meanings. When it doesn't signify a flag or a rallying point
(as in these debates it well might) it is used to indicate 'an
accepted or approved example'. So, those who speak
Standard English as natives are to be the model for others.
As we know, some members of this group, aware of their
superiority, do not hesitate to excoriate, in newspapers or
other public media, those who speak the other dialects and
languages of Britain.

In the past, teaching about language in school was mostly
instruction in the formal patterns of grammar. Both of the
new reports emphasize that this teaching was based on poor
models of linguistic structure long since abandoned by
linguists. In its place they propose that pupils should learn

'some form of analysis (which may be more or less explicit)' which is 'part of the interpretation of texts and of the production of accurate writing; a grammar which can describe language in use.' The Cox Report devotes most space to this topic so as to make plain the principles underlying the programmes of study. The emphasis is on the pupils' own linguistic competence and what they implicitly know about language. The teacher's task is to 'help children to systematize knowledge which they already have on evidence which they collect.'

It all seems reasonable, except, of course, that children's understanding of language, spoken or written, implicit or explicit, is never neutral, never detached from the feelings of the users. Those who do not speak Standard English as 'natives' are not bound to find rational the arguments of others that they should learn it. Children will learn Standard English if they want to; experience makes this plain. Their parents will want them to, because they know what depends on it. But there may be a great deal of confusion ahead for children, especially if the intricacies of the Kingman model and the Cox Report become a series of attainment tests. Parents who take their children to school for the first time knowing that the language they speak is not the one that counts in school have different views of entitlement to Standard English from those for whom the official language is part of their inheritance.

Knowledge about language, however described or made mandatory, implies at all times that speakers, readers and writers have intentions and purposes for its use which are living acts of communication. The teachers' basic task is not to examine children's language, not even to invite children to examine it, but to extend and enrich children's experience of it in both speech and writing so that their *intuitions* about language use can be transformed into more developed awareness. All teachers, at all levels in school, must engage in this kind of activity where English is the language of learning or teaching. If not, their teaching will be unsuccessful.

Advanced awareness of language is related to its meaningful use in a variety of contexts. To be literate in terms of language awareness is to be able to differentiate genuine meanings from spurious ones; to understand others' meanings; to observe and describe the way language is used to persuade and to seem 'reasonable'; to conduct arguments, and to confront with confidence difficult experiences of speaking, writing and reading. Schooled literacy depends on pupils' understandings of language in interaction with social behaviour. To learn about language in use, pupils have to engage with different kinds of analysis and interpretation. In this whole area, questions of *gender*, the differences between girls' and boys' learning, assume particular importance.

In the course of time, the official documents which outline the National Curriculum will become historical documents for students of literacy. But those who read them as archives may never know that many teachers, on whom the whole enterprise effectively depends, are dismayed by the conservative, conformist nature of the model of language thrust upon them. They are critical of some of the standard attainment tasks (SATS). The Curriculum as it stands cannot by itself guarantee that children's language is enriched and enlarged, or their literacy made effective. This is a quotation from the Cox Report.

> *A democratic society needs people who have linguistic abilities which will enable them to discuss, evaluate and make sense of what they are told, as well as to take effective action on the basis of their understanding . . . Otherwise there can be no genuine participation but only the imposition of the ideas of those who are linguistically capable.*

This reads like a statement supporting our notion of critical literacy. Now, ask yourself what you understand by: *what they are told* in terms of *the imposition of ideas*. Who are the *linguistically capable*? For all its apparent reasonableness, the National Curriculum with the documents that define it, support it and make it mandatory have to be read in the context of what kinds of literacy-as-results are expected from it. As always, these will depend on measurements used and what counts as evidence.

Attainment and Assessment

One glance at the proposals for English 5–16 in the National Curriculum makes plain that never before in our history of mass education has such detailed attention been given to what children are to learn and how their progress is to be assessed and monitored throughout their time in school. A specially commissioned Task Group on Assessment and Testing has identified the key stages: age 5–7 (stage 1); 7–11 (stage 2); 11/12–14 (stage 3) and 14–16 (stage 4). (At present, the General Certificate of Secondary Education (GCSE) examinations remain as the exit mode for pupils leaving school.) These stages have within them ten levels of attainment, each describing what pupils should be able to do in order to reach the attainment targets set for them. These descriptions are linked to programmes of study which are expected to form the basis of what teachers will teach, or what, at ages 7, 11 and 14, will be examined.[2]

The demand made by parents that they should know what is expected of their children has been met. In English, the attainment target for speaking and listening is: 'the development of pupils' understanding of the spoken word and the capacity to express themselves effectively in a variety of speaking and listening activities, matching style and response to audience and purpose.' From level 7 (key stage 4) pupils should be using Standard English, whenever appropriate, to meet the standards of attainment. In reading the final target is: 'the development of the ability to read, understand and respond to all types of writing, as well as the development of information-retrieval strategies for the purposes of study.' For writing it is: 'a growing ability to construct and convey meaning in written language, matching style to audience and purpose.' There are targets also for spelling and handwriting at the earlier stages.

Are these sound definitions and exemplifications of being literate in terms of school? In the years to come, everyone involved will have to decide. The schooling of all children will be overshadowed by the processes of 'delivery' of these competences. In the closely detailed proposals for attainment levels in the Cox Report, *should* is the word most used. The chapters which deal with Standard English, knowledge about language, linguistic terminology and assessment are much longer than those chapters on literature, drama, media education, bilingual children, equal opportunities and special educational needs.

It is not the purpose of this book to comment at length or in depth on the National Curriculum. But since for years to come it will define schooled literacy, it is important to see some of its limitations. It will also be the prescriptive source of Standard Attainment Tasks by which children's schooled literacy will be weighed and measured because of the statutory requirement that literacy in school must be seen to have been 'delivered'.

Here lies the crucial difficulty. No language process develops in a linear fashion, incrementally, step by step. Children may learn mathematics in this way, but speaking, listening, writing and reading develop *recursively*, in a spiral. Noteworthy research confirms what we all experience. We are all learning language and literacy all the time. So, if language development is recursive, *levels* of attainment can be only a rough guide. Parents need to understand this. Throughout their children's time in school the records relate to ripening language functions; they cannot measure exactly the size or weight of the final fruit.

Teachers know this. So the challenge of the National Curriculum lies in the opportunity it offers to teachers to assess and record what they see as their pupils' progress. Ample evidence of the kind that no formal examination produces and no standardized test admits is already available and thus has to be made to count as evidence of how children come to be literate. The incentive for teachers is to make this evidence *count*.

Here is an example borrowed from Dennis Carter, a teacher and writer, who is head of a junior school in Wales. He believes that

> Language is not normally learnt outside of the life which it serves. A language course cannot be successful if conceived of as a sort of greenhouse or coldframe to bring along linguistic seedlings before transplanting them into the real world . . . In this class we had two nine-year-old twins, one girl, one boy, who came into my class from another school on the opposite side of the country. She was bright, lively and good at getting things right. If I'd taught to a programme with an 11+ assessment test, she would have registered a high score. Her brother, on the other hand, was lazy, acted silly and sat there, grinning when referred to. The test would have condemned his English. Two children, from the same womb at the same time, arrived in my class as diverse a pair of children as could be imagined. True to expectations, the girl began to succeed in my class and the boy to fail. During our walks, however, new things began to emerge about the twins. Out of school in field or village the boy was animated. It was a common practice for the children to settle down and write about objects and places of their own choice. This became a much loved activity. The girl soon got cracking and produced pleasant little pieces very quickly. The boy would stand staring at things for long periods. Was he lazy? Was he confirming all the reports, written and spoken, that had arrived in his wake like messages of doom? This was clearly not the case from the very first walk when he wrote:

> *Kissing-gate*
> *Along by the kissing gate*
> *surrounded by nettles*
> *blackberries are kissed*
> *by tempted wanderers*
> *for their lips are dark*
> *but also delicious.*

There are other examples kept by Dennis Carter, an observant, highly skilled teacher who records and understands language, life experience, and growth as learning. This young poet's sister has discovered what counts as schooled literacy. His verse outstrips it. So when we think that a tighter legislative grasp on reading and writing, listening and talking, will get better results, better literacy in the world, we must also ask if it may not. But more examples of this kind of recording, such as we haven't yet seen, might make a difference to our understanding of the recursive nature of language processes and how their growth may be promoted and nurtured.[3]

The first sign of such evidence is already so clear, so powerful it must be included here. By 1988 a group of London teachers and advisors in the Centre for Language in Primary Education had devised, piloted and published a Language Record for use in primary schools. Its function is to help teachers to structure their observations of their day-to-day encounters with children's talking, reading and writing. They also record interviews with both parents and individual children where their views of the task of learning to read and write are explored. The activities of bilingual pupils are given special attention. This cumulative record describes the details of progress which come from the children's activities in learning, from the parent's help and from the teacher's understandings. It also encourages the children to assess their own development. As a result, teachers discover how to observe their own interactions with pupils, the particular texts used in class, and to reflect on the nature of children's progress in reading and writing from the efforts of all who are involved. The Primary Language Record will change what comes to be regarded as evidence of what literacy is, not least because it comes from where the evidence *is* in the reading and writing lives of children, their parents and their teachers.[4]

Evidence of this kind has been available before now only in specialized research. Now it offers a means of both assessment and forward planning related to the actualities of learning. The words of children count. ('The story here stayed in my head all week, even when I was playing with my friends, even when we were singing a pop song.') Fluency, in both reading and writing, so necessary to explain and yet so difficult to describe, can now be distinguished in terms of the teacher's longitudinal observations of children's literacy experiences both at home and in the classroom. Everything in this kind of record-keeping is explicable to parents. The appraisal sheets of the record itself demonstrate that, in these terms, teachers are willing to take great pains to be accountable for schooled literacy. Indeed, in this account of teaching and learning, the barriers between school literacy and the uses of literacy in the world outside are already crumbling.

Records of teachers' assessments will be kept in conjunction with the national results of Standard Attainment Tasks. The Curriculum recommendations for the assessment of language competences are that 'the widest practical range and types of tasks and setting should be used'. But the adopted form of any universal test is that which is cheapest to produce and easiest to administer. From experience we also know that standardized tests of any kind have a direct influence on teaching procedures, and bring about a concentrated parental focus on results. So the paradoxes and dilemmas of schooled literacy may be changed or lightened, but they are rarely removed by different approaches to teaching, learning or assessment.

There is no doubt that school literacy is, again, at a crossroads. The effects of centralized administration of the education system and the control of teaching and learning by a National Curriculum with its emphasis on assessment (payment by results) may be offset, in some degree, by increased parental involvement and the wisdom of the advisory services. But the ideological stranglehold of Standard English betrays a strange indifference on the part of those responsible for the National Curriculum to the powerful actuality of language diversity in Britain. When the Kingman Report says that 'Standard English is the great social bank on which we all draw and to which we all contribute', the metaphor leaks out the old idea that public education must, above all, be both cheap and efficient. As one commentator remarked, 'Why is it that some people are forced to borrow at exorbitant rates while their own currency lies valueless in a sack underneath the mattress?' In this context, entitlement seems something of a hollow promise.

Nevertheless, there is evidence that schools can actively intervene to reduce cultural inequalities by organizing themselves for literacy in something more than the minimal sense. Partnership with parents, a revised kind of accounting, and an understanding of the ways by which children learn all kinds of social and literary discourses and texts will make a difference.

Every school has a view of literacy. If it isn't spelt out in a prospectus it can be discovered in the classbooks, the materials used in lessons, the state of the library and the book stock, and in the school's understanding of children's growth in language. The institution itself is decipherable, to be judged by the state of the notice boards, the lists and the writing on the walls. Whatever the head teacher says, children learn what counts as literacy in the place where they are expected to learn it. It is crucial, therefore, that teachers, parents and children know and discuss what they believe are the important reading and writing lessons.

CHAPTER 6

Important Lessons

If the beginnings of literacy have important consequences, should we not be able to make sure that, in the early stages, all children should experience the kind of success which will give them confidence for the rest? If stories are special, are there special ways of making them part of reading experience? If schooled literacy is what counts in the public estimation of literates, what must parents, teachers and others do to ensure as well as to demonstrate each child's competence? Can the partnership of school and home be collaborative enough to keep good records of children's progress? But if, as is indeed the case, there is no single common literacy, and no one way by which literacies are acquired and developed, what, then, are the important reading and writing lessons that secure, powerful literates have learned? Is the standard of literacy that politicians and those who write letters to newspapers say should 'rise', always just out of reach of most people and likely to remain so?

These questions are constantly being asked and answered. No one can guarantee literacy in advance, like interest on a bank deposit. I persist in believing that there are important and discernible reading and writing lessons which have to be learned for literacy success, although not all of them are taught in school. Joy, pleasure, delight in reading seem to be the best guarantee that a confident beginner will continue to thrive. But in the recursive processes of all learning there are breaks and gaps. A disappointing experience in school, mocking by less enthusiastic adolescent peers, for example, can turn the reading of novels or writing a diary into secret activities unnoticed by teachers who write reports. Confidence is easily shrivelled by 'don't tell me you read *that!*'

Tests and examinations play their part in constraining literacy. Those who learn they can fail are often difficult to encourage. Official tests are not designed to let as many pupils as possible do as well as they might, but to discover what proportion of the population does well, averagely or badly. No one is surprised when the children of the poor, the disturbed, the homeless, appear at the bottom of the results table, although many of this group also succeed against the odds. National statistics on literacy standards are always related to policy decisions about money for education.

Those who, like me, want a high level of literacy for all, however this is envisaged, have to confront this question. Do we believe that there should be a significant advance in the *quality* of modern literacy, in the new competences and skills to be displayed by the population as a whole? Or do we expect that an already established high level of literacy— that of specialized literates in the learned professions, of the international business élite with its scribal entourage and publicity experts, and of senior Civil Servants—should be made available to more people? This is where the continuing debate about what are the important reading and writing lessons is at its most acute.

What, then, can be done to help children to read and write as effectively as possible? The first thing is to recognize that no lessons, no teaching method, no special books will be effective without the learners' own will to use reading and writing for what seems to them to be important in their own context. At first, children learn to read as part of the more general business of being at home in the world. This includes pleasing adults who show, in significant ways, their enthusiasm for their children's achievements. Later, children have to learn to read and write both to please themselves and to achieve what they desire. After they have learned to read, many people choose to do no more, and yet are not visibly, or in their own estimation, illiterate.

What do adolescents who are about to leave school willingly engage with as literacy events in the contemporary world? Journalism, mostly: the fast-moving, constantly changing writing that they read as if it were talk. Watch them flip through magazines, listen to chat shows, interviews, commentary, know-how as speech. They seem to read with greatest ease and confidence the prose that implies a *knowingness* in its readers about the subject matter—pop records or sport, conservation, politics or fashion. In the same context, pictures, photography, design images and the immediacy of computer text (which the readers' acquaintance with television has made 'natural') connect readers quickly with information. So swiftly does all this happen, with boredom kept well at bay, that readers are not easily made aware of all the writing in the back-up that generates this quick-fix literacy; the managerial files, the plans of electronics engineers, the book-keeping of bankers, the editorial skills of producers, publicity designers and printers.

Young people are exasperated by the plodding textual grind of some school reading. They respond most willingly to invitations to engage with adult topics. They learn to sample and to reject reading matter. If they are encouraged, they experiment with writing, socially or secretly. If they are ever impressed by skill in reading and writing they show very little sign of it, probably because they rarely see their elders being glad to write even letters. Occasionally they may take note of confident fluency. 'How do you know what to say when you write to someone you've never seen and don't know?' I was asked. With twinges of conscience I wonder how my children learned to write cheques, letters of praise or complaint, job applications. Where did all this word-processing competence emerge from? Do all adults forget how literacy in adolescence is a whole networking of skills held in common outside both home and school, derived in part from popular literature and culture?

Many teachers are curious to see the children they taught to read emerging, unexpectedly sometimes, as confident adult literates. A shy, stammering, hesitant six-year-old I knew who desperately wanted to be a footballer but had little physical prowess now writes much admired match reports in a national newspaper. He went to more games than seemed good for him in his teens and read only the sports sections of the press. Someone helped him to read and write more than I did, but it was his passion for the sport that kept him going long enough to learn the important lessons.

Not all reading is solitary, not all writing is a lonely grind. Some of the excitement of a publishing house, a newspaper office, a television studio can be generated in a classroom if the tasks, the talk, the information, the interests of the learners are linked to the production of something written to be read. Confident literates learn their lessons in the company of those who share topics of concern. They read one another's writing; they lend each other books. They argue. In the end, as the result of reading all kinds of written language they acquire skills that are *textual*. That is, they read on to the end of a story, an article, a book, and thereby discover how these texts are made, built up, organized, constructed. When they learn to write, they keep going past the end of the first sentence, paragraph or page. They understand that written language is cohesive; it links ideas, events, thoughts, in different ways, creating worlds for readers to remake as they understand what is meant. Different contexts, they know, produce different texts. Even when alone, readers and writers are in a dialogic relationship with writers and readers. Why do I persist in repeating these things? Because I know, only too well, that these are the lessons the inexperienced readers put off learning, or are never helped to grasp.

Will you believe me if I suggest that the need for textual understanding is inherent in picture books we have already looked at, those that children read with adults before they go to school? The child who understands that she and the author of *Rosie's Walk* know that the fox is chasing Rosie but Rosie may not know, has already begun to learn the distinctive kind of sharing that readers and writers engage in. However, if some well-meaning adult were to attempt to

explain this to a five-year-old, the result might be bewilder-
ment.

Informal Lessons

Children *feel* reading; first as the closeness of the reading
adults, later as a heady independence. In the beginning,
adult and child withdraw to the world of the story, where a
tiger comes to tea, bears eat porridge or toys play in the park
in the dark. To keep this reading world intact, the story must
go on to the end. The important lesson of how to deal with
continuous prose is learned from the desire to discover what
happens next.

Writing, which begins as drawing, creates patterns that
turn into both words and worlds. The early important
writing lessons begin with the exploratory handling of tools:
pencils, crayons, markers, brushes, paint. Children then
move in two directions: to reproduce the print they see in the
world, and to move their fingers experimentally in order to
see what shapes may become. The lessons of early writing lie
in the balance of trying to represent the world in pictures,
and learning the rules, the alphabetic notation, to make
words *appear*. When Ben writes his name at the bottom of a
picture he has drawn, he indicates that he knows how both
kinds of writing work. Incidentally, names are more than
writing; they are sympathetic magic. Children practise
writing their names and those of others as if they are calling
into being the people they represent.

Reading and writing come together in patterns of language
that are memorable. Children begin to learn them as body
rhythms. Think of how cradles and lullabies complement each
other. (Why did we ever give up the beautiful economy of
someone singing, rocking the baby to sleep with a foot while the
hands do something else?) Here is Sam at eighteen months
fully intent on the delight and desire that take over a young
child as he listens to the rhythmic tale of how Parrot told Snake,
Snake told Bear, Bear told Giraffe, Giraffe told Crocodile,

Crocodile told Lion, Lion told Elephant, and they all told the Hunter, 'Go home'. As the last page comes near, Sam tenses his muscles, holds his breath, then relaxes, and says 'Again!'

Children are wound into the enactment of the events of the story by the formality of the text. For beginners this works by repetitions: *Little pig, little pig, let me come in. No, no, by the hair of my chinny chin chin.* The lessons are about two kinds of dialogue: the talk of the characters in the story, and the more subtle, less explained dialogue of the reader and the storyteller. Children learn both kinds as they begin to read a known text on their own. First of all they join in with the reading adult to keep up the momentum of the story. Then they try it by themselves. We have already touched on the important reading lesson by which children become both the teller and the told. Everyone who has done this successfully knows what it means. The problem is to ensure that it has been learned. The quickest way to discover if children understand how a story goes is to give them all the time they need to retell it to a sympathetic listener.

Before they go to school children implicitly know that what occurs in stories needn't be part of their expectations of what happens every day. Pigs do not go to market; the cow does not jump over the moon. But it is possible to say that they do in the comfort of the nursery-rhyme word play. The research spotlight has again fallen on nursery rhymes because they offer significant examples of the spoken sounds of our language, and the different ways of spelling them in writing.

Children who have heard many stories and read picture books with adults learn the most important lesson of this stage: what a story *is*. They learn it as they learn to play games, by discovering the rules. Some stories are predictable. 'Once upon a time' means 'don't expect this story to work as the ordinary world works'. But five-year-old Marie who is looking with her teacher at a picture of the old woman who lived in a shoe hasn't yet learned it. 'Is that your Nan then?' she asks. Confused by the child's unexpected suggestion that a nursery-rhyme character could be her grandmother, the teacher brushes aside what she sees as a distraction. Marie is left with her puzzle about the relation of story people and events to those of everyday life.[1]

Why is this important? On the day that my research colleague told me about Marie and her teacher I saw a political cartoon which showed Members of Parliament crowded into a large old boot. The assumption of the artist was that readers knew the rhyme of the old woman who lived in a shoe as part of the culture of their English-speaking childhood. That understanding, central to making meaning of the cartoon, is a cultural assumption. Learning to read includes becoming acquainted with the materials that a culture uses to construct its worlds of fiction. Less obvious is the fact that some children are actually *taught*, informally, but directly, by parents or teachers, to interpret stories as *stories* and not as the world. Marie needs to know that there are old ladies in stories as well as in her family if she is to understand what her teachers will expect her to. At this stage Marie knows that print makes meaning, but isn't sure what kinds of meaning she is expected to make. More stories would make the conventions clearer. What Marie teaches adults around her is that reading involves a particular kind of *knowledge* of these conventions, of the rules of the game.

The concern of the most interesting writers for children is to distract their readers from an over-reliance on the traditional rules. In Anthony Browne's picture book, *Bear Hunt*, there is a page on which two colonial-style hunters are creeping up on Bear, a white teddy with a secret smile, who is walking in a luxuriant forest. He is carrying a pencil. The hunters are poised to snatch him. Young readers don't seem to want to know what the hunters are up to, but why Bear has his pencil. The words on the page are 'Look out, look out, Bear!' The children now ask, 'Who says that?' The reader didn't make up that cry; it's there, on the page. But the hunters didn't say it. Who, then, knows what to write that Bear needs to hear?

It is possible for the adult to explain all of this fantasy in everyday terms: what hunters do, that Bear never goes anywhere without his pencil, and so on. But that's not the *communicative act* of the story. The force of the sentence is not to make these strange story activities familiar in terms of everyday life. Instead it is to alert the *reader* to the fact that the next page will show something unexpected: Bear will draw a tripwire for the hunters to fall over. The correct resonance is, 'This is a trick kind of story'. Thus the reader acquires a particular kind of knowing-about-a-story that can be learned only by reading this text and these pictures.

This is the discovery of the *multiconsciousness* that fiction makes possible. Readers progress as they become more aware of the nature of this kind of knowing. When adults read and share stories like *Bear Hunt, Come Away from the Water, Shirley, The Little Mouse Who Got Lost in a Book* and *The Park in the Dark* they seem to know, instinctively, what the inexperienced reader needs to understand. They don't overload the learner with explanations that distract from the complete act of reading the story, the most important lesson of all. What the reader has to learn is *how it goes*. This is the play for real we have already discussed.

Writing, we know, begins as play, experiments with scribbles and drawings. Somehow this is always more relaxed than reading. Parents are more content to wait for schooldays to begin, before they worry about 'real' writing, although now, with the pressures of attainment reckonings in mind, more children are being urged to form letters correctly before they go to school.

The important lessons of schooled literacy, 'getting it right', are in the teachers' demands for performance. But many children come to school with quite clear understandings of reading and writing which school lessons do not confirm. In the transition from home to school the learners' confidence, the feeling of 'I think I'll be able to do this', is the lesson, once learned, that lasts longest.

Formal Lessons and Classroom Informalities

Schools still seem very formal places to those who aren't used to them. The buildings give this impression; the classrooms, timetables and rules of behaviour do the rest. Although parents are now seen more often in classrooms and corridors (I doubt if I ever saw mine inside my schools), and cups of tea appear in meetings with the Head, school learning is still expected to be structured according to a pattern that has children's development, progress, increase of knowledge at its heart. Where teachers say that they have a formal style of teaching reading because 'the parents expect it', they are right if they mean 'we must show that we take reading seriously'. They may also be saying that children's orderly behaviour in class makes their teachers feel more secure.

Learning in classrooms can be both formal and informal. Children who are new to a school listen to what the teacher tells them to do. They also look to see how other children behave. They enter into reading and writing activities by matching what the teacher says with what their friends actually do. Classrooms are little communities; the ordering of the life of the group is marked out in social terms. New pupils want to know if they are being recognized as learners.

As soon as reading lessons start, children sense a new seriousness. Now the teacher's instructions have a different tone. The rituals for handling books, opening and shutting them, are more precise. While the teacher wants the learners to do what she says, her pupils are trying to discover 'what counts as reading in this class'. If they think that what they already know won't appear as significant, they hear the instructions and think 'Perhaps I won't be able to do this'.

Early formal school lessons include knowing how the lessons are organized, what the seating arrangements imply (is the green table for the good readers only?), how to read to the teachers, what kinds of questions are allowed. What does 'sound out the first letter' mean? How do you 'have a go' at the story? Alongside formal operations with texts, which come with explanations, there are informal understandings about choosing books, commenting on the story, telling it in the way that pleases the teacher, all of which are culturally transmitted as classroom behaviour leading to independent reading with confidence.

What *has* to be learned? By the end of two school years children are expected to know that written language makes sense. The outward and visible sign of this comes from the reader's reproduction of the text, sometimes as reading aloud the words on the page, sometimes as the retelling of the story or incident. Most children learn to do this in two ways: by matching what they see to what they say, or by increasingly approximating their understanding of the text as a whole to the production of the words of the text. But how they do these things varies according to their view of the task in hand. Those who do exact matching go slowly and avoid mistakes. Those who work from their understanding of the text as story often substitute words in their concern to keep the reading going (*house* for *home*; *girl* for *sister*). They discover their miscues and retrack their reading to get it right. The most influential lessons that teachers have learned in the last fifteen years is that by examining children's mis-matching of what they see and what they say teachers can discover *how* children go about making meaning from texts.[2]

However the first formal reading lessons are organized, even if they seem to be informal, all children come to believe that to read in class is to say aloud exactly what is written on the page. They do this more easily if the text has already been read to them; they know how the story goes. But to be considered a real reader, especially by their parents, children understand they have to show an increasing aptitude for 'getting right' a new text, one where they are to go it alone from the start. The trouble is, very few experienced readers actually do that. Unfamiliar text always has within it, even for the practised reader, the elements of a test.

No responsible teacher would suggest that, in reading lessons, children can ignore what is written for them to read. But many have come to understand the nature of 'approximations' in the beginnings of both reading and writing. These occur in all learning until there is a degree of secure mastery.

There are still fierce debates about how reading should be

taught and learned. Over-emphasis on teaching methods obscures what children actually do in response to invitations to behave like readers and writers. We should turn our arguments about how to teach reading into a consideration of the different ways (sometimes called 'strategies') of approaching different kinds of texts that children need to learn. As the concern of this book is to promote literate behaviours from the beginning of social life, what follows is a simple list of such behaviours in early schooldays. Reading is a child's first significant experience of schooled learning. To fail to read is to fail to learn; therein lies the risk, the danger which children sense even if they do not fully understand it.

I believe that formal reading instruction from specially written, numerically staged materials is *not* a more *structured* way of teaching reading than one where children are invited to read books from a range of different texts. Reading progress shows itself in many ways, not least in the children's confidence, in a diversity of linguistic abilities, the different ways in which they approach or tackle different kinds of texts and in all that is listed here. Remember, our belief is that language learning is recursive not linear. In the end, the most important lesson children learn is that they can read and, therefore, that they can learn.

Here are the lessons formally or informally learned that *begin* in the first two years of primary school and appear recursively at later stages:[3]

— A growth in independence: picking up a book and behaving like a reader in ways that are recognizable, such as turning the page, and 'reading' a picture book through to the end, and knowing the contents as a story.

— Asking questions of an adult without fear of rebuff.

— Making appropriate responses to books read to the class as a whole.

— Retelling the story with increasing fluency.

— Expecting a text to make sense; not hesitating or having difficulty because the meaning is totally obscure and only to be grasped with effort.

— Re-reading a known text.

— Attempting an unknown text with the help of an adult without fear.

— Asking their own questions: taking the initiative in discussions.

— Understanding that there are different tones and ways of reading that correspond to different kinds of writing.

— Showing interest in print forms: capital letters, italics, bubble print (in comics and elsewhere).

— Making stories from pictures in sequence; following the line of print from left to right.

These are not in any developmental order, nor do they all appear every day in every lesson. Some children show strengths in particular understandings: some are more specially confident. But like all other learning, reading has to be a continuous activity where different aspects of the process interact with each other. Without confidence, readers cannot gain experience. Without interaction with many kinds of texts, they do not know that there are many different ways of approaching different kinds of writing. If there is no growth in their understanding of print in the world and in books, and of the nature of the dependence of the one on the other, how will they ever have reading adventures? Without reading adventures and surprises, when will they think about what they are doing? The child who asks 'Who says that?' about 'Look out, look out, Bear!' has taken at the very beginning, the first step in the kind of inquiry that turns all learning into knowledge, conscious reflection or *reflexiveness*.

After two years of formal schooling the most significant differences in children's learning are those of reading *style*. Some learners want to find out how the story *goes*; what happens to the characters and whether or not all is well at the end. They explore many books and different kinds of texts with the same involvement. They are prepared to take risks with unfamiliar words so as to deduce the sense from the complete reading act. Others seem to move more slowly, or to be interested in different things. They want to be sure what the words 'say' because they believe that the words, the letters, the print are important. Their satisfaction lies in discovering patterns: what turns 'go' into 'going' or 'love' into 'lovely'. They take fewer risks and tend to unlock meanings by reading in a linear mode. Both roads lead to reading competence because, in the end, good readers know that both the complete text and the parts of it are important for the meaning. The teacher's problem is to know how to use the different strengths of each reading style in order to match her instruction to children's different views of the task she has set them. To believe that a single teaching method will always do for all is to ignore what best helps children to learn.

By the time they are due to leave their primary school all children should have a wide experience of different kinds of books. The supply of these usually depends on the parents' interest or the school book fund, but children are adept at seeking books out for themselves. Local libraries and bookshops should also be part of the scene. Those who know what reading is good for are usually enjoying books at three levels of competence *simultaneously*. They know which books they can read without difficulty. They return to their favourites, the books that represent reading pleasure. They follow the class texts with moderate ease, fitting what they read into the topic of the lessons, or varying their sources of information to discover new ways of expressing what they know. At the same time they are looking ahead to the books they will read next: something they want to know more about, or a book recommended by someone whose opinion of them they value. Again, the teacher's task is to keep in mind where the pupils' satisfactions come from, to enlarge the range of books for current lessons, and stretch the readers' confidence that they will be able to make the next step.

Given the range of these kinds of reading, here are some things that children on their way to secondary school may have learned on their own from contact with the writers who have their interest and reading at heart:

— If the beginning of the story is not clear, the best thing to do is to keep going.

— The words do not always mean what they say. Writers make jokes, puns, refer to other books and texts or sound ironic. In the allegorical *Narnia* stories, for example, young readers know that there is more at stake than in other adventure stories. Sometimes the author takes sides, is unfair, or puts words into the mouths of characters that make the reader uneasy. Enid Blyton is unfair to gypsies; boys or girls may be discriminated against. (Children detect prejudice, racism and intolerance before they fully understand the implications of these things.)

— Books about different school subjects are written in ways that define the subject. There is a special vocabulary for geography, a different style for history, although both can be written as stories. Information texts have *reference* parts for 'looking up' built into them: contents lists, diagrams, charts, an index, a bibliography, all of which readers learn to handle.

— Good reading teachers know about different reading styles and different texts. They encourage their pupils to experiment in reading and give them instruction when they need it, confidence when they flag or are bored. They also know that evidence of pupils' accomplishments in reading is complex. Their best performances are never recorded in the results of reading tests which confine reading to a single activity.

— At this time when the nature of reading is rapidly changing we cannot be sure what the literacy of the 21st century will demand of children now in school, but it is more than likely that it will outstrip any method as yet devised to teach or to examine it. Enthusiasm for reading, a range and depth of reading experience are the best guides we have to what the important lessons are.

Reading is what has to be learned for the learner to become officially literate. The test comes at the end of school with formal systems of examining. These have changed. When newspapers in 1988 were full of gloom and doom about the baleful workings of a new examination, the GCSE in England, parents were telling each other how their sixteen-year-olds were absorbed in the work they were doing throughout the two-year course and not only in the month before the tests. Where the topics for written work had been negotiated with the teachers, discussed (as all writing should be) with interested others, researched in a variety of sources and presented with responsible care, the results were better than ever before. Adolescents who put effort into school work expect to be taken seriously as readers and writers, with views of their own in the process of formation. For the first time in my long career as a teacher I see in *examination* writing not the dutiful rehashing of accepted answers, but a new vibrancy, the purposive engagement of young people with what literacy is good for and makes possible.

Much of the difference in the literacy of young people lies in their development as writers. The writing the young now do in school is, effectively, a new literacy, something quite different from the dictation which their forebears of 1890 were expected to do to prove their scribal exactness.

Confident Knowing

No list of lessons, however important, can represent what counts as being fully literate in a world community where the practices of literacy are constantly changing. At best, we help and encourage our children to engage with the world's literacies in such a way that they sense they have freedom to promote change as well as to endure it. They will, we know, make the best use of literacies that serve them best. The powerful literates are those who have a kind of confident knowing that they will be able to cope with written language, however unfamiliar, by discovering how it works. They understand the constructedness of texts, and know that behind any writing there is a writer looking for readers.

Some of the recent understandings of confident knowing come from increased advances in knowledge about the patterns of children's language learning. Many excellent new practices now promote young learners' achievements across a wider range of subject matter taught in school than at any time in the past. Particularly, the resources of individual bilingual learners have been supported, appreciated and extended by a new generation of teachers whose awareness of the implications of 'equal opportunities' is a finely wrought understanding of the diversity of our society. From the puzzles which bilingual children have to solve with regard to the hidden metaphors, the allusions and the hidden historical depths of our language, teachers and others derive evidence of the complexities of English which *all* children encounter.

Nowadays all literates are linguists of a different order. Code switching is a lifetime commonplace, even for those whose birthright language is Standard English. Soon, we shall have to include the necessity of bilingualism as an educational priority for all when the open European frontiers include the English Channel. We cannot predict the literacy changes of the next half century, but surely they will be influenced by the rhetorical conventions of our neighbours. There will be more new texts which those with the textual power to understand and interpret will appropriate. Shall we then make sure that our children's learning to read and write includes a strong, *conscious* understanding and grasp of how language, and therefore literacy, helps them to learn?

Writers want readers who are prepared to engage with their ideas and to adventure with them in their writing. Habitual readers go to writers for reading lessons as ways of reflecting on experience. Together they *keep on* creating texts, confident that they will, together, solve the puzzle of how should this *go*.

But language also lets writers deceive readers, subvert their expectations, for better or worse, and say what is not the case. Irony is pervasive. In the public writing of advertising, in the secondary orality of television and in political speeches, persuasion is a highly developed art. So *textual understanding*—how this trick works, which rhetoric this is, what are the rules of this writing game—becomes ever more important. Scrutiny, once seen as a close reading of literary texts by an educated élite, now seems to be increasingly necessary. Study, if you will, the increase in writing and talking about 'Green' issues in popular sources of information. Are all statements about conservation and anti-pollution ideologically pure? How do readers learn to differentiate the opportunist prose of soap producers and politicians from the more ecologically rooted understandings of serious environmentalists? How do writers deflect cynicism and ignorance? These may prove to be very important lessons indeed, where textual understandings may, without exaggeration, be a matter of life and death.

CHAPTER 7

Literate Behaviour and Literature

Learning From Written Text

The most strongly held and the longest lasting conviction about the importance of being literate rests on the belief that by learning to read and write we can all read and write to learn. This is not a foolish idea. The lives we lead are the result of its implications. The notion that access to books and records brings enlightenment to human understanding would not have persisted if we had never benefited from the writing and print that kept for us the thoughts and discoveries of our forebears. Our cultural traditions of seeking wisdom by constantly reinterpreting the words of dead poets and of writing down what we believe should survive our mortality show no indications of going out of fashion.

Sustained and continuous learning from written texts, maps, drawings, screens and musical scores as well as prose, is commonly thought of as study. The required concentration involves a period of induction, usually in school, where the young are taught how to go beyond the kind of knowing they acquire by knocking about in the world, the 'common sense' everyone is credited with. Study is also the deliberate act of problem solving. It includes thinking about understanding what we know, and judging our judgements. No one does it all the time, and some enjoy it more than others. In the last two years of school, girls and boys sustain and encourage each other through the examination days when reading and writing are more toil than pleasure.

Learning from written text needs application. The voluntary kind is always best.

Our local cultural myth is that those who study (the French and the Germans have no hesitation in calling them 'intellectuals') are solitary individuals who voyage through the seas of thought alone in well-stocked private libraries. This notion is the result of our education system which has tended to keep intellectual development as a privilege for those who can delay earning their living. A more homely fact is that, during the winter months, thousands of people go from a full day at work to voluntary evening classes where they study together. Students of the Open University set their alarm clocks for unsocial hours. They watch a television performance of *Prometheus Bound* after midnight and give up their holidays to writing essays. Those who leave school before they discover how to make written texts yield the information they need look for new learning opportunities in adult literacy centres. In crowded gaols prisoners pass recognized examinations. The rewards of study are generally understood.

The popular view, that we learn to read and write first and acquire knowledge thereafter, is not, in fact, what happens. Children are not awakened to understanding by learning to read. Long before they engage with books their active curiosity about the world impels them to explore it. A passion to find out is not the result of literacy but part of its cause. The need to be informed is empowered by literacy. What literacy adds to learning is not simply more information from written texts, but, more importantly, an awareness of how our minds work.

This is school business and part of every teacher's responsibility. Learning from the written word is only one aspect of the general human desire to know by asking questions and finding out. Study begins when learners think about what they are doing so that they can extend their present knowledge. They develop learning plans and strategies for obtaining new experiences, from books particularly, which lead them to a plane of understanding where they reflect on how they got there. This begins early. Children who, right from their first experience of being read to, have some idea of what reading might be like, also have a parallel awareness of what they are trying to do and how they might be successful. If you listen to an eight-year-old helping a six-year-old to read a story, you know that the older child can already work out part of the reading process.

Books have been impressive tools for learning since the invention of printing. We refer to them as to authorities; we line our walls with them. A dictionary, an encyclopaedia or an almanac represent the learning function of 'looking up'. Behind different beliefs about the nature and value of 'book learning' there lurks a powerful sense that there are personal, social and practical advantages in having access to the kinds of information that books store. Reading them seems to be the obvious way to retrieve what is known. But modern electronic storage systems far outstrip the accumulated information of texts. Thrumming with artificial memories and devices for almost instantaneous recall, they impress us with their usefulness. Yet they still need readers. And neither books nor computers, by themselves, generate ideas, thinking, judgements. Those who devise the programme and make use of the data are always more powerful than those who know only how to make the machines work.

To be useful, or important, information has to make a difference to the person who retrieves it. Readers go beyond common sense when they not only learn what hitherto they did not know, but also discover the difference that learning makes. Then there is a new view of a topic, a situation and the prospect of going forward. The simplest response to this kind of awareness is 'Oh, I *see*'. For a moment at least the learner becomes a kind of visionary, someone whose thought is original. Everyone, young or old, knows what this feels like. Being literate extends this kind of activity.

Books make it possible for each of us to learn at our own rate, by asking our own questions, by putting what we discover into what we already know. They also encourage joint learning, shared understandings, extended awareness.

Where a number of people read the same book, discussions promote different kinds of reflection, the taking on of another's viewpoint. In this, pupils and teachers have the advantage. It is easier to explore learning from the written word in a group than in solitude. Good teachers encourage developing readers to interrogate texts, to ask 'Do I believe that?' before they are confident enough to do it on their own. The best of schooling is the taking of judicious short cuts with an expert guide, in literacy as in everything else.

Children learn early that texts are organized in recognizably different ways. Stories are not the same as 'books about . . .'. Information books for the very young represent the world in pictures, they name objects, functions, categories. *The Baby's Catalogue* does this: the pages say 'Shopping', 'Toys', 'Dinners'. The illustrations show how, although everyone has breakfast, not all breakfasts are the same. Other books are plainer, less subtle in their present-ation of 'animals', 'toys', 'colours', 'shapes', where the representation of a single object appears above a single word. The context of the contents of these books is the presence of objects in the world. The reader is to relate the world to the book and the book to the world.[1]

Here is Jenghis, seven and a half, restless, impatient with adults, and one of the best readers in his class. He wants to read a book about tractors because he spent his holiday on a farm where there were three different ones. On the last day he was allowed (probably against the rules) to sit beside the farmer as he drove across the field. Jenghis reads: *'Tractors let them (ploughs) work on rough and muddy ground. Tractors can pull, lift and provide power for many other machines. Because tractors can work much faster than humans or animals, they help farmers to grow more food.'* As he looks at the picture he talks about how these tractors are the same as, or different from, those he saw. He discovers what tractors can do that he never saw: pulling a plough, a rake, a trailer with food for snowbound sheep. So he fits his particular recollection into the generalized form 'Tractors can . . .'

Near the end of the book, on a picture of a large, tree-less, dusty field, the text has: '*Tractors can plough up land that used to be too difficult to farm. Sometimes the soil is then blown by the wind and nothing can grow on the land.*' Jenghis comments: 'Then they won't need the tractor any more, will they?' As he reads, Jenghis is in charge of his learning, although he has, as yet, nowhere to put the writer's information about soil erosion. His teacher explains that there are no trees in the picture. They have been cut down to make it easier for the tractor to make straight lines with a plough. This sometimes means that the earth dries up and blows away. The teacher's comment links what *causes* the soil condition to the *effect*, that of becoming less good for growing, and offers Jenghis a coherent reason for the writer's statement, and a model for explanation.

Next to Jenghis sits Ludmilla, a little older. She has chosen to read a book about stars. As she rarely sees any stars where she lives she is happiest with the pictures of the moon. From television programmes she knows that astronauts (her word) went there in a rocket. The text explains how the light from the stars we see *travels*, a word that Ludmilla associates with aeroplanes. She has difficulty with the names of the stars. Around the word *Orion* is a curious dot-to-dot drawing labelled 'the Hunter'. But the page that excites her (and the reason for her choice of the book) is the one that has the signs of the Zodiac, another word she knows. She then picks out the planetary signs. Her aunt, she says, is an expert on matters astrological and gives advice to others by 'reading' the stars, which may be what Ludmilla now thinks she is doing. She instructs Jenghis about his temperament ('you're very curious') as one 'born under Capricorn', and explains her own good luck in 'being Pisces'. Her coherence impresses Jenghis, as does her skill in argument. Jenghis' puzzlement about how 'under Capricorn' relates to the fact that his mother told him he was born in the London Hospital spurs him on to expressions of his disbelief. Together they are sorting out what must be the case to make sense. How can they both be right?

Jenghis and Ludmilla are engaged in what their teacher

calls a *project*, for which they have chosen *topic* books to provide them with information. They are invited to find out what they can by reading, talking, drawing (or copying—the legitimate kind that is related to gathering evidence, as in research) and, finally, writing. Jenghis may seem still to be light years away from the kind of school learning that counts as physics, mechanics, soil ecology and economics, mathematics and engineering. Ludmilla's view of the universe will have to undergo some transformation if she is to pursue astronomy instead of astrology. Nevertheless, their *intent to know*, at this stage, is strongly rooted in what Douglas Barnes calls *action knowledge*: the kind that is so integrated into our picture of the world that it influences our behaviour and our understanding.[2]

In their primary school Ludmilla and Jenghis are still concerned, and encouraged, to make what they are discovering fit what they know. That is why they and the rest of their class have arguments. They are also working out how they can be in charge of their learning, and at the same time making 'lessons' part of the collectivity of their classroom. They do not know it, but they are at a crossing point, a transition between inquiring and being told. Later, even before they are eleven, they will be expected, forced even, to give up these open, seriously playful discussions and to attend to their books or papers as something to be remembered in the words of school.

'The traditional role of a learner in an academic curriculum,' says Douglas Barnes, 'is as a receiver of knowledge constituted elsewhere for purposes that he or she has not yet had the opportunity to grasp.' As you read that sentence, do you think 'receiving knowledge constituted elsewhere' is what your children should learn to do in school? My argument is that reading to learn what is known must include the habit of freshly wondering; knowledge must be *reconstituted* by the learner. Turning school knowledge, the content of books, into action knowledge is a function of critical literacy, the habit of reflection. It is learned where children are encouraged to invent and discover and to think *about* what they read and write.

Textbooks and Other Resources

Fifty years ago, whatever had to be learned in school was in a book, on the blackboard, or dictated by the teacher. The books represented the body of knowledge to be transmitted, reproduced, examined. The rest was précis or comment, the teacher's little jokes or asides, the mnemonics and tricks for remembering chemical formulae and Latin pronouns. The authority of the textbook was unchallenged, even when what it contained was ill-informed (my school science was all pre-Einstein), racist (as in history), changing (the map of Europe), ethnocentric (everything). I even had an English exercise book with model letters for writing to persons of authority: 'Dear Sir, etc.' Imagine the fury of my Presbyterian grandfather on finding that my homework, on one occasion, consisted of the of task writing a letter to a *bishop*, beginning 'My lord'.

Durable hardback textbooks are still found in classrooms where teachers are bound by a fairly rigid programme of work which the book has been written to match. My experience of schools in the United States suggests that the elementary and secondary school texts in use there define school knowledge in yearly packages of information and accompanying tasks. In this model, learning is sequenced, linear, cumulative. It leaves little room for querying, dissent, alternative points of view. If the pupils have difficulty in reading the textbook they are given special forms of reading instruction. To study such books is to complete the given assignment. The reader is at the greatest possible distance from the writer; there is no 'voice' in the pages. David Olson says that this is 'the authorized version of valid learning'.[3] It does not encourage thought or speculation, the important version of 'Oh, *now* I see'.

Unlike storytellers and artists of picture books, textbook

writers are constrained by publishing formats and the selling price of a 'series'. The presentation of information and pictures is regularized. The readers' task is to collect information on topics which interest them. This usually means copying from the text and drawing pictures, which become the standard form of information retrieval. It is, in fact, the last dregs of the clerkly condition of literacy because it can be done without thinking. It is also very boring.

When readers are bored by stories they stop reading them, but with textbooks they are expected to plough on until they have learned what has been 'set'. I shall have more to say about boredom. Here I simply note that boring textbooks are usually either too difficult or too easy for the reader. Some books which begin with a concern for the learner by presenting 'facts' in small segments for easy assimilation become ludicrous. I have a book about motorbikes designed for inexperienced readers. There are two pictures on the first page; one with the caption 'This is the back of a motorbike'.

The main problem for pupils using textbooks is how to fit what they read into the pattern of what they already know and understand. I clearly recall, at a distance of more than half a century, a sentence in my first history book: 'The death of Mary Queen of Scots was a stain on the reputation of Queen Elizabeth.' I worried about that 'stain', how it could resemble what had to be cleaned from tablecloths, carpets, clothes. In situations like this, bilingual learners are often at a special disadvantage if they have no contextual way of discovering the meaning of special terms in subjects like science (heat and temperature), the technicalities of European news (what is an 'ally'), and the storehouse of dead metaphors in the English language. Books of information offered to the young often have statements so condensed as to leave them no alternative but to copy out the sentences as they stand, hoping that the person who reads their writing will accept this transfer as evidence of an effort to learn.

Confusion often arises between children's 'being interested' and 'becoming interested'. When they simply reproduce the sentences they have read about molecules, river basins, economic movements and religious wars, without the information making any difference to them, interest is at its lowest ebb. Yet the pupils are then encountering one of the crucial problems of literacy, the move from information to understanding. How does information become 'the difference that makes a difference'?[4]

Learning from the written word is never straightforward. With our different learning styles we make different meanings, create varied understandings. The 'ordinary means' of language which brings this about is, most often, talk, especially shared, collaborative talk, teacher to pupils, pupils with pupils. Even then there are difficulties.

A class of eleven-year-olds is exploring a topic common in geography lessons—Artesian wells and porous rocks. The text they are reading says that porous rocks 'hold water like a sponge'.[5] The learners apply their everyday understanding of sponges to what is, in fact, a formal concept in physics. Their talk reveals that some of them believe that the water passes through the rocks, as water passes through the holes in a sponge. For those pupils the rocks are porous because they have tiny holes. Others believe that the water stops in the rocks because a sponge 'holds' water. The teacher's problem is to sort out what 'in' and 'through' mean in this situation but it is a subtle linguistic confusion which she may not even notice.

The pupils are struggling with their notions of *porosity*; they half-grasp ideas of what is *permeable* or *pervious*. Single definitions are not helpful. The learners are moving to concepts where the word meaning has to encompass more than a single instance. They need experienced help. Yet, ever since their days in the nursery class, they have known that water passes through sand more quickly than it does through clay.

Competent reading of non-fiction school texts depends on much more than can be defined as reading *ability*. The comprehension of texts in special subject areas involves an understanding of the rules by which they are written, the agreed vocabulary of the topic and the inferential moves that relate language to logic. Many an intelligent reader, failing to see the implied negative in a sentence ('Never has there been so much rain') has made the wrong assumption. Irrelevant responses confuse the reading of any text. (It is not always useful to assume that the writer is a man.) In an exemplary article, *Comprehension: bringing it back alive*, Bob Moy and Mike Raleigh show how understanding needs discussion, negotiation, speculation.[6] Meaning isn't given in texts; it emerges, grows, is redefined, devised, revised, reformulated. As long as the reader-talker is interested in the topic as the writer presents it, these processes are effective in learning.

Before the arrival of the National Curriculum teachers in British schools were responsible for the programmes of study and the choice of materials. In many schools this led to innovative and successful teaching and learning. In others, too little money for resources and a continuing erosion of teachers' confidence and morale meant that worksheets replaced books. Some worksheets supported genuine enquiries which the pupils were encouraged to follow; others were simplified writing tasks which acted as a form of classroom control. Short prose extracts with 'comprehension' questions modelled on examination papers were, and perhaps remain, the meanest form of this learning device. I have seen pupils answer the questions by filling in blanks in sentences after the most cursory reading of the passage. And yet, parents are often quite content when children are engaged in mindless repetitive exercises of this kind.

Everyone knows that school reading and writing in most subjects includes repetitious practice: learning the grammar of a new language, the memorizing of facts, events, operations, results. Some European schools now use packs of 'modules' for 'mastery learning'. The pupils work through the examples on their own while the teacher gives her attention to those who have difficulty. Many new paper-and-pencil exercises outrun my experience, but everyone who has 'mastered' a process knows that, in the end, it is the desire for mastery that makes the repetitions purposeful and successful.

Libraries and Study Skills

All secondary schools in Britain have a library. Since 1936 the School Library Association has promoted and encouraged the use of libraries as 'powerhouses of learning'. The state of the school library is often a clear indication of a school's commitment to effective literacy, independent and collaborative study and the promotion of learning from a variety of resources.

Primary-school libraries usually depend on the interest and skill of a designated teacher. Although most children read more story books than books of information, most school collections are predominantly 'non-fiction'. Some children are inducted into the simplified Dewey classification system as soon as they are allowed to use the library. Others never discover throughout their time in school how library books are arranged.

At their best, school libraries offer pupils the resources that study requires: access to reference books, information in different forms, a place to read socially. Children who learn to browse amongst books, newspapers and magazines, glancing, page-turning, pursuing ideas or idling, come to be at home in a library. They learn the secret that confuses inexperienced readers: that you can take out a book, read it, return it, and still, in the most significant sense, *possess* it.

As the use of single-subject textbooks has been gradually replaced by 'topic-centred' learning activities, school libraries have become 'resource centres'. Sometimes they are renamed as such. This move acknowledges that no single book can encompass all that is known about a subject area; not all the facts, inferences and arguments on each topic can be confined in one volume. In the information-laden contexts of new curricula the library plays a central role in what is now called 'resource-based learning'.

Librarians have always been a special breed of literates. They now mastermind a range of resources unknown to their predecessors: charts, film loops, micro-bibliographies, summary pages. They guard copyright from the users of photocopiers. They study the different ways in which information may be presented, including computers. They are also experts on the matter of study skills, to which they often induct pupils in lessons given when they introduce them to the library or help them with assignments.

Here is a library lesson for eleven-year-olds. The librarian shows the class how to operate the card index in the little drawers, or the microfiche index with its cunning little glass slide, to find a book, provided they already know the author or the title and how to apply the extended subtleties of alphabetic order that they probably learned from the telephone directory. The librarian instructs them in the use of encyclopaedias and shows where the subjects are. The class is then given a worksheet with which to prowl round the shelves looking for answers to questions such as 'What was the date of the Battle of Trafalgar?', 'How many titles have you found of books that deal with Dogs?'. The operation is also called 'study skills'. The children are not, at this point, studying anything. They are finding out about finding. As an introduction to orderly library behaviour, the lesson is a useful one.

Although looking for information in books is a complicated business, young learners master it quite quickly if their interest is engaged and their desire to know makes them patient. I have seen eight-year-olds use the AA Handbook with confidence and success, while botanists of the same age scorn beginners' books of wild flowers, preferring the adult kind with good pictures. But when learners actually need information to fill a gap in their knowledge—'What's a gazelle?'—their instinctive move is to ask someone who is likely to know the answer to their question. They have done this since they could talk. To be told in class that they should 'look up' the meaning of a word comes as a surprise. For some this is the beginning of a lifetime's addiction to Scrabble, crosswords and reference books; for others it can be a dreary chore. I remember with gratitude all those who helped me at various times with reference sources, filing boxes, contents lists and the mysteries of listings. My experience suggests that where the need to know is para-mount, the skill of discovery is powered by it. My concern for the young is that they may be given lessons in how to use a library or a dictionary before they have real need of either. I cannot believe that study can be taught apart from the topic to be studied. So study skills can be effectively learned only in a context of genuine enquiry, a necessary knowing.

Nevertheless, many people are greatly helped by learning how to be *systematic* in their researches, to order what they find out by reading, to explore what they want to understand by writing. But facts never stand alone, not even the time of a train or a telephone number. The rules for 'looking up' information apply only to the practice of getting it, they do not determine what has to be done with it.

The most difficult early lesson for young enquirers is that facts, information, do not come from books or other sources as neutral substances. They bring with them the presenter's, the writer's assumptions, judgements and understandings: the context of their origin. This is the hardest part of reading to learn. When a fourteen-year-old told me: 'They said I should read *The Origin of Species* to find Darwin's theory of the descent of man, but I can't find it anywhere in there', I knew I had to do more than tell her to read it again and try harder. To help her I needed to know that she was anxious to sort out what she described as 'the Genesis problem', which she presented to me as 'Which is right, religion or science?'. Young people's desires to learn are universally connected with big topics. The teachers' puzzle is how to save them from the pursuit of unhelpful details.

Just how complicated this can become was made plain to me when I hired myself out as a research assistant to a group of girls who were sorting out the meaning of events related to the Pope's visit to England in 1982. The starting question was: 'Why are some people pleased the Pope is coming and others are so strongly opposed to the tour?' What began as a fairly routine enquiry soon became a mass of handwritten notes, cuttings from newspapers and a pile of history books. The pupils eagerly interviewed local clerics whose responses were often both vague ('He is the Holy Father') or disturbing ('He is Anti-Christ').

After two weeks of 'looking up' and asking questions the girls had a confusing collection of unsorted data over which they haggled in their concern to write their report on this, the topic of their choice. They weren't simply bored; they were genuinely confused.

Suddenly, in the middle of a discussion, the girl who had found the whole affair most onerous and unsortable suddenly asked 'Who *is* the Pope, anyway?'. The silence that followed showed that she was asking the basic question: the one that not only puzzled her friends but had also provoked debates, wars and massacres down the centuries. So we began to investigate what we all knew, believed or imagined about the Pope, and where our understandings came from. The enquirer showed that she was struggling to sort out what she had seen on television about the Borgias, her history lessons about Henry VIII and Anne Boleyn, what the local priest had said, and her agnostic father's beliefs about the troubles in Northern Ireland. Her question led her classmates to share their bits and pieces of knowledge and to move on to the sorting out of their material in terms of what they understood of *oppositions*. In doing so they became more explicit about their own opinions. Meanwhile, their research assistant was helping them with the historical sequence, to read the books with more interrogative understanding, and to discard what wasn't directly related to their enquiries. When the writing was completed, it was possible to review what had happened.

The pupils agreed that getting information does not consist of copying difficult prose that will satisfy the teacher. It begins with a good question. In the course of my encounters with these girls, I asked them how they decided on the topic. One of them said: 'There is hardly a day goes by when I do not wonder how I got on earth, why I am here, and how the universe and the world were made.' The learning problem is to reduce this to something manageable while keeping the 'wonder' that provoked it to power more than another class exercise. The teacher's role is more difficult than giving good advice or instruction. She has to be a co-learner, a collaborator.

Ask any expert how he or she learned to study and the answer will be: 'by reading and thinking, and talking and writing in ways that were related to my purposes and intentions, and fuelled by my desire to know, to find out.' They admit that their teachers helped them when they allowed the learners to express doubt or difficulty and gave them time not only to pursue their established interests, but also to *become* interested in related topics. Good teachers also let their students be tentative, perplexed, uncertain, and don't always know better than the learner.

Adolescents confront deep and serious puzzles. They respect those who take the trouble to help them towards some understanding of where they may look for enlightenment. So the resources from which young people are expected to learn, in school or college, should be ample, well selected and reviewed, and generally available. Guidance in book selection is crucial. Nothing frustrates learners more than the unreliability of source materials. We know that to promote literacy is to provide the means of becoming literate to more people and to decrease boredom. We understand the purposes of literacy. How do we will the means of its increase? We could begin by turning school libraries from being book museums into workshops where all kinds of texts are actively, continually, used and replaced. Study is not only individual search in silence, but also talkative and listening collaboration. The written word offers young learners a wide range of purposes for their learning. They need help to get started, to carry on, to think about it.

Literature

Throughout these pages the importance of being literate has, I hope, never been in doubt. I have tried to show my conviction that all children and adults should have access to the kinds of literacy that give them the greatest degree of control over their lives. As literacy promotes and refines ideas, so it advances what human beings have always called freedom. Beyond that, literacy supports our passion to know what it is to be human, a passion that is much older than writing, embodied in the ways by which we make language memorable.

As we looked at what reading and writing are good for, why stories are important, which early lessons let children experience reading and writing as ways of making worlds; as we encountered the pluralities of language and the differences that are inherent in schools and learning, you may have picked up, in the forest of my explanations, some markers for the next topic to be discussed. We are bound now to consider what literacy brings, as our language lets us doubly say, *into play*: literature.

We know that the relationship of literature and literacy has deep cultural and historical roots. Here our concern is with children's discovery that some kinds of writing are to be read differently from others. They are not for 'looking up', but, simply, for reading.

In the primary-school library the chief distinction is between fiction (stories) and non-fiction (topics). In the secondary school children encounter 'literature' as a category that is rarely explained, only exemplified as more stories and poetry, with a hint of its greater significance, value, difficulty, and its relation to 'the imagination'. Before a year is out, most secondary-school pupils distinguish reading matter which has certain formal properties from writing directed towards a practical end. In this scheme of things a poem is literature; a railway timetable or a geography textbook is not.

The underlying problem of the study of literature in the secondary school is one of ownership. Those who never 'get on with' poetry, plays, or narrative fiction are not sure how to be part of the group that enjoys reading specially selected texts and knows how to talk about them. Literature seems to belong not to everyone, but to those who make their living by reading and writing, who debate what counts as literature and describe their particular reading acts as 'criticism', which to the less experienced means 'finding fault'. To pass from reading a novel or a poem to *interpreting* it, saying what it means, is a significant move for all literates, and one which depends a great deal on the teacher's understanding of how to encourage a young reader or a would-be writer to possess a text and not simply to read it.

Those who are exclusive about literature, whose concern for special kinds of writing seems to downgrade the reading that ordinary people do, are not helpful to those needing to know that literature is *not* reserved for specially trained readers belonging to a club that keeps the secrets of texts. The definition of literature comes from those who read, and that means anyone who is literate. The little girl or boy who says 'Again!' at the end of a story and a scholar writing about the art of the novel are both part of the same enterprise.

If we want young readers to engage with interpretive reading of books which offer different kinds of reading experience we have to remove certain misconceptions about literature which have blocked their way in the past. Literature is not old books, not a list of specially chosen great books which represent an unchanging heritage, conferring on the reader the distinction of showing taste and discrimination. There is no way of saying that a text is literature by inspecting its sentences or its formal arrangement. We should dissuade the young from believing that literature is a privileged form of reading reserved for those who stay at school long enough to claim literature as a possession or to qualify for access to antique poetry. What counts as literature will always change as the technologies for its production change.

Yet most parents who encourage their children's reading want them to encounter 'the classics', to know literature as hard-won, effortful and demanding reading. I know I find it difficult to accept that my grandchildren may never read most of the books that formed my literate history, but I hope they will discover some of them. The reason why old texts survive to be continuously reckoned with as literature lies in the fact that they are recurrently *re-creative*.

Instead of keeping the secrets of literature to themselves, writers reveal them. Shakespeare tells us what it is like to be a poet and a dramatist; Henry James writes about writing novels, Milan Kundera tells us that 'all novels, of every age, are concerned with the enigma of the self'; Borges says that reading is 'guided dreaming', and poets never cease to describe poetry. Literature is clearly literate *activity* that can bring everyone a fuller enjoyment of life, beyond usefulness, beyond, even, the worthy notion that it is nourishment that makes us grow. It is its own kind of deep play. For all that the books I have called literature at various stages of my growing old have joined me to the history and language of my forebears in ways that plumb my very depths, and taught me who I am, for all that they have also added wondrously, immeasurably to my understanding of humankind, myself and the world, I think of them as something I have *enjoyed*, in the richest sense. Descriptions stop short of the teaching-knowing of what happens in this reading and writing. The uninvestigated parts of these activities are the second before the reader or writer begins, and the minute after they stop. There are the words on the page. The reader and the writer have, somehow, changed places. To read a book is, in a sense, to rewrite it; to write it is to be its other reader.

The creative and recreative properties of anything called literature are experienced by children when they sing, dance, bounce about in the playground to chants and popular songs. Poetry is never better understood than in childhood when it is felt in the blood and along the bones. Later, it may be intricately interpreted, explained and demonstrated, as something made of language. To enjoy poetry is to revel in it, to explore sadness, loss, in ways that language makes possible. Poetry is also about language as a *plaything*. *Pop Goes the Weasel*, scatological parodies, children's versions of Michael Jackson songs, all the memorable ways by which words deal with varied, troublesome, irrational, unnameable aspects of sense and feelings are also threaded through our literate lives in poetry, sometimes without our being fully aware of it. At the same time poetry shows us that language makes and remakes *texts*, in ways that relate that word to *texture* and *textile*. The attractiveness of any poem includes its shape, its constructedness.

In the past two decades, teachers of literature have extended children's awareness of what language makes by introducing into their lessons a wider range of reading matter to demonstrate that 'high' culture (what has hitherto seemed selective or exclusive) and 'popular' culture (enjoyed by all but not always deemed to be literature) both need and feed off each other. In so doing, they have given their pupils a wider range of literary competences. In their campaign to demonstrate the pluralism of literature, teachers in inner-city schools have taught Black literature by engaging all pupils in a discovery of how English is used by those whose history in it began with the songs of slaves.

Similarly, adolescents as well as adults have become aware of feminist literature. Men and women read and write differently; they have different histories in reading. Everyone knows that, during their years in school, girls read more than boys; they are more practised, and look to reading for different kinds of satisfactions. Yet, until recently, the visible history of literature, and the sources of judgements about the worth of texts, were seen as a male preserve, despite the number of women poets and novelists. Now, who could think of the release, growth, power of feminine (not only feminist) consciousness cut off from the revelations that come from women's writing and reading? Literature written by women became the site for its analysis and struggle.

As I read with my students Maxine Hong Kingston's autobiographical novel, *The Woman Warrior*, in which a bilingual Chinese girl growing up in California struggles to make internal sense of her confusions about where she belongs, which language she speaks and how to relate the stories of her Chinese ancestors to the white 'ghosts' of those who walk the streets with her and sit next to her in school, I re-read my own past, as my students do theirs. In so doing we all come to know two good things about reading: the nature of literature and the essence of being female.[7] Boys have the same chance. The books that favour them in this way have always been more numerous. But now, unlike Jane Austen, the Brontës, George Eliot and George Sand, girls can read and write in ways that do not have to be hidden, faked or excused.

If the relation of literacy to literature is not just private preference about what to read or the good luck of being published, how are we to engage the young in understanding it? The National Curriculum for English is judicious in its claim that 'the exploration of literary texts is not an élitist activity, distinct from the study of other means of communication'. The writers of the Cox Report admit that good teaching practices abound, and that the pupils' pleasure is a guide to their engagement with the many excellent books available. They also say that literature and language are 'inseparably intertwined'. But, like all promotions of what is seen to do children good, including those things which involve 'social and cultural diversity', there is little depth in the advocacy of 'novels from India or Caribbean poetry' to match the actual experience these provide. A Utopian plan for teaching literature now must, as all Utopias do, employ the latest technologies of literacy: cassettes, films, two-way videos, fax machines for international exchanges of school writing, drama studios for role play, radio links, desk-top publishing. Why not? All these help the rewriting and reading of poems, novels and plays, and can be extended to creating television scripts, cartoons, broadsheet poems, satires in mixed media, magazines. The young are at ease with these technologies and could well use them to discover, in Kundera's words, 'some answers to the question—what is human existence and wherein does its poetry lie?'[8]

Whatever else we do, we may well begin by re-reading with our young tales in all traditions: fables, folk stories, legends and myths, where heroes are often simpletons, or the proud and argumentative are outwitted by the plain and practical. In every school classroom lurks an expert young storyteller who enriches local knowledge with her or his inventions and exotic retellings. The spellbinding of the oral tale is a necessary prelude to 'being lost in a book'; new readers align themselves with characters by being concerned about the outcome of their adventures. The richness of cultural and linguistic diversity can be tapped from the traditional tale from the beginning to the end of school life. We know we tell tales, to ourselves and others, until we die. So narrative remains as the important way of thinking that literature makes possible. The point is, we have to collect, understand, rework, celebrate and extend the riches of stories so that in us and in our children their form and function become well set as literary competences. These include mimicry, dramatic enactment, telling and writing.

Recent research makes this plain. I have already mentioned Carol Fox's account of her son Josh's early narratives which show how he moves from the simple inclusion in his story of a character from a story book to the introduction of book language into his ordinary speech, and then the incorporation of book techniques and forms into the stories he tells. When Josh was eight he wrote a story called 'The Last Chime of the Bells'. *'One winter night in Wales these children were at home. Just then the bells started to ring. The bells of the church, that is. That was the first time in three years that the bells had rung. So then the boys ran out of the house that they lived in and went to the church.'* This textual power, this handling of time sequences, is no individual freakishness but a kind of Proustian certainty. Evidence of this kind alerts us to possibilities in all children. We are simply excusing our-selves if we don't find literary competences in most of those we know. Our failure to expect that children can acquire power in written language derives, in part, from too great a preoccupation with their spelling and punctuation—the power we exert over them—rather than a sufficient concern for their productions—their skill in using language and in making plain what they are reading and writing *about*.

Here are some things that poems, stories and plays of all kinds help children to learn about the nature of literature. (Television also helps.) First, that language and ways of using it change according to what is being told. Children

185

discover the differences between prose and verse quite early. They find out that there are some written forms of language that are rarely, if ever, spoken. 'Yours sincerely' does not trip off our tongues. Words used in churches seem to stay there. Once they have met *The Owl and the Pussy Cat* they may look for a *runcible* spoon but never find one ('Why,' said a little girl, 'does the owl sing to a *small* guitar?'). The particularity of words, the nature of appositeness in a context, are learned where they are seen to advantage.

Next, *multiconsciousness*, that awareness of sharing with an author the knowledge that another character lacks is learned early and grasped consciously much later. As they watch television dramas children know how they must end: the good are blessed, the wicked punished. But as the story goes on they have to interpret the moves of the characters, good and bad as each sees the scene. The reason I return to *Rosie's Walk* time and time again throughout this book is simply that no reader I have met aged five or over fails to grasp that Rosie never turns round to look at the fox; she may, or *may not*, know he is following her.

Then, for the next literary competence, I need the word *heteroglossia*—many languages.[9] Children demonstrate in their play that they know how to 'do the voices'. They imitate those whom they want to mock. On a school bus you will hear them giving an impression of Miss X trying to keep order in class. Exaggeration of the salient features of texts makes the parodies they greatly appreciate. When they discuss television programmes they re-invent whole scenes with perfect mimicry, pretending that they are not taken in by the skilful producers. With the vicious rapier thrusts of experienced satirists they are able to assassinate the characters of their elders.

Literature extends both social and personal learning. Part of my argument—that literacy is enhanced, made strong by readers and writers entering the alternative worlds of prose fiction, drama and poetry—depends on our agreeing that the experience of all readers, but especially children, can be extended by entering the alternative worlds of prose fiction, drama and poetry. To read Mildred Taylor's *Roll of Thunder, Hear My Cry* is, for a white child, a way to understand *being* Black. Gillian Cross's *A Map of Nowhere* shows a teenage boy, whose family lives with easy forms of individualistic self-gratification, meeting another family whose uprightness keeps them in social isolation. Alan Garner's *Stone Book Quartet* takes 'spots of time' in the lives of his ancestors to show how children enter history and language and in doing so remake both.[10]

By trying to use literature, in school or in the wider domain of the books which we specially designate as being 'for children' or 'young adults', we often fail to match what language makes with what children can do with it by themselves. We may have played down (that word again) the ebullience of the young, their gift for parody and excess, their necessary explorations of the boundaries of sense and nonsense, their ventriloquisms, escapology and their appreciation of the seriousness of comic relief. Whatever they learn about literature, they should find all these things in it.

Although I have read honoured and moving texts with all kinds of young people for our shared pleasure, amongst my most effective lessons were those when I simply asked twelve-year-olds to make books for children to read in a first class of the local primary school. I gave them no instructions. Within a week the older pupils produced a variety of alphabet books, counting books, new folk-tales, all with illustrations. There were pop-ups, serious and funny poems, some in the modes of current commercial productions, others in forms remembered from childhood. There were no 'simplified' texts or babyishness. The secondary pupils had written into their texts what they best remembered of their early reading and much of themselves. A funny book about whales was also 'about' ecology and Greenpeace. A fairy-tale in black and white had nothing banal about it. The counting books were in four languages.

In making these books for the young children the older ones discovered the *textuality* of writing, the content-in-form of something made. The writers were also demonstrating that they had mastered the connections of different *genres*, the frames that hold the text as text. Even better, they showed that they could mix the kinds, break out of the frames, change the rules and the conventions. They invented different ways for an author to negotiate meanings and reading skills with a reader as a form of exchange. Having done all of this, the older students were then able consciously to describe what they had been up to, in shaping a book about a fish like a fish, in drawing the playground as the scene for the counting rhyme, using the hopscotch grid that is there permanently, decorating the flower poems with flowers, and so on. For me, this kind of undertaking matched my firm belief that literature is the same kind of activity in the early classes of the primary school as in the sixth form or in the discussions of literary theory in university seminars. In all we find what the young choose to read to please themselves and what they are expected to read to please their elders. No one has yet proved which of these two sets of texts has played the greater part in their readers' literacies.

CHAPTER 8

Causes and Cures

Signs of Change

The fate of adults and children who fail to learn to read and write, or who do these things less well than others think they should, becomes a testing ground for what it is for the rest of us to be literate. Our success is the measure of their failure. We are secure, so we comfort ourselves with the idea that if we could find out what caused the difficulties some learners experience, we could also devise the cures.

Since the setting up of various adult literacy schemes during the past twenty years or so, more than 100,000 adults have sought help to learn to read and write in order to make their daily lives less burdensome. Those who try to help them know that most people who cannot read have other problems, that illiteracy is part of a broader social picture of deprivation, discouragement and the ills that afflict the poor. Some have had broken or inadequate schooling and are fiercely angry when they recall what they see as time wasted when they might have been learning. Others have had every possible advantage, including early experience of being read to. Their difficulties are interpreted as other kinds of failure: of 'motivation', of the brain or, more particularly, of school. Whatever the cause of their ineffective literacy those who suffer from it long to be relieved. The agencies which are there to help them, in school or outside, know that they can make a difference, but they cannot call back the youth of the learners, nor reconstruct the schools. As usual, the tangle of theories, practices, institutions and the needs of individuals makes generalizable solutions impossible. So when television programmes, magazine articles or promotional campaigns bring to public notice the 'fate' of so-called illiterates, emphasizing their inadequacy or the inefficiency of their teachers, we should ask ourselves whose view of the situation is being presented in this way. It is not always that of the sufferers.

When I helped to set up an adult literacy centre in the Sixties I discovered that many people who came there had encountered some kind of crisis involving print. Most of them had to sort out the formal writing of official documents: how to find their birth certificate, get a driving licence, apply for unemployment benefit, confront the legalities of divorce. Young men in trouble with the courts came at the direction of the magistrates who saw their stealing as directly related to their inability to read. Given my literate history, the social optimism of the time and my inexperience, it was perhaps inevitable that I should urge all those who couldn't read to become 'real' readers as soon as their immediate problems were solved. My identification with their state also included the feeling that they must all have been suffering a loss of self-esteem by coming to seek help from a group of middle-class teachers. At that time I did not know how to make explicit, even to myself, the differences between my view of literacy and that of my students.

In my early lessons with adults in difficulty I made some discoveries. Literacy *is* related to self-esteem, even if not in the ways that teachers believe they can predict, and texts—what is read—change the learners' view of the task of learning. It was salutary for me to find out how difficult it was to read the *Daily Mirror* if you didn't already know the codes of football journalism, and there my students had the advantage. It also became clear, after a series of turbulent trials, that the students felt I was withholding from them the secrets of reading, while I wanted them to *try* to do it. Only later did I realize how hard it was for those who had appeared to fail so often before to risk failing again. Sometimes late readers are startlingly successful when they discover that they need *more* text, longer passages, stories, articles—not the snippets that they have been fed since they were first proclaimed 'poor' or 'backward'. Many more times their peers diligently performed useless exercises in 'special' lessons, in the hope that if they were successful they would receive a gold nugget of reading wisdom which, if added to others of the same, would one day be traded for complete reading ability and literate confidence.

With the arrival in the inner cities of numbers of adults whose first languages were not English and whose social and ethnic diversity was greater than anything hitherto known in schools or in work places, it became evident that a single model of literacy teaching would not do for everyone. The new arrivals needed help to learn English. Some were literate in their mother tongues, others were not, but wanted literacy above all things for their children. Many needed help to learn a different alphabet and a new writing system. The facts of world literacies: their differences of form, structure, construction and cultural significance, were suddenly there. At once there were signs of change. The adult learners formed cohesive groups, of Vietnamese learning English with attentive care, of young mothers studying child care, of too-early school leavers, British and others, changing jobs at thirty or over.

Gone is the older view of those who seek literacy help creeping to evening classes believing that they should not draw attention to their disabilities. Besides learning to read and write in their changed situation, these learners now want access to new technologies. They have their own view of entitlement, believing that a society which needs their skills as workers should provide them with modern retraining in the literacies of the future. They have no lack of self-esteem. Having been about in the world they know that literacy should help to make them more at home in it.

To respond to these needs, the Adult Literacy and Basic Studies Unit (ALBSU) has created a number of 'drop in' centres in British cities where anyone can come to get help for their 'perceived needs'.[1] In these places adults are *clients*, as with lawyers or the Citizens Advice Bureau, not pupils, as in school, or patients, as in hospital. Clients seek advice because they want to use literacy as an activity in their lives. They are also choosing their own ways into literacy, becoming responsible for their own learning, planning and setting their own goals for literacy development. This is altogether less wasteful of everyone's time and efforts than earlier operations which tried to mop up all illiterates at once by means of a step-by-step television programme based on a school model of teaching and learning. I hope that these new centres will also support the community publishing ventures now well established as the result of local efforts to encourage those who want to write in ways they never discovered in schools, by finding their own voices as *writers*.

The 'perceived needs' of late arrivals in literacy change dramatically when they learn to read and write. Their involvement in society becomes different; their views of themselves change. Brian Street, who knows and shows how all models of literacy are, at bottom, related to cultural values, believes that there are positive aspects of the 'provide what people want' approach to literacy teaching of adults which also challenge the nature of literacy in school. But he is also convinced that if people are to use their literacy to make changes in society, these changes have to affect the whole system, not just parts of it.[2] Nevertheless, significant groups which have grown up around consumer advice agencies and organisations to protect the environment have had local roots. Those who join with their neighbours to protect or protest find themselves sooner or later writing letters in order to give their views the status of documentary evidence. Linked to new technologies, which are the most visible signs of change, writing still counts.

Misalignments

The experience of helping adults to read and write was both exhilarating and depressing. With all their different experiences and expectations, their competences and their lack of confidence, they always believed their teacher knew more than they did; they always underrated themselves. Some groups, especially of women, encouraged each other to read children's books that they could then read to their children. Men found this difficult. The books that 'worked' with them in some contexts were hopeless in others. Generalization about the condition of those who fell through the school literacy net is usually inaccurate and always unhelpful. What remains with me of that early teaching experience—it lasted for ten years—is the persistence of the learners and the devotion of the helpers. The clearest memory is of the frustration and anger of those who believed school had cheated them.

With these thoughts in mind, and a belief that all teachers should share responsibilities for literacy, I went back to the beginnings of children's learning to see if there were early moves that could be made to prevent later disappointment. At about the same time I joined a group of skilful and perceptive colleagues to try to find out how to help inexperienced readers in secondary school become critically literate before they went to work.

The first thing I discovered is the gap between those who study reading problems and those who teach children, and, more surprising, the gap between those who teach and those who learn. Academic investigation of reading is extensive, but it is also overwhelmingly a study of reading failure, a pathology of problems. Given that far more pupils succeed in learning to read than those who have difficulty, it is strange that we still know so little about reading success. The tradition of remedial teaching in schools, based as it is on the medical model of looking for symptoms of breakdown, diagnosing the condition and offering treatment or remedy in order to restore the patient to health, has resulted in the persistence of the metaphors of *illness* in ways of looking at children whose progress is not as steady as parents and teachers expect. We have no comparable studies of reading success to match. Sometimes, in descriptions of children believed to be 'gifted', details emerge of what successful learning looks like, but again, these are seen to apply to children who are regarded as special. Very rarely has the special teaching of gifted children been regarded as the best way to deal with the remedial class, but common sense suggests that the two groups have much in common.

Children's reading difficulties, as these are generally understood, are described in terms of *misalignments* or failures of matching. For example, parents will tell you, and so will Frank Smith, that children who are not at ease with their teacher do badly in reading lessons, as in all other kinds of lessons. 'To get on with' a teacher usually means to be successful in the subject.[3] Recovery from reading difficulties can then be described in terms of realignment of teacher and learner. A simple misalignment occurs when a reader doesn't like the book he or she is expected to read, and where a simple change of text may make 'all the difference'.

Mismatchings of learner and teacher, learner and task, context and text, situation and explanation are frequent. Usually the breakdowns in understanding, knowing what to do, or what the teacher wants, are quickly repaired. But, unfortunately, some pass unnoticed by the teacher and are not expressed by the learner.

Suppose that two children arrive at school on the same day, both able to name the letters of the alphabet. One of them can recite them confidently and pick them out from an alphabet book. The other knows the letter names but can't recite them in order. But she can write her name. Neither child is at a particular advantage if both of them have also learned that reading is an interesting thing to do. If, however, one knows that words written down are conveying a message and that the world is full of such messages, and the other one continues to write her name and repeat the letters, then the former has discovered something more useful, the purpose of print to convey messages. This is social learning, the kind that links school to the world outside, the kind I want teachers and parents to understand. But if the skill of reciting the alphabet remains unconnected to reading for meaning, the child who can do this will believe she has learned it to no purpose or has failed to grasp what it is for.

Likewise, any child who arrives in school without much experience of how a book works *seems* to be at a disadvantage if her teacher assumes that this is common knowledge, taken for granted in all her pupils. Note, *seems*. If the teacher makes no effort to check this out, the child will probably do one of two things: imitate the readerly behaviour of the rest of the class and ask her friend what's involved, or decide that she cannot take the risk of trying to discover what the others all seem to know. When a teacher understands that she must quickly help the child to know what the others know, she may also discover that the situation of *not* knowing is more prevalent in her class than she had realized. The common alignment of 'what counts as reading in this class' is what all children seek to grasp. The worst teaching scenario is when a child decides she is not able to find out what she has to do, and the teacher is unaware of her need to know.

Being in line with the others in agreement about 'this is how we do writing and reading in this class' has a powerful cohesive force in all early teaching and learning. It sets the bounds of children's dependence on what they are told and makes clear how much they have to find out for themselves. They begin to show reluctance to take learning risks when they believe that what they know doesn't fit in with what the teacher treats as knowledge. Children's decisions about their alignment with classroom learning is often expressed in terms of whether or not their teachers like them. 'They only taught the kids they liked,' complained one inexperienced reader of fourteen. 'We just kept quiet, for if we made mistakes, she (the teacher) always said, "I've told you before that's wrong".' When they feel hurt by real or imagined insults, many children turn away from the tasks that threaten them, with the result that they expect less and less 'fit' between what they know and what they are told.

The case of bilingual pupils highlights this problem. Those who are at the first stage of learning a new language

often speak very little, even when they are given encouragement. The risk of making mistakes is then at its
highest, but their listening is still very active. Monolingual
teachers who do not understand these silences sometimes
feel threatened by what they interpret as the children's
'stubbornness'. True, the pupils may not want to be there.
But when they do not speak much in class it is not because
they have nothing to say.

Children may be misaligned in the accomplishment of
school tasks in many ways we know nothing about. 'When
you ask me what it *says*,' complained a brave child to me
once, 'I don't know what to tell you because you've read it
before and you know. So I don't know how to say what it
says.' When learning to read and write seems unnecessarily
repetitious (boring), when, as another child said, 'The story
ain't so good', learners of all ages turn their attention to other
things, back away from difficulties, and hope that, somehow,
it will all come right. Quite often it doesn't. Then there are
frantic searches for the cause of failure.

Making sense of reading is never a straightforward task
for children who do not teach themselves. They have to let
others help them while still acting on their own account. The
successful are those who synchronize their understandings
with their teachers', which is why alignment is important. As
Margaret Donaldson says: 'It's our very knowledge of what
children have to learn that blocks the realization of precisely
what children have to be helped to see.'[4] The teacher's view
of the child's view of the task is sometimes based on a false
premise of what that particular child actually knows. What
saves the situation in reading is a joint agreement to make
sense of a text that genuinely interests them both. But if the
teacher demands that all the answers to her questions must
be exact, correct in her terms, then the learner assumes that
the important operation is to do as she is told. If this means
abandoning her own understanding and engaging in a
procedure she finds unhelpful, the learner gives up trying to
make sense of the text and performs the actions of 'doing
reading'. It is at this point that children usually lose

confidence in their chances of success and, actually, learn to fail. Those who suffer from acute and prolonged reading difficulties have, at some time, told themselves 'I can't do it.'

Two further misalignments inhibit success in children's learning to read. First, children often have implicit understandings which their language may not yet match. That is, they know more than they can explain in the words their teachers want from them. Here is a girl reading in her first science book an account of how a drinking straw works. The teacher asks her to tell the others what she has discovered. 'There's nothing pushing down the lemonade on the outside,' says the reader, matching what she knows about straws with the description of the diagram she has studied in the book. 'That's not a very good explanation,' says the teacher, and passes on.

In many school reading lessons, instead of negotiating the starting point more exactly, teachers take for granted what children have to be helped to understand. The same is true in classroom discussions which surround the exercises in reading we have already discussed as 'comprehension'. The less experienced readers are not the least experienced understanders of what goes on in the world. Yet, if they are not allowed enough time to put their viewpoint because they stumble when they read aloud, they will reject their teachers if the teachers seem to have no time for them. The relation of speakers', listeners', writers' and readers' meanings to the social worlds from which they come and which their words imply has to be teased out in a patient and rich exchange of perceptions and understandings, not simply tested in class reading exercises. Those whose learning to read does not seem to have gathered momentum often need more reassurance that their understanding of the world still counts. They often get the message of a text, even when they are ill at ease with the medium, the writing on the page.

Children sometimes find it difficult to explain what they know about reading, especially to their parents. They see the hurt in their eyes if they fail to identify a word on a page to command. They hear such conversations as, 'What *is* the matter with him? The other three learned to read with no trouble. Why can't he recognize letters? We've done everything the teachers say: read to him, let him read on his own. We've taken him to the library, fixed his reading light, read *Learning to Read*. Why don't they teach him to recognize letters and words at sight? We'd better have him tested.' Indeed, parents often *have* tried everything, except, perhaps, to understand what the child understands, namely, that he or she isn't coming up to scratch, and somehow it is his or her own fault for not discovering the clues that everyone so earnestly tries to give them to the reading puzzle. Bamboozlement is what they suffer from; that strange conflict and confusion of instructions, overloading their view of the act of reading, draining it of any pleasure it may have, turning it into something threatening.

What puzzles me most about my own difficulties in understanding psychological investigations of children's reading is that, search as I will, I find so few studies that analyse in any depth what children think they are doing when they read. What is their view of reading as a learning task? Here, again, their boredom is a clue because it manifests itself in their disinclination to continue. When they are bored, they shut the book. That seems to me the moment to enquire: what made you do that? What turns you off about reading? What, exactly, bores you?

If we are to look closely at what happens when children say they are bored, we begin by distinguishing the state of boredom from its ancestor, *accidie*, the condition of torpor or sloth or indifference which has been known since the thirteenth century. I don't believe that children learning to read are lazy or indifferent. We are sometimes told that they 'lack motivation', a psychological definition of 'not wanting to'. The only motivation for reading that really works is the pleasure of the text or feelings of increasing success, and these depend on the reader's own activity. When I invite young readers to estimate the degree of boredom they are suffering from ('How boring is this book? Give it a mark out of ten') they are usually clear about the reason for their decisions. ('Six: it's all about boys and I've had enough of them.') When they disagree with their friends about how boring a book is they offer keenly observed judgements and criticisms which usually suggest that the set tasks are either too easy or too difficult. I believe that children say reading bores them when they have to take risks or make special efforts to understand a text, and their teachers have not made it clear to them what the risks are, or what counts as success. Readers are quite prepared to 'have a go' at making their way through a text on their own, but they want to know what depends on it: a mark, more hard work, their future, our good opinion of them as readers, our belief that they can be literate.

What Hinders: What Helps

Some hesitation always impedes my making direct statements about teaching reading, because, as I have said many times before, there is no one way to do it. Nor is there ever a single reason why a learner should fail, so no single teaching method will serve to recover all children whose reading has become an encumbrance to them, their parents and their teachers. Think again of what we now know about literacy as *recursive* learning and you will see that, if we believe that learning to read occurs as a spiral progression, we cannot judge progress as a straight line. We cannot keep on subjecting our children to different ways of being taught in the hope that we will eventually find the one that works. We may discover a teacher who is more patient, more sympathetic, more inventive, but I believe children fail when they lose confidence in their own ability to succeed. So my solution is to engage them, in any way we can, in the process of *discovering* what reading is and not in worrying about how to do it. Literacy is always both experimental and developmental. Sometimes I think they can't know what reading *is*, because everyone—parents, teachers and others—is too busy telling them what to *do*.

Here are some things that never seem to help unconfident, inexperienced readers and writers to make progress. They are based on the work my colleagues and I did when we were with adolescents who had given up all hope of becoming literate because others had judged them hopeless. First, most teachers and parents are always sure that they know best what is good for the learner and entice the learner into doing what they provide as help. Next, it is difficult for helpers not to *collude* with those who are disinclined to read and write, to find excuses for them when they are tired or have a headache. While readers in difficulty seem to warrant our sympathy, they don't really need it. If you are helping someone to read or write, think of the physiotherapist who helps by turning the pain of an injury into the different pain of exercise to make it better. Most readers have, at some time, found reading an effort; all writers certainly have done the same. Then, over-praise, unconditional acceptance of half-heartedness isn't helpful. Learners know when they are not getting ahead, and to be told they're wonderful when they know they are not makes them worry even more about the seriousness of their case. If we say that their inability to read and write as well as they want to isn't their fault, we reinforce their conviction that they will never be successful because there really is something *wrong* with them. Above all, we must resist giving those who have come to dislike reading or writing more of what they failed to do or enjoy before. My heart sinks in remedial classes when I see children working away at exercises that seem to have nothing to do with real reading.

Now, here are some things that usually make a beneficial difference. First, the teacher (parent, helper) should be convinced that the inventive intelligence of learners is not a problem. Their view of school, as well as of reading and writing, may be *part* of the problem. Their view of the task of learning is always a problem if it is misaligned with that of the teacher. Next, learners should be told helpful things about reading and writing. They need to know, clearly, that 'getting the words right' is not the task. They are to interpret the meaning beyond the signs. Understanding what is coming and where they have been needs to be made clear from their interaction with a text. What does that involve for the teacher? Not letting the learners struggle with words when their understanding of the world is there to help them. If we encourage children and adults to make texts mean in the contexts where they are to be understood, we have no need to emphasize *skills* at the cost of reading and writing as *activities*, things that people do in a literate society. Then, we have to create lesson contexts where reading and writing let the literate world into the literacy of school. Reading and writing are linked to ideas of 'growing up', being responsible, having a point of view, setting the task and discussing with others how to get it done and thought about.

Right from their earliest lessons children should be helped to reflect on what they have been doing and what they want to bring about. 'The trouble with getting to the end of a chapter in this book,' says Daniel, 'is that you don't know if you really mind what happens to these people or not.' 'How is it,' asks May, 'that this author doesn't seem to mind how often she changes a line of a poem? How does she know that she has got it right?' These are questions that growing literates ask at different stages of their awareness that images and print make meaning.

One thing more. To get better at reading and writing also implies reorganizing what one has learned. If, as I have insisted, progress is recursive, then from time to time any child may seem to stand still or even go backwards. 'Her reading isn't nearly so good as it was' is never a helpful judgement if the reader has just begun to go more slowly with more demanding texts. (There is usually one old favourite book still being read, quickly, somewhere else.) Until the learners get the hang of what will really help them, their teachers and other adults have to be patient as well as active when they seem to dally on the way. With everything else we care about—health, money, progress of all kinds—we want our children to achieve quickly what in fact needs to grow at the rate of understandings that cannot sprout overnight.

There are no miracle cures for those who have reading and writing difficulties. There are helpful conditions, including, sometimes, the withdrawal of over-anxious adult interference, but no single solutions. Some baffled learners need only to know that they do not have to *identify* words by a series of secret rules, when they need only *recognize* the ones they know. Others need help with texts they cannot manage on their own, but not total takeover of their problems. No adolescent, no adult learns to read and write in a vacuum. The context must be supportive as well as the teacher, whose particular task is to insist that reading matters, not as a sign of intelligence but as a normal activity.

Dyslexia: a *Special* Special Need?

One of the GCSE examination tasks in English is the preparation and delivery of a short talk on a subject chosen by the candidate. In order to learn how to assess these performances, examiners are trained by watching videotape recordings of pupils talking. Then they give marks, and discuss their judgements with other, more experienced examiners. In one such training session I saw and listened to a sixteen-year-old boy address his camera audience about how he 'suffered' (his word) from dyslexia. He gave details of his inability to recognize words, the problems he had with spelling and writing, and, in passing, he explained that he had 'something wrong' with his brain. He then went on to describe the teaching which had proved helpful and his feelings about it. He could, he said, now read quite well, and his spellings troubled him less as he knew now how to check the words he was uncertain about. The trainee examiners were impressed by the confident coherence of the presentation, the boy's cheerfulness and poise. Here was someone who had worked hard to overcome the most stressful condition of illiteracy. He also justified, by his competent handling of his topic, the inclusion of oral work in the examination routine. He got a high mark.

What impressed me most in this episode was the boy's statement about his brain. How could he be so confidently cheerful about it? This led to a further inspection of the words he used about his condition and an interpretation of what he actually said. (There was no problem about his mark; the examiners' view stood firm.) None of the descriptive words he used could have come from him in the first place: 'lateral dominance', 'spatial difficulties', 'letter reversals', 'poor visual memory', 'hemispheric differences' are not terms sixteen-year-olds use instinctively to describe their reading problems. The words themselves are taken from the diagnosis of the condition by experts and were used by the boy as the official description of his condition as dyslexic. Significantly, his greatest emphasis in the entire presentation was on his intelligence, which, he said firmly, was 'normal'. As I watched him, over and over again, my respect for him grew, especially when he detailed his poor performance on a range of psychological tests which confirmed his disability. Yet I was also very disturbed. He seemed to be living in a house from which the scaffolding couldn't be removed in case the house fell down.

Discussions of dyslexia, its nature, its implications and cure are full of confusions. Yet those who are part of the movement to make others more aware of it have no doubt that it not only 'exists', and is a serious problem, they also say that it affects one child in ten, and that these children ought to have special teaching which addresses this diagnosed condition directly. There is no doubt at all that the children need help and should have it. Why, then, does dyslexia stand out from other reading problems? Why are claims made that children who 'suffer' from dyslexia are in a particular, separate category? Is dyslexia a special Special Need which only special teachers can alleviate in a para-medical fashion?

Dyslexia and, indeed, dyslexics have been around for nearly a hundred years. Hinshelwood, an eye surgeon in Scotland, was sure that some children had a special difficulty in remembering words and letters. His was the first medical investigation into children's reading problems. Like many others since, he looked for what was missing in the array of physiological activities that make up reading. While we now know that Hinshelwood's theory about the eyes is wrong, his idea that there is a special, separate group of people who are poor readers because they are affected by conditions not shared by the rest of the population has persisted. Dyslexics believe themselves to be such a group because they have 'brain damage' in common.

Those who insist that dyslexics are different are usually parents. They know well what an individual child finds difficult and are alarmed by signs of wayward progress in literacy. When they discover other parents with similar anxieties they are reassured that their child is not abnormal, but only distinctive, so they look for teachers who understand the teaching of reading in these cases, pinning their faith on the 'method' used to 'cure' them.

In fact, some children who are designated 'dyslexic' have the same difficulties as other children who are considered 'normal': reversing letters in writing and failing to distinguish phonological differences in reading—*weigh* and *weight*, for example. But dyslexia has become a matter for investigation on its own for a number of reasons, including those of the social class to which most dyslexic children seem to belong.

There are also different kinds of dyslexia, which different diagnostic tests reveal. Psychologists differentiate between 'acquired' and 'developmental' dyslexia. Within 'acquired dyslexia' there is 'deep dyslexia', 'phonological dyslexia' and 'surface dyslexia', all of which are defined in terms of features that have appeared in the reading of individual children. The evidence is not in doubt. But, as Bryant and Bradley, the acknowledged Oxford experts in this area, say in their book *Children's Reading Problems*, it is not just a matter of proving backward readers to be curious cases; they must also be shown to be 'curiouser' than other children. Thus comparisons between poor readers and acquired dyslexics should also include details about the skills and behaviour of normal children.[4]

Those who engage with dyslexia as an educational cause or movement have certainly drawn attention to the needs of some children. They have also been disparaging of the competences of those responsible for the teaching of reading in schools. But, in the context of universal literacy, there are other implications which go beyond the diagnosis of individual difficulties. Since the Warnock Report of 1978 suggested that children with identifiable special needs should be taught in mainstream classes of ordinary schools where provision could be made for teachers to help them, pressure has been exerted by private dyslexia groups to have dyslexia classified as a 'special need'. In this way, private lessons paid for by parents would become part of local education authority provisions. What most parents of dyslexic children want particularly, however, is that the teachers should be those who have been specially trained in the medical units established in hospitals where dyslexia is considered a condition best dealt with in a medical context. Hinshelwood's ghost stalks this corner of literacy. The vocabulary of dyslexia experts is distinctly that of doctors: *diagnosis, treatment, remedy, cure, strephosymbolia, laterality, syndrome.* The reading tests are usually devised and administered by psychologists who still retain an interest in nonsense words as a technique for isolating reading difficulties. The special nature of dyslexia has always been claimed by those who begin by insisting that their child's intelligence is not in doubt, but that their reading is a particular problem which teachers in ordinary schools are not trained to deal with. Despite this curious élitism which particular kinds of reading failure seem to produce, all children in difficulty can now benefit from the activity of dyslexia groups which has resulted in 'special referrals' to psychologists for all parents anxious about their children's reading. Note, however, that those who prescribe the remedy are not always those who know about the ordinary difficulties of children who can't read.

We should always pay attention to well conducted researches into children's learning difficulties, but we should be wary if they suggest universal failure in education. At present the research literature suggests that 'difficulty in reading' is the only common characteristic in all children described as dyslexic. The real cure is that they learn to read by experiencing success. The common wisdom now is that there are a few rare children whose reading difficulties persist when all causes for them have been eliminated, but they are few.

Most of the children I know who have or have had reading difficulties are constantly in conditions of great stress. There is always something else wrong. Most experts in dyslexia are agreed that early diagnosis of the condition offers the best hope of early remedy. What seems to me to go beyond remedy in these cases is the loss of what Judith Graham called 'the elusive joy' of reading when she described how, after many years of lessons, her pupil could read effectively but approached written texts with less enthusiasm than he had shown in the early stages when he could read much less.[5] If reading is troublesome, children will avoid it and fall behind. To help them we must keep their interest in the pleasure of reading, encouraging them to discuss what we read with them, making relevant their interpretation of the world to the words they will surely come to understand. We must not let them be isolated, which, for me, is the saddest aspect of those whom dyslexia turns into *patients*. The word, after all, means sufferers. The first move in their cure is to get rid of the pain, the anxiety. Deep dyslexia is best treated by deep reading in the company of those who do a lot of it.

CHAPTER 9

New Literacies

Old Habits: New Challenges

Throughout these pages stalks the idea that what counts as being literate changes in every generation. The history of literacy confirms that there is no single line of progress from oral societies to literate ones. Compulsory scholarship didn't bring with it a natural increase in logical thinking or upward social mobility. Children are not necessarily wiser than their parents if they stay longer at school. Being literate, like all other aspects of social life, is re-made and re-conceptualized in new settings. What seems to stay the same is that the literate have definite advantages over the non-literate, which as a result give them more power and influence, a greater range of choice in their lifestyle, what they think about, or do, or how they re-create themselves in what they enjoy.

For all that literacy began with writing, reading usually occupies the foreground in discussions of being literate because most people read more than they write. But in the division of literate labour, the writer is still the powerful one. There is also abundant evidence that from now on, the meaning of 'reading' will continue to expand, to describe what people do in contexts where what is read is not, evidently, writing, script or text. Television is the obvious example. Do viewers *read* what they see? If so, how? There are advertising print, Ceefax titles, sub-titles of foreign films, headlines, logos, and incidental writing. But what counts as reading pictures both on screens and in modern newspapers? As writing changes, so does reading. But what about images? Are we re-learning to read these?

'Will the need to be literate become defunct in a technologically advanced society?' was how a young secondary school teacher asked about new literacies. Part of what she meant was 'will the children I teach eventually compose on screens instead of paper, without pens or pencils, so that they won't need to worry about spelling because the "checker" will clear the mistakes?' Will we then judge the presentation of their work in terms of printing style? These are reasonable queries, but there's more to new literacies than the technologies that represent them.

If literacy includes, as I believe it must, *reflection* on what is written to be read, then irrespective of changes in the technologies of the new literacies, the composers and receivers of communications and texts, of words and images, will have to be more *critically* literate, not least because of the amount of information that will circulate simply to justify the existence of the machines. Our children will still have to read texts in contexts and in ways they will need to understand. Perhaps we have to remember that the increase in universal literacy did not bring about either general highly specialized literate capabilities, or, and this is more significant, any marked decline in the general level of competence, no matter what the doubting say. Teachers will still be at the heart of the matter, however, for they will be the first professional group to have to deal with *generalized* changes in popular literacy and the new channels for its conduct. On them will fall the obligation to encourage those who use word processors and cameras for the new kinds of essays to think about the nature of their composing.

New literacy technologies are always extensions of older ones. Where once scribes made copies of texts to be more widely read, today photocopiers do this at the speed of light. For all their comprehensive adaptability and usefulness, computerized networks are still, generally, print-based. Analysts and programmers are still in the business of keeping records. The second Gutenberg revolution may be in the hands of 'knowledge engineers' as we are now to call the technologists of information systems, but, at the same time, strict laws protect the composers of texts.

In this expanding situation, the literate seem to be those who are at home with sophisticated screenery, who know their way about in the computer culture, using its vocabularies with confidence. *Compatible* has added to its meanings of harmonious existence or the possibility of self-fertilization the notion of machines which have interchangeable parts. So the *language awareness* which the National Curriculum wants all children to have will doubtless take account of these innovations and others, such as 'wraparound', 'cursor' and 'boot', in their new contexts. Another fact related to our education system is that men dominate this brave new electronic world; with a few notable exceptions, women are the handmaidens of the machines, as in an earlier period of social change, when they learned to type. Once in place, computer-based literacies create a need for new 'generations' of hardware by defining new reading habits, writing formats and roles for their users. Newspaper prose changes as journalists type their copy directly into the production system. Does a poet compose differently if she or he changes to a word processor? What becomes of the early drafts?

This is a period of exciting transitions. All schools will have to take account of innovations such as desk-top publishing. The abundance of writing opportunities, the plethora of data, suggest that more, not fewer, imaginative understandings can result from their use. Pupils in secondary schools will join those at work in expecting to have 'hands on' experience of many different communication systems. Schooled literacy will be adapted to accommodate what learners want to do with their competences as well as to continue what teachers think they may be good for. The traditional power of the academic essay, the claim that it has a privileged place in promoting reasoning, logic and reflective thinking will be loosened.

One particular strand that joins the pre-history of literacy—the paintings in the caves of Lascaux, for example—to the most recent technological advances is the perceived relation between writing and *images*. Our lives are thronged with pictures, signs and symbols whose meanings we read without words, but which are an inherent part of our contemporary culture. Those who create double-page colour advertisements or films about expensive cars can shut their minds to the fact that very few people can actually afford them compared with the number who wish they could. New technologies bring new paradoxes, new challenges to our critical awareness. We still have to remember, however, that there never has been, in Raymond Williams' words, 'effectively equal access to written and printed material or anything like effectively equal opportunities to contribute to it'.[1] One of the changes that the new literacies should make us contemplate is that of access. Not all the advertisements for computers will, by themselves, make computers available to all who might profit from them. My limited experience of software about literacy does not fill me with confidence about the quality of its messages. One of the great virtues that still remains from our oral tradition is the kind of scepticism that saves us from the importunings of novelty. 'Garbage in, garbage out' is as good a warning as the old adage, 'If you believe all you read you'll eat all you see'.

New technologies of literacy highlight the problems which stem from the amount of writing that now exists to be read. Most competent literates complain about the trouble they have 'getting through' a day's amount of print. Students in school and college are bombarded with bibliographies which are swollen by the writings of those who must be seen in print if they are to be promoted. Again, the machines are used to sort out what needn't be read, to process information into manageable chunks. Language becomes terse, snappy, self-referring, immediately graspable.

At the same time, public print is full of secrets, working on the literates' need to be 'in the know'. When the gas supplies were being privatized I saw huge letters, B.G., everywhere. Before I'd realized what was afoot I saw *British Gumption* and, thereafter, other two-word slogans with the same initial letters. By the time you read this, the contexts and the texts of British Gas will have faded; you will be reading something else which depends on your social awareness more than your literacy. As this process continues, new literates will need encouragement to look closely at the ways by which others use words to control people's lives. It is the same old problem, but a different kind of challenge, because the very lack of certain kinds of information, and the more general, propagandist presence of misinformation makes 'who knows what' a constant social preoccupation. This is an education-al matter for the young, their parents and their teachers. A literate awareness, the skills of reading *against* the texts of power will have to be a particularly important new literacy.

What else? Too well entrenched in my bookish habits to change very much, I am nevertheless curious about and fascinated by the kinds of reading and writing my grand-children will learn to do. Without laying too many obligations on their generation or claiming any prophetic skill, in what follows I have made a purely personal selection of new literacies that might make learning to read and write pleasurable, enjoyable and recreative as well as useful and profitable. I have chosen these as alternatives to older traditional models of schooled literacy because we are most concerned about the generation shift in being literate when our children begin to read and write in the traditional social setting of school. There the old alphabetic elements meet new media *and* new pedagogic processes. So we begin with the most traditional literacy of all.

Children Writing

Amongst my collection of writing done by children is this letter, on yellowing paper of good quality, in faded but impeccable copperplate handwriting. Each upper case letter is one and a half centimetres tall; each lower case letter exactly five millimetres. The ascending lines are thinner than the descenders, the slope is regular throughout. The writer is eight years old.

24 Gower Street
London.
the fifteenth of December 1876

My Dear Parents,
    The Misses Robinson desire me to convey to you their compliments and to say that the date for the commencement of the next school period will be Monday, the twelfth of January.
I remain,
Your ever-loving daughter,
Joanna Wolf.

As Joanna Wolf went to a day school for young ladies she presumably saw her parents often enough to tell them the dates of the school holidays. But her alert teachers made the letter-writing exercise serve a number of purposes. It taught the conventions, including those of punctuation, of this kind of communication. The words themselves exemplify important spelling rules. Besides, it meant that each individual letter displayed the writer's expected level of attainment and also saved the Misses Robinson from the expense and tedium of sending notes about school term dates to all parents. Joanna demonstrates the social competence of 'pen*man*ship'. The formal wording is not of her composing. She is acquiring what the Cox Report calls the 'secretarial' aspects of writing. (The gender implications are there too.) How many times did Joanna write the first line, I wonder. As a scribe, she exhibits the controlled social behaviour expected of her. The drill, exactness and neatness were also the accomplishments of the intermediate male clerks in her family's bank who used steel pens to write in ledgers until well into the next century.

As she copies the message, Joanna could be thinking of something else. What she writes demands nothing of her; the communication is that of her teachers who believe that before they can say anything of their own in writing, children have to master the skills of handling the tools. This has changed fundamentally in the past twenty years. Now we know that, long before they come to school, children compose. In speech, in play, in drawings they represent their view of their world.

By watching adults who read and write, children discover that message-making is different from making pictures. They begin to reproduce the print they see in the world, sometimes to copy it. At other times they want to make their own meaning visible and permanent. Experts who examine children's early writing claim that they, the children, act like authors in that they generate texts. They make decisions about what they want to write, and take responsibility for its format and production. To look at only one aspect of this complex set of processes, spelling, for example, is to treat their writing too casually. In so far as children invent spelling they are rarely making random guesses. What they put on a page shows how their awareness of letter combinations is being reproduced. Other conventions, sentences, punctuation and speech marks all make their appearance neither haphazardly nor as the result of direct instructions, but in response to the young writer's growing attempts to control this powerful process of making oneself understood.

Although teachers may know how coherent messages are carried in children's early mapping and their hypotheses about letter strings, parents have to be reassured about these approximations to conventional spellings. Paul Bissex's written question to his mother who was not paying attention to him: R U D F ? (Are you deaf?) showed her that he knew what writing was for. Myra Barrs discovered a budding linguist who made a small book, unbidden, which displayed her five-year-old's awareness of language to be already at the level expected of teenagers by the National Curriculum. Here is what she wrote:

mY NAN   SEIɲ SАhɾ
SEi5   TEe 4Ɛ
irEs   SAΝ5
              SEiꝭTO.T
              4 Ʀ

('My Nan says Irish. She says 't'ree for three. And she say 't'irteen for thirteen'.) The picture of this original script also appears in *Patterns of Learning*. Adults who remember the constraints of their own early learning want to be reassured, however, that conventional writing will still be taught and learned.[2]

Many children learn the fluency of writing before they can spell and punctuate. This fluency is experienced as *power*. The feeling is important because, if it lasts long enough, it carries the learner over the business of learning the necessary *control*, the constraints that the conventional alphabetic system lays on the composer of any text. Recent studies of children's writing, especially the National Writing Project, show that if children experience the power of writing they will submit to the discipline of 'getting it right' by means of revisions, redrafting and proof-reading. As they engage with the writing process children discover that they can report what they know of the world and, in stories and poems, change it. When children write they make choices. They are ready to look for alternative versions of what they are expected to call 'real'. This is a new literacy, something not envisaged by those who have tested children's scribal efficiency with dictation exercises or spelling tests. It implies an ownership by the writers of what they compose.[3]

This ownership of writing becomes even more important in the case of children whose mother tongue is not English and who nevertheless want to do well in the school system. The language of their literacy may not be the language spoken and used at home, so they need to be guaranteed confidence and help. The language-dialect Sylheti is spoken, but its speakers read and write in Bengali; Panjab-speaking families write in Urdu, the first language of Pakistan. Muslim children may be learning Arabic for studying the Qur'an. Exotic as these examples seem, they reflect the experience of many children in our inner cities. The more homely instance, perhaps, is Welsh. We have not taken nearly enough advantage of what we could learn from those bilinguals, including the effects of belonging to a distinctive community with its own rich literature.

We must stop underestimating what children in secondary school are capable of writing. In adolescence, writing either takes off or is turned off. The grudging exchanges that accompany essay-writing are now being replaced by more imaginative interactions, wider contexts, important contents. Young people who watch television are neither ignorant nor uninformed. They have strong visions about how the world might be. Often muddled, confused and in need of more explicit information, perhaps, these young writers are certainly not indifferent to events in Eastern Europe, the fate of Nelson Mandela or their social interactions with their peers. They don't write about football and *Neighbours* if they believe that what they have to say will not be taken seriously. I have never forgotten the anger of an exceptional student who said: 'They asked me to write about something that was important to me. I told them about my Gran's funeral and all I got was a C.'

My experience is that in discussion, talking and listening, the complications of the moves to abstract thinking can be sorted out in writing *if the learner is not made to feel stupid*. When young people attempt to deal with more complex topics they often begin to be aware of ambiguities in their lives. Their writing reflects the tangles of their thinking. At this point the teacher may know how to sort out the writing, but it is sometimes much better to give the learner help first in sorting out the saying. Talking, listening and reading are always part of writing, but these new texts of new writers are sometimes dealing with topics scarcely a generation old. At other times they are the site of struggles everyone has known. Adolescents nowadays know better than their parents that writing can be a collaborative act and that talk is its necessary framework.

My conviction is that more young people write better, more coherently, interestingly, powerfully than at any time in the past because they begin as authors not as scribes. Parents accept this idea if it is explained to them and if they are helped to see what progress looks like. But as a community, we still keep too many writing secrets away from those who would be helped by knowing more about, for example, the relations of writers and readers. Contemporary literates of all kinds are gregarious; published authors talk about their own writing and that of other people, when invited into school. They also talk to the young who ask them better questions than their teachers do.

Television

Do we *read* television? If so, how do we do it, and are we right to suggest it is a new literacy? Television technology, the workings of the set, comes from scientific adaptations of light and sound. We speak of TV as a medium, which links it with films, newspapers and radio as a way of bringing to us – right into our homes, in fact – representations of the world we live in. Television offers us versions of life that we are invited to look at. 'You sorta listen with your eyes', said a nine-year old child to Bob Hodge and David Tripp when they set about discovering whether the effects of TV on children were as baleful as many people insisted they were.[4]

Television becomes a literacy when those who examine its succession of visual images as if they were verbal texts borrow the words that linguists and literary critics use to describe language. Analysts of TV look for rule systems in the 'messages' that viewers see. So to be literate in terms of TV you have to know what you are doing when you look. Most children discover how to do this without any lessons, which may in part account for adults' distrust of children's familiarity with the medium. 'Watching too much television' has a warning sound, while 'reading too many books' is a kind of shy praise. One thing is certain: children become adept at watching without the intervention of adults. They give themselves lessons alone, with adults or older peers. Just how quite young children learn to make sense of TV we do not exactly know, except that they clearly distinguish *images* at an early age. (They recognize their parents in photographs before they are a year old.)

Television is usually social watching, especially in the home, where conversation goes on around and about whatever is being seen, with a lot of commentary. There is a possible comparison with the oral tradition of children listening to familiar stories being read from 'chapbooks', the popular print of the seventeenth and eighteenth centuries, before the young were separated from their elders and had books of their own. These 'grimy little productions were everywhere by the middle of the 18th century' says the historian Harvey Darton.[5] They cost a penny, tuppence or sixpence and were read to bits. They were despised by the skilled literates of the day in the same terms that, later, people were to use about comics, and then about TV. As the interesting feature of the chapbook was the illustrations, of Saint George, Bevis, giants, dying Christians, bears and dragons, I am persuaded that children learned to read from these in ways that are matched by their reading of TV pictures. **Images** are the common attraction.

Some people set TV and print literacy in opposition to each other and hold TV responsible for a decline in reading. We have no way of knowing that, if they were not watching, children would be reading. My guess is that they would still be doing something else if it held more fascination for them. But I wonder if we still secretly fear the power of TV, its hold over viewers who choose its more sensational productions, just as readers of popular journalism seem to prefer scandal to news and serious comment. If we are unwilling to regard TV as a literacy because to read it is a metaphorical extension we disapprove of, then we are bound to remember that what we see most constantly on the screen is faces. We read faces all day long to know what others think or feel. Children learn to do this before they can talk; even in infancy they distinguish a cross parent from a smiling one.

The belief that, if not closely monitored, TV will oust traditional print literacy is not so widely held as it was. Perhaps the serious immediacy of important political events seen on TV routed any suggestion that TV viewers are concerned only with entertainment. In some quarters however, the notion is still prevalent that constant TV viewing does more harm than good, that children watch indiscriminately, become moronic, illiterate or disinclined to read. So far, convincing evidence for these calamities is lacking. Just as comics did not deflect children from other texts, TV is unlikely to persuade committed readers to abandon reading. Perhaps we are beginning to speak of 'TV literacy' so that TV may be considered in the same way as print literacy, as a serious, interpretive cultural medium which people use to examine their world and not only to escape from it.

The belief that TV stops children who have learned to enjoy reading from doing as much of it as they should is unfounded. There is also strong evidence that TV-watching helps beginning readers. It is easy to see why. TV programmes are episodic; they are rounded off in organized time slots, so that watching becomes a complete act with its own conventions, the very thing we say children have to discover about reading and writing. In addition, TV teaches children to keep the story going, just as readers learn to do. What's more, over the years, TV programmes have created audiences and taught them *how* to watch. Serial plays adapted from novels are now televisually different from the earlier adaptations. Audiences are more sophisticatedly aware of the techniques of presentation than those who saw the Coronation in 1953. Screen reading is not taking over or replacing traditional print literacy. It is developing contexts and styles of its own for which the term 'literacy' is appropriate only as a metaphor because of the role TV plays in most of our lives.

British TV for children has always been strongly book-based. (Sales of *Thomas the Tank Engine* increased from 20,000 copies a year to 40,000 when the series was shown on ITV.) In reverse, TV has a stimulating effect on those who write books for the young. Determined to create a new generation of readers, artists and authors invent new literary conventions that cannot occur in moving pictures. They invite children to look closely at details in picture books so that they discover ways of seeing. Look at the two boys in the first picture of Anthony Browne's *Piggybook*. Examine their folded arms, then their hands. Adults usually miss the resemblance of fingers to pigs' trotters, but children learn to pause to look.

In children's novels the storytellers no longer have to

describe a setting into which the characters will walk. Instead, they can begin with a fast-moving dialogue, or monologue, because TV programmes have taught the young to read – again in the extended sense – the plot and the characters from the conversation. Here is Janni Howker opening her impressive novel, *Isaac Campion* and making use of what TV teaches children: to hear the voice behind the words and then to see the character in the mind's eye.

> *Now then, I was twelve, rising thirteen, when our Daniel got killed. Aye . . . it was a long time ago. I'm talking about a time of day eighty-three years back. Eighty-three years. It's a time of day that's past your imagining. I'm talking about a different world. You may as well say it was a different planet, the world I was born in.*
>
> *No radios. No television. No World Wars. They'd not even built the* Titanic *let alone sunk her.*

This passage expects a lot of the reader who has to sort out who is the 'I' of the story, what the world was like eighty-three years ago, and to read on till 'how our Daniel got killed' becomes clear. The author lets the reader supply images for the gaps in the text, a habit that TV watching sustains and even makes ordinary.

Although both watching TV and reading a book involve children in an imaginative dialogue with what can be called, in both cases, a text, we are bound to admit that TV fills the lives of adults and children in ways that books and magazines have never done. There is no comparison between the audiences for *Neighbours* (15 million) and *Eastenders* (13 million; but some people watch both) and the readers of best sellers. The figures are instructive. In 1989 the estimated sales of *The Satanic Verses* were 103,000 copies; for *The Guinness Book of Records* the number is 240,000 and the bestselling paperback, *Rosemary Conley's Hip and Thigh Diet*, sold 450,000. While any author would like to top the charts, these figures are quite low when compared with the number of children who watch the current soap operas. The *Narnia* stories, in the most recent TV production, may have reached more children in their TV form than in the books when they first appeared in C.S. Lewis's lifetime, although the nature of the encounter is quite different.

Some sophisticated children can make detailed comparisons about the treatment of the narrative in both forms. When this happens we see a parallel between children's growing competence in interpreting print texts and their ability to look at TV programmes beyond the events of the narrative. This is a new critical literacy, and like the early 'reading' of TV, it is often learned but rarely explicitly taught.

In schools, television is widely accepted as making learning more immediate, more resourced than anything teachers can do or textbooks can explain. In secondary schools where media studies are part of the curriculum, pupils acquire a critical vocabulary for describing different kinds of programmes and the techniques used in making them. When this happens, young watchers move from easy looking to more discriminating seeing, a move which is matched in the process of reading literature as interpretation and literary criticism.

'Every television viewing occasion is a potential source of learning about television, and hence about media forms generally,' says Maíre Messenger Davies, whose book *Television is Good for your Kids* should be required reading for all who pontificate or agonize about children's viewing habits or the activities of programme-makers. She makes it quite plain that what children get out of television (and what they bring to it) 'is often quite different from what adults assume they get out of it'. Her research shows that children's tastes are broader than those of their parents and teachers. Their approach is exploratory; they are not yet gripped by the issues that worry their elders about the effects of popular media.[6] As in their contacts with print literacy, they are involved in narratives which offer them adventures with the possibility of surprise, and a significant kind of deep play. Their relations with television over the whole period of childhood are very complex, and suggest that we are still making much too simple generalizations about what actually happens when children watch at different stages in their learning. Television competences cannot be explained by references to the 'skills' of 'decoding' visual images, nor by matching the social class of children with programmes they watch. Most viewing goes on in family groups and generalization about these is notoriously difficult.

Television is a new literacy because of its capacity to make us look directly at how we use signs, symbols, pictures and words as message systems for meaning-making. But the effect of these is not always benign. To be intrigued by advertising techniques is to be manipulated by the designers. We see a skilful piece of photomontage which catches our imagination before we know it's about banking. We enter the lives of coffee drinkers, thrifty savers, clothes washers and watch an entire episode about a caring father rushing to his wife's bedside in hospital even when we know the intent of the film-maker is to sell cars. We worry about the manipulative effects of TV as we marvel at their seductiveness. More equivocal are the faces of those who make our laws, run our public utilities, spend our taxes, threaten our health. TV can make lying seem easy. As the young grow in viewing sophistication they discover how TV tricks work. But the speed of the passage of the film, the lighting impressionism, works against thoughtfulness, consideration of alternatives, reviewing and revisions. I know that the mechanism that stops a video film in its tracks is a help in looking critically and closely at message systems. But I am not persuaded that this is what people do. The TV equivalent of being 'lost in a book' is, I contend, a different kind of consciousness, the kind that lets us believe in magic even as we know it's a trick.

We understand that the ostensible role of TV is to present to us the *actualities* of our lives, the now-ness of news, the current debate, the instant awareness of 'being in the know'. It also gives us chances to confirm and extend our understandings of our social lives, alternative ideas and new discoveries. In one evening, we can see the effectiveness of a well constructed argument in a discussion, experience an unexplored depth of feeling in a story or a play, enjoy the pleasure of relaxation with diverting talk and music. Almost simultaneously we may see the dazzling diversions for selling things, the inequalities of news bulletins, and hear the din of clamour without form, the gabble of those whose job is to distract us from what we need to know.

We have to learn the *critical* literacy of TV if we are to judge it on its own terms as a force for social cohesion that book literacy has never been. As the novelty of viewing wears off we shall have to look at TV in terms of its history, its propagandist as well as its informing effects. Meanwhile, we have to acknowledge that its economic base, as well as its universality, has made TV an attractive proposition for some of the best creative talents of our time.

Computers

With this important new literacy I am, in several senses, out of my depth. But I know that anyone who takes being literate seriously has to attend to the consequences of computers. My children seem to be computer literates. They use the technology with confidence, producing on desk-top screens complicated diagrams with calculations and 'results' at the speed of light. Sometimes these are about their professional concerns: chemistry and engineering. At other times they are checking on their bank balances or the date of their nephew's birthday. I often wonder how they communicate ordinarily with computer semi-literates, like me. They are sure that their own children, at three and a half can 'get the machine up and running' to print their names and addresses as Ron Scollon predicted.

Baffled I may be by the speed of microchip advances, but I read articles in the *Guardian* like this one (July, 1989):

> *Multi-media technologies will change the world as much in the 1990s as personal computing changed it in the 1980s . . . they will make their impact on education, presentation tools (including advertising) and entertainment.*

The multi-media pack which drew my attention was: '*The Magic Flute—set of three CD ROM discs from Warner New Media. Contains music, libretti, analysis, glossary, self-test, etc. CD ROM and HyperCard.*'

Multi-media technologies have invented new languages and therefore, in some senses, a new world literacy. Before I discovered that 'self-test' meant that the system will check out its own functioning, I wondered if the HyperCard was a kind of worksheet with questions like, 'Do you believe that the sound of the female voice singing *Ach, I fühl's* is one of the great human miracles?' Clearly, I have grown old without knowing half of what I ought to know about this opera, and I recognize new enlightenment in these coded messages. The cost of the pack (£500 or so) would probably pay for seats at nearly all the live performances I might go to for the rest of my life.

As computers are, for me, a latterly acquired literacy and not an initial tool, I wonder about the gap between the children's expectations and competences and those of their teachers. Many children who are now ready for school have experience of keyboards and screens; they may also be able to read. If so, they are doubly indemnified against literacy failure. Others in their first school class will lack these experiences, but will certainly want them. If there is only one computer in the class the task of the teacher will be to let the children teach each other, just as they do when they watch television together.

It is easy, common even, to speak of computers and literacy as if access to the technology were equal for all. It isn't. The chances are that advanced computer technologies will extend the power and wealth of those who are competent to realize the potential of the machines they invest in. So, as far as learning to write is concerned, children need the techniques of pen-pushing where the alternative technologies are not funded.

As soon as word processors became available in schools I was persuaded that children could make good use of them for composing, re-drafting and publishing. My student, Bob

Moy, showed me how his TRAY, a computer game where the players have to reconstruct a text in which only the punctuation marks are visible, works. The claim is, this helps them to understand how they read. In my work I derive enormous relief from computerized bibliographies, my own and other people's, while ruefully noticing that the current academic game is how to make them as long and as comprehensive as possible. (The computer also lets me calculate how long it would take to read all the books and articles listed.)

I believe that computers help us to learn about learning and about language and other symbol systems, their nature and functions. The focus should not be on the machine, but on what we think we are doing with it. As a literacy tool, a computer depends on who is in charge. Word processing has made children less afraid of making spelling mistakes and of getting going in writing. But not all novelists or writers of articles use word processors. Given a choice between picking up my pencil and preparing the machine I know which I do more often. Word processors have made me into a frenetic re-drafter, chiefly because I can't see enough of the text at once, and as soon as the page looks neat I stop noticing the repetitions.

Computers give us more information and more choice of what we do with it, different ways of communicating and changing what we want to say. I doubt if they will replace the ancient scribal tools of pens and pencils—there are more of these about too. The partiality of new technologies and their dependence on sources of electric power restrict their use to particular places.

Those who want to use word processors for writing need the advice of an expert who also recognizes the computer's limitations. Daniel Chandler's encouragement comes with his understandings that 'writing done on a word processor obscures its own revelations'.[7] We have already noticed that first drafts disappear. We are also sensitive to the fact that, as yet, no one is likely to write a letter of condolence to a friend on a machine.

The advent of computers in common use made me

reconsider what I believe literacy is all about. Here are these machines of unbounded practicality, letting us store and recall, change and reproduce all that we know and regard as important and useful. To be literate has always meant to be at ease in a literate society, so, in some senses, we have to learn, as our ancestors did when steam trains and factories, crop rotation and power stations changed the lives of millions, that we brought about this new literacy with its paperless publishing, its international efficiency and its new language. In practice, we need to learn to use the machines *imaginatively*, to re-create what we understand, and not simply, in the old scribal tradition, copy from one disk to another facts and figures which we do not understand. We know we can be manipulated by writing and television; how much more then by the selective procedures of those who know how to use computer information to keep us in the dark. Already there are 'viruses'; screens collapse, disks are wiped out. Computers are not beyond the reach of human error, as anyone who has lost a file will tell us.

We are confronted by new paradoxes. Computers, like writing, keep secrets. The contents of disks are locked with passwords which ensure that they cannot be read by the uninitiated. Then, the whole computer 'science' is structured inside a rhetoric, words which are incomprehensible outside the world of the users. Here is an example, from a newspaper article called 'Model Making for the Real World' by Ralph Cowes.

Screenfields are grouped to match the structure of the data-base instead of input documents, screens are commonised to reduce programming rather than screen management, the impact of numbering series on manual filing is ignored, in-house standards are bureaucratically applied to dissimilar operations, and ad hoc interrogation isn't tailored with default options for common queries, default options are largely ignored on input, error messages refer to information which is miles away, and so on. So manual procedures have to be changed for the worse.

Apart from a feeling that there is something wrong, I cannot sort this out, although I have meaning for every word in the passage. New literacies create new illiterates.

In a remarkable essay in a collection called *The State of the Language*, Michael Heim described the 'dark side' of word processing while still acknowledging its revolutionary effects of word production. Fixed vision stare and Repetitive Motion Syndrome (inflamed hand and arm tendons) seem to be common. Heim's main anxiety is about what he called '"infomania", a growing obsession with data without a concern for significance.'[8] Word processing makes us information virtuosos, as the computer transforms all we write into information code. But human we remain. For us, felt language always depends on the felt context of our own limited experience. We are biologically finite in what we can attend to meaningfully. When we pay attention to the significance of something we cannot proceed at the computer's breakneck speed. We have to ponder, reflect, contemplate. New literacies do not, by themselves, generate what we once called wisdom.

Contemporary Journalism

All the features of new literacies come together in the matters, modes and techniques of modern journalism. This is the most obvious kind of new writing, born in a printing revolution of competitive ferocity and subject to the infomania and key-hitting data-entry techniques of ephemeral publishing. Producers and consumers wade through a morass of paper. Every morning the owners of our local newspaper shop, first-generation Londoners from Bombay, sort out the piles of print that are dropped at their door at dawn. Sunday brings the most. They neatly organize newspapers and magazines in surroundings which include other local necessities – milk, bread, sandwiches, beer, cigarettes, chocolate and ice-cream. Wedged in between freezers full of ices and birthday cards the pictorial journals are, like the other things, renewed as an unending stream of consumables.

Those waiting to pay for what they have selected flip over the pages of magazines and read the headlines of newspapers other than the one they have chosen. The variety of presentations is astounding. Photographs, often of superb quality, fill the main space on the outside. Inside, articles, advertisements, cartoons, crossword puzzles, announcements of a line or two, serious comment, all invoke reading skills unthought of when popular literacy became enshrined in law. The multiple kinds of typeface, from which we take our reading directions, have been deliberately chosen. As space is money, the machinery must be set to save it. The second Gutenberg revolution is most visible in the everyday reading and writing of productions which soon disappear, except in libraries and places where records are kept. When the microfiche takes over, the paper can be pulped.

Consider the range of topics over a week in the 'heavies', the *Guardian*, the *Independent*, *The Times* and their Sunday counterparts. Journalistic skill is no longer the immediacy of reporting. Television has taken on that function. Instead, writing for a newspaper is a particularly focused expertise in making available the ways in which the chosen facts of specialist matters can be interpreted. So the journalist's literacy is to transform exclusive rhetorics – law reports, government decisions, economic forces and trends, disaster inquiries, social moods, reviews, fashion, ecology and health – into a fact-cum-comment immediacy. The skill is in the *ellipsis* of the telling: the headline condensation that makes memorable the content of the column and the attitude of the writer. Technology takes care of the presentation.

In popular newspapers and magazines photo-journalism cuts down the number of words to be read and relies on the impact of the images, as in much television. The result is that extremes of feeling – outrage, compassion, curiosity and daring – are whipped up to accompany each reported incident or 'scoop'. Although appearing crude to sophisticated readers, the form creates its own literacy. Readers are to believe they are getting the heart of the matter with none of the verbiage of 'if on the one hand . . . whereas on the other'. They may not know that they are often deprived of both fact and the possibility of comment. The editor's concern is not to match the content of the report with the style of the prose, but to create a context for either agreement or indignation among readers. The words and pictures tell the readers how to respond, either by agreeing or arguing.

The versatility, variety and, in an ambiguous sense, the cleverness of current journalism in western countries is displayed in its scope, and in its use of all kinds of discourses that represent our dealings with the world. Journalists break down, for common perusal, the impenetrable speeches of judges, the reports of doctors, the researches of scientists, even the new arcane speech of computer-buffs, and present their findings and opinion to both the expert and the lay reader, with a finely tuned perception of their audiences. The travel section of one newspaper will discuss hotels in Spain; another will report on Samarkand. Unease comes when readers discover what has been omitted. But to discover this is to learn to read critically, and then to write to the editor in reply.

In many demonstrable ways, for better and for worse, journalism represents what it is to be literate in our time. To know our way around a newspaper generates a feeling of belonging. We know what we needn't read. We turn confidently to what we expect to find: the women's page, the sports results, the favoured commentator. Journalism appears to be socially responsible. It begins by taking account of people's lives. It offers for reading, in a way that also teaches readers, most of the ways of writing with which we are bound to be familiar if we are to use our literacy critically. Newspapers feed and feed off our longing to be in the know. The array of specialized journals that circulate through mailing systems and the display in the railway bookshop (itself a creation of the history of literacy) which offers information on subjects from angling to Zen, as well as the full range of novels, biography, history and information, are evidence of the extent of common literacy. We define our individual literacies by the company we keep, the books and papers we read, and what we choose to write or avoid writing. Our attitude to the papers and magazines we don't care for is also part of our literate behaviour.

Ephemeral as they are, newspapers, magazines and journals keep alive, by their very disappearance, the possibility of *revision*, of our coming back to a topic in the light of subsequent information or discussion. Journalism offers opinions for us to consider in ways that television cannot. It offers us a chance of learning new vocabularies which we may never be expert in, as, for the length of an article, we join famous gardeners, cooks, brain surgeons and astronomers. We may, if we read more than one newspaper, weigh one report against another.

New literacies appear to be related to new technologies. But when we watch children learning to write, curling their fingers round their pens and crayons, enduring the struggle because they are impelled by the passion of what they have to say, we realize that at the heart of the matter is language in writing as *desire*. The dialogic imagination is at work. Later they will learn both to use and to resist the language manipulation of the writing done by machines. Even if their faxed greetings merge with banking transactions, there will be, I hope, a chance that they will write to their grandparents on their birthdays. Meanwhile we can use what critical literacy we have to know what we needn't read in the mass of information which threatens to swamp us.

CHAPTER 10

On Being Literate

This book grew out of a very simple idea, to set children's learning to read and write, together with some recent understandings of these processes, into the context of what it means to be literate in a modern society. As soon as I began to think about it, I wondered what kind of an obligation *is* literacy that we impose reading and writing on our children earlier and earlier in childhood?

At first, the plan seemed reasonable enough. Undoubtedly, the nature, uses and consequences of literacy were changing in response to some fundamental shifts in communal living. Schools were about to undergo fairly radical upheavals in management and curriculum. Parents would be obliged to understand and to be involved in their children's learning by forming a partnership with their teachers who, in their turn, would produce new kinds of assessment of children's progress. To offer some kind of guide to the differences in literacy and in education which we should all, young and old alike, have to live with, was the initial intention. Part of it involved a belief that literacy itself would have to be re-described, at least as *literacies*, in order to match the new, emergent contexts and kinds of literate behaviours that are prevalent in modern society.

As always happens, the topic grew under my hand. Literacy is labyrinthine, a maze of studies to match a multitude of practices, full of contradictions and paradoxes. History, anthropology, sociology, philosophy, linguistics, psychology, social and cultural theories all contribute to understandings of literacy, but still it eludes any final description. Every publisher, politician, writer, editor, scholar, citizen and beginning learner has a view of what it is to be literate, a view that grows out of what they think literacy is good for, and where, in the social world, they practise it. All definitions of literacy are located in the system of beliefs which characterize those who use language. Part of everyone's literacy is the history of how they learned to make sense of reading and writing, and why they believe, at any given time, that literacy is important.

How then, I wondered, could I get a purchase on all of this? As I thought about it, the United Nations declared that 1990 would be International Literacy Year, as if to bring to a head the ever-increasing preoccupations with the subject. Predictably, there have been more publications, meetings, conferences, statements, the emphasis on national statistics and league tables of achievements. We now know that, in countries such as East Germany, people turn to literature when the newspapers are organs of state propaganda. But they also watch TV. There is 'still' a shifting population of approximately six million illiterates in Britain. Children still go to school for the first time, and adolescents leave with different kinds of qualifications which describe new literacy, or lack of it. What difference does a year's focused attention make to this hydra-headed subject? It demonstrates that literacy is an issue of human rights.

Two things seem to be important; we have, in a simple way, dealt with them. The first is the history of literacy. All literate societies are influenced by the writings that remain from their past, however these are regarded in the present. To look at the relation of literacy to culture and history is to make a start in understanding that there is no single, neutral literacy that contrasts directly with illiteracy, or non-literacy; no great separation of writing and reading from talk and listening. There is no high literacy that guards each high culture, only a continuum of social practices on which social attitudes depend. Our new situation is characterized by mixed, hybrid modes of talking and writing that include pictures and looking, as in television.

The second seminal idea is that children enter their culture at a given point in history. Language and literacy are there when they arrive; they change both. As they learn to act and talk in their world they also learn to read and write so as to find their way around, to map their world. As these things happen before they go to school, we are now more aware of the literate and literary competences children bring with them when they get there. In class, their view of schooled literacy is tinged with the response that their teachers make to these earlier, local practices. I believe that children are members of a literate community before they go to school, though some parents and teachers believe that they are literate only after they have been in school long enough to prove that they are. It is this difference of viewpoint that lurks behind some of the statements made in the foregoing chapters. It also influences what now follows.

As I began to clear a path through the maze of literacy studies I was struck by the apparent indifference to their own literate history on the part of many scholars and researchers, most of whom wrote wisely and well. Unlike poets and novelists who confront their struggles with words as part of their resource material, academics who write about literacy are notoriously reticent about how they learned to read and write. Yet everyone knows that no scholar, researcher or essayist chooses a topic at random. To write about literacy always implies more than a passing interest in its nature, as I perceived at every stage in this act of writing. Whenever I needed to clarify a point, a position or a procedure in these pages I was driven to reconstruct the experience (or something like it) in my own literate history. Now I hope that the occasional references to my experiences, random and muddled as they must seem, encouraged you to reflect upon your own. My insistence that this is a good and helpful thing to do comes from my knowing that, when they talk about the reading done by children, teachers and parents are drawing on their own experience without raising this fact to the level of consciousness. If a mother says, 'I could read before I went to school' she means, 'I hope my children will do the same. It will save me much worry.'

Literacy is determined by the literate. I have assumed this by drawing you, the readers of these pages, into the group that I have created by saying 'we' and 'our', imagining thereby that we have views and interests in common. Sometimes I have given you a parent's consciousness, sometimes a teacher's, as these are the visions I most easily share. You are encouraged at all times to exert your right to read against this text, in the mode of critical literates whose competences I have tried to describe.

Perhaps you are also concerned to protect literacy, to keep whole a tradition that you see in your own history as something you want your children to inherit safely: the reading of good books, the thinking of clever thoughts. I am sure they will do these things, but their literacy will still be different, as their lives will be. So, if you see that their school books and lessons present reading and writing to them differently from your experience of learning, there is no need to assume that they will fail to reach a standard which will give them a good life, even a better one than yours.

I have deliberately separated myself from those who see literacy as some kind of neutral device for gleaning inform-ation or acquiring higher education, and from others who believe that children will be lost if they are not taught the alphabet by rote, to spell correctly before they are five and to write a fair italic hand. All of these are desirable, perhaps important, accomplishments, but useless if the writer has nothing to say beyond the sending of party invitations. I do not believe that 'real' literacy is a thing of the past or the achievement of a favoured few. What is already past is the possibility of thinking of literacy in general terms of reading-and-writing. To see it thus is to regard literacy as a depreciated legacy, which it is not. This book promotes the idea that literacy, now as always, is dependent upon *contexts*, the nature of different kinds and uses of texts, especially where language is related to power and, at the same time, to our ordinary passions to know and to feel, to the stories we read, tell and write.

Come then. What is it to be literate? We have to draw our own maps, trace our own histories, acknowledge our own debts and consider ways not taken. Our literacy auto-biographies reveal riches and gaps, but these narratives are not tales of solitary journeys. We were always in dialogue with others—those who taught us to read, those for whom we wrote, who lent us books, shaped our preferences, encouraged us, forbade us even. They were dead poets, living authors, cynical critics. We remember them as friends who made our world more habitable, who helped us, as we read and wrote, to discover who we were and could become.

As memory reveals literacy as a series of dialogues there are always significant encounters. My argument with Miss Macdonald about the spelling of *friend*, when I was seven and she was straight from college, revealed the abstract nature of English orthography. How, I asked, could it have an 'i' if it didn't sound? The dictionary was on Miss Macdonald's side, so I demanded one of my own. The first page of Chaucer, of Molière, of geometry, of David Hume, of *Little Gidding* in its flimsy paper cover still return like a warm wind from a far country if I think of them. My first experience of a book in manuscript was Norman Kemp Smith's study of Descartes. I helped to make a copy of his first draft (oh, the solace of remembering that his hand-writing was even less legible than mine). He wrote on the back of thick sheets of fine mourning writing paper, black-edged in the old style, left over from the death of his wife. Here was writing and thinking. As I struggled to reach a coherent understanding of that fine text I re-read Descartes, who became a 'familiar compound ghost'. Once experienced, such encounters are actively sought.

Looking back I realize that literature, however described and certainly not claimed, in my case, as a privileged activity, is at the heart of my concern about literacy. I do not expect my children and grandchildren to recite ballads or read Walter Scott. I am not persuaded that reading, necessarily, is good for them because it has been, verily, good for me. Only, I do know that, like the Wyf of Bathe with whom I have little else in common, literature has been one of the important ways by which 'I have had the world as in my time', because encounters with writers and other readers have been active and life giving. Yet, at the back of all that recollection is the fact that neither at school nor as a student did my teachers and tutors encourage me to think I could write. Only my old philosophy professor, addicted as he was to detective stories, was benignly encouraging about my occasional verse and the stories I wrote for women's magazines to earn enough to buy my own books.

Some of my most important dialogues have been with children. The firstness of literate encounters, which I so prize, is visible in every classroom. For a certain space children are not trammelled by the need to make the right response to situations, social and literate. They are exempted until they learn. So when they begin to write, to cast their ideas in their language, they relate their world directly. 'There was once a little girl who loved chocolate. I have three cats at home.' It is in seeing children master the rules of reading and writing that I have come to understand, bit by bit, what it is to be literate. This next part of the account is not complete, not universal, but perhaps the beginning of a way of looking that takes us out of the tramlines of our expectations.

Autobiography again. For all that my growing years were full of books and texts, there were also other voices: on the radio. The part that radio played in pre-television childhood, and especially during the Second World War, is a powerful recollection for those who experienced it. The voice of Neville Chamberlain hasn't faded in my inner ear where it lurks with a symphony of national anthems. But there were other voices too. Cricket commentators: what were they describing with 'slip', 'long leg', 'run out'? My uncle understood and tried to explain when Len Hutton broke a record one lunchtime. Then, jokes, comic programmes with repeated phrases I both understood and didn't: 'Can I do yer now, sir?' There were sermons, not in fiery Scottish words but in a delicate English, and a strange way of reading the prose psalms with singing in between. How did anyone *get into* these languages? How did Churchill make his speech style match the events of Dunkirk and the Battle of Britain? He sounded like a mixture of Milton and John Bunyan.

Part of the answer came in my first year as a student. I went to a class in *rhetoric* where I was taught occasionally by Herbert Grierson, the great editor of the poems of John Donne. The drift of his argument seemed to be that language is always a dialogue. We speak to, and are spoken to. So with reading and writing. (Remember the young readers who have to learn to become both the teller and the told?) Thus, as we put our point of view into what we say, we take account of the surroundings and the person we address, fitting our words to both. We have a repertoire of speech forms to suit the contexts; the rules of the game are what we learn. It all seems obvious, yet the idea is very old. The Greeks, as ever, made different rhetorics a close and detailed study. Looking back I now see that Grierson's audiences were worthy men who would enter the kirk or the lawcourts where persuasion in both speech and writing was paramount. For the rest of us, learning to write in the style required was what it all seemed to be about.

These old lessons re-surfaced as I thought about being literate. To be at home in a print-crammed world; to deal with the new hybrid forms of TV commercials and junk mail; to find our way around the *Radio Times* and the new shopping centres we have to act as those who are classed as literates. Once we know how words, phrases, texts relate to situations, occasions and contexts, in both speech and writing, we respond in language, in act and gesture, to the language used towards us. This is as true of reading a book and writing a letter as of listening to a parliamentary debate or writing a legal document. The new technologies extend our range and our competence but, in both speech and writing, the one who speaks and the one who is spoken to are joined by the utterance. To be literate is to know the rules for the joining of one to the other in the particular context of the language event.

So here we are, back with the children in school, in the first stages of their schooled literacy, trying to discover 'what counts as reading in this class?' The answer is not in the teacher's method but in the text and the context for understanding it. The pupils do what they are told as far as they can, looking to see what other children do, and making the most of the help they are given. They are not single strugglers up the smooth face of the rock of learning. They adapt their ways to include the habits, poses, words, hypocrisies even, of the readers and writers round about them. They take over the rhetorics of the wider community. They 'do the voices' that they discover on a page; they write 'in the role of' writers. When professional authors visit schools children ask them if they write in pen or pencil. The answer is important for the apprentice.

So if we are to help our children to be literate, what should we do? Informally, every day, we induct them into ways of behaving of which language is a vital part, especially in narrative. 'What did you do at school today?' If the answer is 'Nothing much, just played', we have to wait until we overhear them discussing their teacher with a classmate, imitating her minatory phrases: 'John, put that *down*.' The stories come when the time is ripe, and they come with rhetorical flourishes. 'And do you know, he said that is a very *immature* thing to do.' Formal reasoning is not delayed until adolescence; it begins as the special pleading about bed-times. 'If you let me stay up I'll put my toy box away neatly.' Any child who knows a story as 'what if. . .' has begun the processes of logic. Arguments are visible in stories that children tell before they go to school. They practise for themselves what they hear others doing. 'You won't get a whole family fed unless you have more money,' says a four-year-old to a doll.

This understanding of different kinds of language use and of ways of persuading others and responding to their persuasions is part of all social life in the world. So, in one sense, children cannot avoid contact with its literate forms. Why, therefore, are we so worried in case they fail to master the rhetorics of writing and the dialogues of reading? We know the answer; some children are tongue-tied, or, in writing, *hand*icapped, in the powerful dialogues of our hierarchical society. We cannot be sure that they will be 'up to' dealing with the literate world unless we see to it that they get a head start early in their schooldays, for, when they leave, their level of attainment will attest their fitness to belong to, or to be excluded from, the group of powerful literates who dominate the dialogues of others.

This *feels* like reality, so, as parents and teachers, we do our best to extend the language competences of the children we know to meet the so-called *demands* of society as they encounter these. But we should also remember that children have time on their side. Literacy, however defined or acquired, or used or sought, is never static. As language and art, it changes and is changed by those who find uses for it and who, like the artists who create new books for children, actively seek to play the games of reading and writing and to change the rules.

To be literate we have to be confident that the world of signs and print, in all the different mixtures and modes of meaning that surround us, is a world we can cope with, be at home in, contribute to and play with. If it is simply mysterious, threatening, unreliable or hostile, then we feel at a disadvantage, victimized, inadequate. There is no guarantee that literacy makes the world a more benign place, but it helps everyone to consider how it might be different. But, as Harvey Graff said, when I began this inquiry, 'Literacy is neither the major problem, nor is it the main solution.' It can be, however, the difference that makes a difference, in all our dialogues with our world; an adventure with the possibility of surprise.

Postscript

This book is full of debts: obvious ones, to scholars such as Brian Street, Harvey J. Graff, Robert Pattison, Jack Goody, Walter J. Ong, L.S. Vygotsky, Jean Piaget, and all those who write about children's language, literacy and literature whose work shadows whatever makes sense in these pages. The support and tolerance of my friends and colleagues in the Department of English and Media Studies in the Institute of Education, the inspiration of groups of teachers in the London Borough of Brent and in the Centre for Language in Primary Education are beyond praise. Other sources I have acknowledged where I can, knowing that there are bound to be omissions. My students have always been my teachers, especially Henrietta Dombey and Carol Fox. To Sharon Grattan and Freda Bailey I owe the transformation of my old-fashioned handwriting into modern text, a formidable task. Above all, I thank and acclaim Margaret Clark for her friendship, skilled editorial help and most generous encouragement.

Notes

CHAPTER 1

The history of writing and of what people in the past have done with written language is both fascinating and complex. The British Museum has examples of the early scripts; the Rosetta Stone is there. We all enter that history, and are part of its continuity. Here are some books which have contributed to the thinking in this chapter:

Cippola, C. *Literacy and Development in the West*. Harmondsworth, Penguin Books 1969.

Clanchy, M. *From Memory to Written Record; 1066–1307*. London, Edward Arnold 1979.

Goody, Jack, (ed) *Literacy in Traditional Societies*. Cambridge University Press 1968.

Graff, H.J. *The Labyrinths of Literacy* Lewes. Falmer Press 1987.

Ong, W.J. *Orality and Literacy* London. Methuen 1982.

Pattison, Robert *On Literacy: the Politics of the Word from Homer to Rock*. New York, Oxford University Press 1982.

Street, B.V. *Literacy in Theory and Practice*. Cambridge University Press 1984.

1. The snippet of monkish text comes from the first volume of *Monumenta Germaniae Historica*, series *Scriptores*. It is translated and quoted by Hayden White in his article 'The Value of Narrativity in the Representation of Reality' in *On Narrative* edited by W.J.T. Mitchell, University of Chicago Press 1981.

2. T.S. Eliot's lines are from *East Coker*.

3. Raymond Williams gives the clearest short history of the use of 'literacy' in *Keywords*, Penguin Books 1976.

4. The Poem in the Underground is by Shirley Geok-Lin Lim from *Modern Secrets*. Dungaroo Press 1989.

5. To 'practise language (and therefore literacy) as a doctor practises medicine' is an idea of James Britton's. He is the author of *Language and Learning*, published by Alan Lane in 1970 and still one of the most influential books in its field.

6. The quote from Jonathan Culler comes from *Structuralist Poetics: Structuralism, Linguistics and the Study of Literature*. London, Routledge and Kegan Paul 1975.

7. At the heart of most of the ideas in these pages are the writings of L.S. Vygotsky: *Thought and Language* (first published in English in 1962; re-edited and published in 1986, M.I.T Press) and *Mind in Society*, Harvard University Press 1978. A.R. Luria, his colleague, investigated the new literacies of the Soviet Union in the 1930's. His book is *Cognitive Development*. Harvard University Press 1976.

CHAPTER 2

1. The relation of literacy to social life is now widely explored. Brian Street, in *Literacy in Theory and Practice*,

explains how social groups adapt to new ways of reading and writing. Kenneth Levine's book is called *The Social Context of Literacy*; Routledge 1986. Other important writings and researchers include *Ways with Words* by Shirley Brice Heath, Cambridge University Press 1983; *Literacy, Schooling and Society*, edited by Suzanne de Castell, Alan Luke and Kieran Egan, Cambridge University Press 1986; *The Acquisition of Literacy*, edited by Bambi Schiefflin and Perry Gilmore, Ablex Publishing 1986; *The Social Construction of Literacy* by Jenny Cook-Gumpertz, Cambridge University Press, 1986. The publication dates of these books show how recently literacy has engaged the interests of social scientists and anthropologists and is not now simply a matter for educators. Investigations of literacy are often comparative, showing that there is no single way of teaching it and no one set of social practices by which it can be defined. The details in these studies are drawn from a wide range of cultures.

The notion that information is 'the difference that makes a difference' is borrowed from Gregory Bateson: *Mind and Nature: A Necessary Unity* (Wildwood House 1979).

2. The dangers of smoking and the threat of AIDS are brought to public attention by means of advertising. But publicity of this kind generates both awareness and scepticism, so that a fairly general response becomes, 'You can't believe all they say'.

3. It is difficult to do justice in one short chapter to the issues raised by class, race and gender in relation to literacy. The differences that result from social 'positioning' seem to be obvious, but we tend to over-generalize these when we speak of 'equal opportunities'. We need much more empirical research in a greater variety of contexts. Two helpful books are: *Democracy in the Kitchen* by Valerie Walkerdine (Virago 1989) and *Read to Me, Now* by Hilary Minns (Virago 1990).

4. The National Curriculum comes into our discussions again in Chapter 5. For detailed information about subjects, programmes of study and methods of assessment it should be possible for parents to consult the relevant documents in any school or in local libraries. They may also be obtained from the National Curriculum Council.

CHAPTER 3

1. Paulo Freire was born in Brazil. He criticized the literacy campaigns sponsored by Unesco for their over-simplification of the process of becoming literate which he links with raising people's consciousness about their positions in the wider world. He sees notions of basic literacy as confining and repressive when literacy should be emancipatory. His writings include: *Cultural Action for Freedom* (Penguin 1972); *Pedagogy of the Oppressed* (Penguin 1972) and *Literacy: Reading the Word and the World*, with Donaldo Macedo (Routledge 1987).

   The beginnings of literacy have become the focus for different kinds of research. Teachers and parents are now aware that children in literate societies explore public writing before they go to school. The influential studies are discussed by Nigel Hall in *The Emergence of Literacy* (Hodder and Stoughton 1987).

2. I am not persuaded that literacy simply 'emerges' from children's interaction with various forms of written language in the environment. They are curious about what writing 'says'. Their active search for meaning is always purposeful. They enjoy the discovery of what adults are up to when they write. But it is the *habit* of intellectual search, a deliberate concentration of the kind that most children can be helped with, that brings about the understanding that teachers and parents want to promote.

3. I am grateful for the examples that come from the careful work that Barbara Tizard and Martin Hughes report in their book: *Young Children Learning: Talking and Thinking At Home And At School* (Fontana 1984). The interactions they record between children and adults make plain, amongst other things, how selective are most enquiries into children's lives, and how difficult it is to be sure what counts as significant evidence of early learning. The point of view of the researcher always influences the analysis.

4. Kornei Chukovsky's book is *From Two to Five* (University of California Press 1963). When his daughter first laughed at a joke – at barely twenty-three months – Chukovsky said he 'understood the reason for the passion children feel for the incongruous, for the absurd, and for the severing of ties between objects and their regular functions expressed in folk lore'.

5. Books about the importance of children's play abound. A good anthology is edited by Jerome S. Bruner, Alison Jolly and Kathy Sylva. *Play: Its Role In Development And Evolution* (Penguin Books 1976). For the relation of play to the beginnings of children's understanding of metaphor see also Vygotsky's *Mind in Society*. Susan Stewart discusses how children 'play the boundaries' of what counts as sense in her book: *Nonsense* (Johns Hopkins University Press 1978). The classic collection of recurrent examples of children's language play is *The Lore and Language of Schoolchildren* by Iona and Peter Opie (Oxford University Press 1959).

6. Myra Barrs' account of Ben is in 'Maps of Play' in *Language and Literacy in the Primary School*, edited by Margaret Meek and Colin Mills (Falmer Press 1988).

7. Tommy Scollon is a 'new' literate in the ways discussed in Chapter 9. His parents' account of his early adventures with the computer are in ']RUN TRILOGY: Can Tommy Read'? in *Awakening to Literacy*, edited by

Hillel Goelman, Antoinette A. Oberg and Frank Smith (Heinemann Educational Books 1984).

8. Donald Winnicott writes about the 'Third Area' in *Playing and Reality* (Tavistock Publications 1971).

9. Studies of children being read to show how complex this apparently simple act really is. Maureen & Hugh Crago's book *Prelude to Literacy: A Preschool Child's Encounter With Fiction And Story* (Southern Illinois University Press 1983) follows the model of Dorothy White's *Books before Five* (Heinemann Educational Books 1954, 1984). Dorothy Butler's study of her grandchild: *Cushla and Her Books* (Hodder and Stoughton 1979) is a detailed account of books in the life of a child whose post-natal development was retarded. Other analyses of children's early reading, including that of Henrietta Dombey, are in *Opening Moves* (edited by Margaret Meek). Bedford Way Papers no 17. Institute of Education, the University of London.

10. Whenever I want to explain how the text and pictures in a story picture book help beginning readers to understand that they are part of the process by which the story is told, I turn to *Rosie's Walk* by Pat Hutchins (first published by The Bodley Head in 1969). The villain of the tale is a fox who follows Rosie the hen round her farmyard, pouncing on her from behind and falling into a mishap each time. The word 'fox', well within the competence of every beginner, never occurs in the text, yet every child understands what is happening. The role that books of this kind play in children's development as readers with literate competences is examined in *How Texts Teach What Readers Learn* (Thimble Press 1988).

11. 'Deep play' is explained by Clifford Geertz in his account of 'The Balinese Cockfight' in the anthology *Play* (details above). The chief characteristic of deep play is risk-taking.

12. Glenda Bissex's account of her son's early literacy is called *Gyns at Wrk* (Harvard University Press 1980). While he was writing, Paul wrote this message ('Genius at Work') on his door. His mother explains how he moved from his own 'invented' spelling to more conventional orthography because he wanted others to read what he had written. Teachers now understand this as a stage on the way to becoming literate, but the process is not one that simply 'emerges'. Parents tend to be ambivalent about accounts of impressive early learning. They always want spelling to be 'correct'. But the evidence is persuasive from both this and other studies in depth, that fluency and correctness come from having something to write about and someone to read it.

CHAPTER 4

1. My copy of *Orbis Pictus* is a facsimile of the first English edition of 1659, introduced by J.E. Sadler and published by Oxford University Press in 1968. There is an introduction by Jean Piaget to the *Selections* of Comenius' writings published by Unesco in 1957.

2. David Attenborough's television series *The Living World* had a marked effect on the early learning of young people who have now become responsibly involved in ecological movements.

3. Helen, Rose and their mothers are in *Young Children Learning*.

4. Carol Fox's collection of oral narratives told by young children between the ages of four and six is a rich storehouse of evidence of how their language and thinking develop before they begin formal schooling. Some of her analyses have already appeared: 'Talking

like a book' is in *Opening Moves* (details above); 'Poppies will Make them Grant' is in *Language and Literacy in the Primary School*; 'The genesis of argument in narrative discourse' is in *English in Education* Vol.24 No 1 1990. Dr Fox's forthcoming book will add significantly to our understanding in this area. I have been privileged to listen to many (original recordings) of Josh's stories. No transcript does full justice to his bright energy and narrative style.

5. Maureen and Hugh Crago *Prelude to Literacy*. Southern Illinois University Press 1983.

6. Jane Doonan's commentary on Anthony Browne's illustrations is 'A new look at *Hansel and Gretel*' in *Signal* No 42. September 1983, pp 123–131.

7. R.L. Gregory. 'Psychology: towards a science of fiction' in *New Society*, 23 May 1977, reprinted in *The Cool Web: the pattern of children's reading*, ed. Meek, M., Warlow, A., and Barton, G. The Bodley Head 1977.

Children's books referred to in this chapter are:

Eric Carle	*The Very Hungry Caterpillar*
Raymond Briggs	*Mother Goose Treasury*
	Father Christmas
	Fungus the Bogeyman
	Gentleman Jim
	When the Wind Blows (for adults)
	The Snowman
Anthony Browne	*Hansel and Gretel*
	Bear Hunt
	Gorilla
	Knock! Knock!
	Look What I've Got
Jan Ormerod	*Moonlight*
	Sunshine

Shirley Hughes	*Up and Up*
	Chips and Jessie
John Burningham	*Come Away from the Water, Shirley*
	Where's Julius?
Janet and Allan Ahlberg	*The Baby's Catalogue*
Maurice Sendak	*Where the Wild Things Are*
Pat Hutchins	*Rosie's Walk*

CHAPTER 5

1. Details of the National Curriculum, its subject regulations, assessment plans and programmes of study may change as the dates for their implementation arrive. The documents referred to in this chapter are: *Report of the Committee of Inquiry into the Teaching of English Language;* Chairman: Sir John Kingman FRS, HMSO 1988 (the Kingman Report), and *English for Ages 5 to 16; Proposals of the Secretary of State for Education and Science and the Secretary of State for Wales.* June 1989 (The Cox Report).

2. The proposals for a system of assessment were first outlined in the reports of the National Curriculum Task Group on Assessment and Testing (TGAT), which appeared in 1987 and 1988.

   Responsibility for the implementation of these proposals lies with the Schools Examinations and Assessment Council (SEAC).

3. Dennis Carter's account of the twins comes from his chapter 'Quaint Moonmarks' in *Learning Me Your Language: perspectives on the teaching of English,* edited by Michael Jones and Alastair West, pp 51–57 (Mary Glasgow Publications 1988). I am grateful for his permission to reproduce it here. I do this in tribute to his teaching and to the anthology as a whole.

4. *The Primary Language Record Handbook* and its expla-

natory sequel, *Patterns of Learning; the Primary Language Record and the National Curriculum* are the work of Myra Barrs, Sue Ellis, Hilary Hester, and Anne Thomas together with a group of Inner London teachers who helped with the early trial stages of this forward-looking way of accounting for and recording children's progress in literacy in their first schools. Both volumes may be obtained from the Centre for Language in Primary Education, Webber Row, London, EC1 8QW.

CHAPTER 6

1. I owe the example of Marie and her teacher to my colleague Evelyn Gregory, whose article 'Do English Eat Octopus?' in *English in Education* (Vol 23 No 3, Autumn 1989) discusses how teachers of children whose mother tongue is not English negotiate a common understanding of learning to read.

2. When they read aloud, children often substitute a word they know for one that is unfamiliar. These substitutions, like other mismatchings, are never random nor, simply, wrong. Kenneth and Yetta Goodman have shown how these 'miscues' are a 'window on the reading process'. They allow teachers and researchers to understand how children use their understanding of language to make meaning. For further details of this process see *Language and Literacy: the selected writings of Kenneth S. Goodman*, edited by Frederick S. Gollasch. 2 Vols. Routledge & Kegan Paul 1982. Sometimes 'miscue analysis' is mistaken for a reading test by those who do not understand the procedures.

3. The summary appearance of this list stems from my attempt to display both the number and variety of modes, acts and understandings that reading and writing contribute to our literacy and of the competences

that we acquire by practising these skills. Very few can be directly taught as lessons from snippets of prose; they come from reading and writing as complete acts. For example, a distinct point of growth is reached when a reader consciously grasps the difference between the author and the narrator of a story. Another is when a reader discovers that the *Narnia* tales of C.S. Lewis mean more than they say. Philippa Pearce shows how *time* is an essential ingredient of all novels. Alan Garner narrates in a distinctive *voice*. Well told stories for children illustrate the complexities of narrative discourse in ways that accord with Gerard Genette's analysis of Proust (*Narrative Discourse*, Blackwell 1980).

Children's books relevant to this section:

Harry Stevens	*Parrot told Snake*
	Fat Mouse
Pat Hutchins	*Rosie's Walk*
Selina Hastings (reteller)	
illustrator Reg Cartwright	*Peter and the Wolf*
Anthony Browne	*Bear Hunt*
	Bear Goes to Town
John Burningham	*Come away from the Water, Shirley*
Monique Felix	*The Little Mouse who Got Lost in a Book*
Martin Waddell & Helen Firth	*The Park in the Dark*
C.S. Lewis	*The Lion, the Witch and the Wardrobe*
Philippa Pearce	*The Way to Sattin Shore*
	Tom's Midnight Garden
Roald Dahl	*Danny, the Champion of the World*

CHAPTER 7

1. Catalogues, like that of *Mothercare*, are common house-

hold print which young children use to turn pages and to recognize representations of everyday things. *The Baby's Catalogue,* by Janet and Allan Ahlberg, copies the conventions to mirror the samenesses and differences in the lives of five families over a single day. For very young children the pictures offer the pleasure of recognition; for adults sharing it with them, the book is a good humoured, intricate analysis of the varied nature of our contemporary society.

2. Douglas Barnes' best known explanation of the importance of group talk in school learning is in *From Communication to Curriculum* (Penguin Books 1976). A stronger statement of his rationale is in 'Knowledge as Action' in *The Word for Teaching is Learning: Essays for James Britton,* edited by Martin Lightfoot and Nancy Martin (Heinemann Educational Books 1988). 'What is required is to give students access to the processes by which pictures of the world are constructed and eventually justified and thus to alternative pictures which might reasonably be adopted. Students would become conscious of what many already understand tacitly: that knowledge is a human construct, perpetually open to revision. This would constitute a critical curriculum.' I would add: it is also critical literacy.

3. David Olson's words are from his essay 'On the language and authority of textbooks' in *Language, Authority and Criticism* edited by Suzanne de Castell and A. and C. Luke (Falmer Press 1988).
    Learning from the Written Word by E. Lunzer and K. Gardner (Oliver and Boyd 1985) shows how complicated 'comprehension' lessons can become.

4. Gregory Bateson also says that 'it takes two somethings to create a difference'.

5. The lesson about porous rocks is common in science classes. The details given here owe much to the

accounts given by Robert Hull in *The Language Gap* (Methuen 1981) and Peter Medway in *From Information to Understanding* (Schools Council).

6. Bob Moy and Mike Raleigh: 'Comprehension: bringing it back alive'. It is reprinted from *The English Magazine* in *Language and Literacy from an Educational Perspective*, edited by Neil Mercer (Open University Press 1988).

7. *The Woman Warrior* by Maxine Hong Kingston is published by Picador (1981).

8. The words of Milan Kundera come from *The Art of the Novel* (Faber 1988).

9. Heteroglossia: two people talking together at a particular time and place bring to even a simple conversation their own experience and also the whole history of their language. They exchange meanings not only in the words they utter, but also in all the multiplicity of understandings that their words imply. The richness of this idea permeates M.M. Bakhtin's essays: *The Dialogic Imagination* (University of Texas Press 1981).

10. Mildred Taylor *Roll of Thunder, Hear my Cry* Gollancz 1977.
    Gillian Cross *A Map of Nowhere* Oxford University Press 1988.
    Alan Garner *The Stone Book* Collins 1976.

CHAPTER 8

There is no need for any child to fail to learn to read except when impeded by severe mental handicap. All children who are deemed to have 'special needs' should have individual help. That said, we must also realize that children do not learn directly from instruction, by being told what to do. They have to form their own understanding of the nature of the task.

1. The official British agency responsible for monitoring and helping those with literacy problems is the Adult Literacy and Basic Skills Unit (ALBSU), Kingsbourne House, 229/231 High Holborn, London, WC1. Local voluntary help can usually be contacted through public libraries.

2. Brian Street: see note in Chapter 1.

3. Frank Smith's book *Reading* (Cambridge University Press 1978) has encouraged many teachers to see learning to read from the point of view of the learner.
   In the same way Margaret Donaldson's *Children's Minds* (Fontana 1980) makes plain how active children are in pursuit of understanding.

4. Michael Bryant and Eve Bradley offer an up-to-date psychological perspective on reading and the problems experienced by young learners in *Children's Reading Problems* (Blackwell 1985). It is particularly clear about definitions of dyslexia.

5. Judith Graham's work with an adolescent boy who was a remarkable story teller is detailed in *Achieving Literacy*, by Margaret Meek, with Stephen Armstrong, Vicky Austerfield, Judith Graham and Elizabeth Plackett (Routledge 1983). Detailed accounts of longitudinal studies are less common than they should be. *The Strugglers* by Tony Martin (Open University Press 1989) has excellent examples. It is difficult to write about children who do not make progress without concentrating on their 'problems', but the resolution of these always has to come from their strengths.

CHAPTER 9

1. Raymond Williams *Writing in Society*. London, Verso 1983.

2. The history of writing and the early stages of children's entry into written language have much in common. Two interesting accounts of beginnings (besides that of Paul Bissex whom we have met already) are: *Literacy before Schooling* by Emilia Ferreiro and Ana Teberosky (Heinemann Educational Books 1979), and *Writing with Reason: The Emergence Of Authorship In Young Children*, edited by Nigel Hall (Hodder and Stoughton 1989). *The Primary Language Record* is also a good source of explanations. See Note 4 in Chapter 5 for details about it and also *Patterns of Learning* where this example of writing is published.

3. The National Writing Project created a network for and engaged teachers in the production, exchange and evaluation of children's writing development in school. Accounts of classroom practice were linked by the understanding that writing helps to shape thinking and is a central process in school learning. Consequent publications: *Writing and Learning* and *Becoming a Writer* (Nelson 1990) demonstrate the ideas and activities now current in British schools.

4. Bob Hodge and David Tripp suggest in *Children and Television: A Semiotic Approach* (Polity Press 1986) that 'adults in their contact with children should take an active part in helping to mediate children's interaction with and ideas about television. Adults should be wary of blanket rejection of programmes which are avidly viewed by children, or which provoke strongly positive responses. They should also acknowledge the role of peer interaction, as vital for a child's normal development.' Since this work appeared more analysts of

children's viewing have reported on their inquiries, especially in school. *Watching Media Learning; making sense of media education*, edited by David Buckingham (Falmer Press 1990) is an example of this kind.

5. Harvey Darton's account of chapbooks is in his classic study *Children's Books in England: Five Centuries Of Social Life*. The third edition by Brian Alderson is a tribute to a remarkable bookman (Cambridge University Press 1982).

6. Maíre Messenger Davies writes for parents and others who are anxious about television addiction in *Television Is Good For Your Kids* (Hilary Shipman 1989).

7. Daniel Chandler's book is *Computers and Literacy* (Open University Press 1985). His concern is to press home the idea that people are in charge of the technology and not the other way round. My understanding of the consequences of computer literacy was greatly enhanced by reading *The Cuckoo's Egg* by Clifford Stoll (The Bodley Head 1989) in which he tells of his discovery of a 'hacker' who infiltrated military intelligence networks.

8. 'The Dark Language of Infomania' is the title of the extract from Michael Heim's essay, which was printed in *The Independent* on 30 December, 1989. The book of essays, *The State of the Language*, is edited by Christopher Ricks and Leonard Michaels (Faber 1990).

Index

AA Handbook, 176
abstract thinking, 44–5, 215
accents, 17, 139
accountability, 7, 128, 135, 146
acronyms, 38
action knowledge, 170
adolescents, 150, 176–9, 183, 214–5
Adult Literacy and Basic Studies Unit, 191
adult literacy schemes, 166, 189–92
adults,
  affecting children's learning, 30–1, 64,
    75–7, 98, 100, 152–5, 201–2, 232
  learning to read, 70–3, 189
advertisements, 5–7, 24–5, 53, 73, 115, 164,
    207, 210–11, 221, 227, 236
Africa, epics, 15
Ahlberg, Janet and Allan, 120, 248, 251
AIDS, 53, 242
ALBSU, 191
Alice in Wonderland, 118
alignment, 192–9
alphabetic writing, 20, 152, 214
alphabets, 4–5, 97, 100, 101, 176, 191, 194,
    233
  learning, 75, 76, 187
analysis, of texts, 140, 141, 164
anthropology and anthropologists, 66, 230
anthropomorphism, 121
approximations, early reading, 157
Arabic literacy, 15, 20, 97
argument, 17, 80–1, 84, 123, 141, 151, 169,
    170, 221, 237
artists, 99, 116, 117, 118, 119, 121–2, 171,
    218, 238
attainment targets, 135, 138, 141–7, 155,
    157, 158–9
Attenborough, David, 104, 246
Austen, Jane, 29, 70, 184
authors, 22, 30, 40, 91, 115, 118, 119, 216,
    218, 234, 237

Baby's Catalogue, The, 120–1, 168, 248, 251
Bacon, Francis, 37
ballads, 234
banks and banking, 52, 150, 222, 229

Barnes, Douglas, 170, 251
Barrs, Myra, 85–6, 99, 213, 244, 249
basic literacy, 30–1, 51
Bateson, Gregory, 88, 242, 251
Bear Goes to Town, 250
Bear Hunt, 118, 154, 155, 247, 250
beginnings, for stories, 36, 106, 107, 111,
    153
behaviour,
  early literate, 110–15, 170
  language for, 237
  learning process, 6
  in libraries, 176
  literate, 165–188, 229, 230
    in school, 124–47, 158–9
  in school, 156–9, 195
Beloved, 41
Ben, early learning game, 85–6, 96, 99, 152,
    244
benefits, to progress, 200–2
best-sellers, 30, 40, 219
Bible, The, 2, 14, 15, 22, 36, 89
bidialectical children, 59
bilingual learners, 36–7, 59, 139, 143, 145,
    162–3, 172, 183, 195–6, 214
biographies, 65, 226–9
Bissex, Glenda, 95–6, 246
Bissex, Paul, 95–6, 213, 246
Blake, William, 121
Blyton, Enid, 29, 161
bookishness, 11, 58, 62, 63, 93, 126, 137–8,
    211
books, 37–8, 57, 58, 63, 71, 74, 151, 165–74,
    233, 238
  and changing literacy, 99, 216, 218–20
  children making, 187
  choosing, 41, 127
  early reading, 75, 77, 78, 93, 100–3, 156–
    62, 195
  influence of, 43
  in school, 124, 132
  uses of, 33, 175–9
boredom, 130, 133, 172, 179, 196, 198–9
Borges, J.L., 182
boundaries of literacy, 49–68

boys, different from girls, 10–11, 61–2, 132, 141, 144, 183–4
Bradley, Eve, 204, 253
Briggs, Raymond, 116, 118, 247
British Museum, 18, 240
Britton, James, 40, 241
broadcasters, 2, 63
broadcasting *see* radio, television
Brontes, The, 184
Browne, Anthony, 117, 118, 154, 210, 247, 250
Bryant, Michael, 204, 253
Buckingham, David, 255
Bunyan, John, 3, 22, 35, 236
Burningham, John, 119, 248, 250
Butler, Dorothy, 90, 245

Caldecott, Randolph, 121
calligraphy, 19
Canterbury Tales, The, 29–30
cards, sending, 50–1, 73
Caribbean literacy, 58, 106, 184
Carle, Eric, 247
Carroll, Lewis, 118
Carter, Denis, (quotation), 144–5, 248
cartoons, 116, 154, 184, 227
Cartwright, Reg, 250
catalogues, 250–1
CD ROM discs, 223
Centre for Language in Primary Education, 145
Chamberlain, Neville, 235
Chandler, David, 224, 255
chap books, 216–7
Chaucer, Geoffrey, 29–30, 234, 235
children,
    and computers, 223
    early learning, 194–5, 235, 237
        story telling, 100–23, 152
    kinds of writing needed, 23, 96
    learning,
        language, 55–6, 140, 187
        literacy, 66–8, 73–99
        to read, 35–7, 64–5, 100–2
        to talk, 57–60
        to think, 44–8
        to write, 94–7, 213–14
    reading to, 110–15
    represented in children's books, 121
    role playing, 108–10
    and television, 216–22
    telling stories, 112–15
children writing, 211–15
Children's Bible, 117
Children's Reading Problems, 204
Child's Garden of Verses, A (quotation), 88
Chinese literacy, 15, 19
Chips and Jessie, 119, 248
chirographic cultures, 19
Christmas, 51, 93

Chukovsky, Kornei 82–3, 244
Churchill, Winston Stanley, 236
Cinderella, 15, 93
civil servants, 63, 149
Civil War, The, and written language, 22
class, school, 124–9, 155–6, 170, 171, 195, 235
class, social,
    and learning attainment, 10–11, 50–1, 132
    and literate confidence, 49–50, 57–60
classics, the, 181–2
clerical literacy, 130, 172, 212
Come Away from the Water, Shirley, 119, 155, 248, 250
Comenius, John Amos, 101, 246
comic strips, 116, 119
comics, 72, 116, 122, 159, 218
common literacy, 226–9
communications networks, 2, 56, 150, 224
competence,
    about television, 221
    achieving, 51, 132, 184–5
    of adult learners, 192–3
    with computers, 223
    demonstrable, 8, 148, 149
    early development, 76–7, 84–8, 112–15, 179–188
    linguistic, 54–7, 140
    with non-fiction, 173–4
    of teachers, 205
    and technological advances, 209–11, 220
    tests in National Curriculum, 135
    and universal literacy, 208
competences,
    attainment levels, 142–3, 146–7, 161
    of children for society, 238
    of children starting school, 232
    developed at school, 58–60, 133–4, 160–2, 183
composing,
    with new technology, 208
    as part of writing, 22, 23, 96, 214, 223–4
Comprehension: bringing it back alive, 174
comprehension, 173–4, 197
computers, 16, 49, 56, 134, 150, 167, 210, 222–6
    changing literacy, 3, 7, 37–8, 60, 99, 166–7, 176
    in early learning, 20, 86–8
confidence,
    of adult learners, 192–3
    with computers, 222–6
    developed at school, 58–60, 127–8, 156–62, 168
    discovering, 66, 148, 214, 215, 238
    and dyslexia, 202–3
    from control of language, 27, 54–7, 141
    of the literate, 3, 5, 8, 25, 32, 33, 71–3, 151, 162–4, 191

Index

loss causes failure, 199
consequences,
  of computers, 222–6
  of literacy, 1–4, 129–30
  and thinking, 45
contexts,
  of language, 55–6, 57, 81, 86
  literate games, 210–11
  for modern living, 236
  of the spoken word, 236
  of study skills, 176–9
  of television productions, 218
  of texts, 35–8, 151, 168, 172, 177–9, 201,
    202, 208, 233–4
  words and pictures, 116
control,
  by powerful literacies, 211
  learned in school, 125
  learning, 214
  results from competence, 54–7, 179–80
conventions,
  of language, 163, 213–14
  of schooling, 125–30
  of spelling and writing, 45, 95–6, 188, 212
  of storytelling, 119, 122, 154–5
  of television, 218
copy-writing, 7, 24
copying,
  learning to write, 94, 212
  as part of learning, 22, 96, 170, 172, 234
core subjects, of literacy, 135
Cowes, Ralph, (quotation) 225
Cox Committee working group Report,
    138–41, 184, 212, 248
Crago, Maureen and Hugh, 90, 112, 245,
    247
creativity, 55, 80–8, 96
critical awareness, 64, 210
critical literacy, 10, 12, 123, 141, 170, 193,
    208, 220, 222, 226–9, 233
critics and criticism, 62, 66, 120, 181, 199,
    216
Cross, Gillian, 187, 252
crossword puzzles, 5, 54, 176, 227
Cuckoo's Egg, The, 255
Culler, Jonathan, 41, 241
cultural behaviour, and early learning, 73–
    99
cultural memory, 121
culture, 4, 9, 32, 44, 57–68, 97–9, 147, 165,
    183, 232
cultures,
  bilingual, 183, 195–6, 214
  literacies of, 35–8, 57–60, 69, 103, 107,
    116, 154, 180, 191
cumulative tales, 14, 29–30
curricula, 128, 130, 170, 175
  common, development of, 134–5
Cyrillic alphabet, 20

Dahl, Roald, 29, 250
Daily Mirror, 72, 190
Danny, the Champion of the World, 250
Darton, Harvey, 217, 255
Davies, Maire Messenger, 220, 255
deep play, 78, 85–8, 93, 182, 220, 245
defining literacy, 230–238
Descartes, Rene, 234
design and designers, 44, 99, 138, 150
desire to learn, 77–9, 177, 229
desk-top publishing, 49, 184, 209–11
developing countries, distinctive literacies,
    69
diagrams, 38, 39, 72, 161, 222
dialects, 17, 57–60, 139
dialogic imagination, 229
dialogues, 219, 235
diaries, 25, 149
Dickens, Charles, 29, 125
dictation, 162, 214
dictionaries, 39, 42, 57, 166, 234
differences, types of literacy, 9–12, 36, 136–
    8, 189–202
discourses, 27, 28, 35, 48, 111, 122, 125,
    127, 228
discussions, 17, 168, 197, 215, 221
divisions, social, 11, 49–68, 97–9
documents, official, understanding, 1, 24–5,
    53–4, 190
Dombey, Henrietta, 91
Donaldson, Margaret, 196, 253
Donne, John, 236
Doonan, Jane, 117, 247
drama, 143, 184, 187
drawing, 74, 152, 155, 170
drawing language, 94
dyslexia, 202–6

early learning, 6, 69–70, 73–99, 102, 152–5,
    184–5, 194–5, 235
  of scholars and academics, 232
East Coker (quotation), 27
Eastenders, 84, 219
economic literacy, 44
economics, 134, 170, 222
education, 11
  authorities, 7, 128
  development of, 32
  government documents on, 17, 131, 132,
    134–7
  and humankind, 101
  policies, 131, 146, 149, 174, 230
  standards of, 31, 50, 132
Education Reform Act, 1988, 134–6
electronics, and modern literacy, 3, 56, 166
Eliot, George, 184
Eliot, T.S., 27, 241
emergent literacy, 73–7
Emil Award, 122

encyclopaedias, 42, 101, 166, 176
endings, for stories, 36, 106, 107, 111, 112
engineers and engineering, 32, 61, 129, 138,
    150, 170, 222
English,
    core subject, 135, 202
    foundation for literacy in school, 135, 163
    lessons, 54–5, 127
    sounds representation, 85
    Standard English, 59, 135, 138–47
    variations in, 17, 58–9, 183, 184
    as a written language, 22
enjoyment,
    from new literacies, 211–29
    of language, 54
    of learning, 73–7
    of literature, 180–5
    of reading, 29–30, 33, 39–42, 206
    of reading aloud to children, 90–1
entitlement, 136–40, 147
epigrams, 106
episodes, 105–7, 108, 111, 113, 218
equal opportunities, 60, 143, 163
essays and essayists, 66, 126, 133, 166, 208,
    209–11, 232
ethnic groups, learning, 37, 57–60, 74, 97–8,
    131–2, 183, 191
Europe, 2, 32, 37, 101, 116
    and languages after 1992, 59, 163
evidence, of progress, 143–7, 161–2, 185
examinations, 8, 60–1, 70, 126, 128–9, 133,
    137, 142, 143, 149, 162, 165
    (see also) tests
experiences,
    learning, 55, 69–99, 91–7, 91–9, 107–10
    reading, 39–42, 65, 117, 121–2, 137,
    186–7
    and school, 124
    of television, 221
expert literacies, 23, 44, 56, 99, 129, 138,
    149, 173–4, 227–9

fables, 30, 105, 184
failure, 189
    and dyslexia, 202–6
    and early learning, 75–7, 185, 196–7
    possibly lessened by computers, 223
    and schools, 128–9, 130–47, 149, 158
    sensation of illiterates, 71, 190
    subject of research, 193
fairy-tales, 30, 36, 47
fantasies, 106, 119, 121, 154–5
Fat Mouse, 250
Father Christmas, 116, 247
fax machines, 56, 184, 229
Felix, Monique, 250
feminist literature, 183–4
Ferreiro, Emilia, 254
fiction, 41–2, 84, 89, 100–23, 122, 154, 186
    (see also) stories

fictionalizing, children's early learning,
    107–123
films, 115, 175, 184, 210, 216
financial transactions, 18, 20, 21, 23, 24,
    52–3
Firth, Helen, 250
fluency, 146, 150, 158, 214
folk-tales, 15, 83–4, 105, 112, 184, 187
forms,
    filling in, 72
    of language, 45–6, 53–4, 55
    of speech, 236
    of writing, 74, 172, 181, 187
foundation subjects, 135
Fox, *Dr.* Carol, 112, 114, 185, 247
Fox, Josh, 112, 113–14, 117, 185, 247
Freire, Paulo, 69, 243
functional literacy, 41, 51
functions,
    of language forms, 55
    of literacy, 3, 54
    of public writing, 24
    of storytelling, 122–3
Fungus the Bogeyman, 116, 247

games,
    based on technology, early learning, 85–
    8, 95, 96, 99
    on computers, 224
    in early learning, 55, 81–2
    played by literates, 5–7, 54, 210–11, 236,
    238
    story telling as, 108–10
gaps,
    children and teachers, for computers, 223
    teachers and learners, 193
    teachers and researchers, 193
Garner, Alan, 187, 250, 252
gender, 10–11, 61–2, 132, 141, 144, 174,
    183–4, 193, 209, 212
General Certificate of Secondary Education,
    142, 162, 202
Gentleman Jim, 116, 247
geography, 59, 72, 126, 127, 133, 161, 173,
    180
Geok-Lin Lim, Shirley, 40, 241
gifted children, teaching, 194
girls, different from boys, 10–11, 61–2, 132,
    141, 144, 183–4
Gorilla, 118, 247
government, educational documents, 17,
    131, 132, 134–47
Graff, Harvey, 238
graffiti, 25
Graham, Judith, 206, 253
grammar, 29, 55, 66, 139, 140, 174
Greek literacy, 4, 15, 18–21, 20–1, 97, 236
Gregory, R.L., 122, 247
Grierson, Herbert, 236

Index

Guardian, The, 227
Guardian, The (quotation), 222
Guinness Book of Records, The, 219

habits,
    of literate behaviour, 5, 100–5, 209–11,
        237
    of reading, 31, 109
handwriting, 10, 19–20, 211–15, 233
Hansel and Gretel, 64, 112, 117, 118, 247
Hard Times, 125
Hastings, Selina, 250
Heaney, Seamus, 27
Heim, Michael, 226, 255
heteroglossia, 186, 252
hieroglyphics, 18–19
Higgledy Piggledy, Pop, 64
hindrances, to progress, 200
Hinshelwood, 203, 204, 205
history, 43, 72, 125, 126, 133, 135, 161, 178,
        226–9, 230
    available through literacy, 48, 165
    created by writing, 2, 18–19, 20–2
    of literacy, 2–4, 13–48, 207, 231
    of literature, 183–4
    oral cultures, 14
    story telling, 103, 105–6
    of writing, 18–22
Hodge, Bob, 216, 254
Homer, 15
homework, 49, 60, 126, 128, 171
Hong Kingston, Maxine, 183, 252
Howker, Janni (quotation), 219
Huckleberry Finn, 62
Hughes, Martin, 80–1, 244
Hughes, Shirley, 119, 248
human rights, 231
Hume, David, 234
Hutchins, Pat, 93, 122, 245, 248, 250

ideas,
    creation of, 2, 40
    dissemination of, 43, 48, 72–3, 165, 221
Iliad, 15
illiteracy, 43, 70–3, 149, 189, 225–6, 231
illustrations, 6, 37–8, 70, 92, 100, 101, 115–
        22, 187, 217
images, 31, 69–70, 101, 104, 115–22, 210,
        216–17, 227
imagination,
    creates literature, 28–30
    and early learning, 79, 80, 85–8, 91,
        102–5
    and literature, 42, 180
    and picture books, 117–23
    in play, 107–10
    and schooled literacy, 126
    in story telling, 113–15
    and technological advances, 209–11, 219,
        225

Independent, The, 227
independent schools, 136
Indian literacy, 4, 15, 184
infomania, 226
information, 24, 41, 52, 66, 103, 175–9, 208,
        215, 226–9
    on computers, 223–6
    retrieval, 42–3, 142, 166, 170, 172
    sources, 33, 54, 124, 150, 161, 164, 166–8
instructions, 5, 72
interactions,
    children,
        and computers, 86–8
        and early reading aloud, 89–94
        and early stories, 100–123
        and text, 200–1
    language,
        and imagination, 40
        and social behaviour, 141
    readers, and writers, 22–3, 34–8, 72–3,
        151, 153, 164, 182, 215, 235
    reading and writing, 27, 236
    speaking and listening, 236
    teachers and pupils, 145, 194–5, 194–7
    writing and thinking, 234
International Literacy Year, 231
interpretation,
    of ancient writing, 18–19
    of experience, 44–5
    of information, 57, 167–79
    of specialized writing, 23
    of texts, 32, 70, 140, 141, 154–5, 164, 166,
        181, 220
inventions, advancing literacy, 3, 18, 23,
        37–8
Isaac Campion (quotation), 219
Israel, literacy of, 4, 14

James, Henry, 182
jokes, 47, 54, 56, 83, 161, 235
Josh, 112, 113–14, 117, 185, 246
journalism, 1, 63, 150, 226–9
journals, 22, 25, 49, 53, 226–9

key stages, 142
King Lear, 105
Kingman Committee of Inquiry, 138–40,
        248
Knock Knock, 118, 247
knowingness, 150, 154–5, 162–4
knowledge,
    available from the written word, 3, 24,
        42–3,
    children's understanding of, 195–6
    pursuit of, 41, 124–5, 170
knowledge engineers, 209
Kundera, Milan, 182, 184, 252

language,
    development in children, 45, 97–9, 124,
        143–7, 185

development of, 13–23
early learning, 79–88, 100–5, 152, 182,
    187, 235
is dialogue, 236
spoken and written, 46–7, 92, 111–12,
    115, 186
teaching Standard English, 138–47
and technology, 210, 224
and thinking, 45–8
understanding, 41, 54–7, 197
varieties of, 114, 185–6
and writing, 95
language awareness, 209
Language Record, 145
languages, variations within, 2, 17, 35–8,
    223
Lark Rise to Candleford, 64
Lascaux, cave paintings, 209–11
Latin, learning, 37, 61, 126, 171
laws and lawyers, 20, 21, 23, 24, 54, 190
learning, 17, 22–3, 44–8, 124
    differences, 10–11, 37, 57–60, 97–8, 131–2
    early experiences, 69–99
    extending, 166–74, 186–7
    learning about, 224
    and reading, 35–7, 39, 168–71
    and talking, 17
    and teaching, 66–8, 194–202
legends, 14–15, 30, 184
letters, 10, 25, 49, 72, 76, 127, 150, 171,
    192, 211–12
    of complaint, 26
    of condolence, 3, 26, 224
    to programmes, 16
levels of attainment, 128, 132, 142–3, 161,
    212, 238
levels of literacy, 11, 30–8
Levine, Kenneth, 52, 242
Lewis, C.S., 64, 250
libraries, 3, 44, 62, 63, 79, 115, 124, 126,
    160, 166, 175–9, 227
linguistic terminology, 143
linguistics, 80, 139, 230
linguists, 17, 66, 216
Lion, the Witch and the Wardrobe, The, 250
listening *see* talking
literature, 28–30, 62–5, 143, 165–188
Little Gidding, 234
Little Mouse Who Got Lost in a Book, The, 155,
    250
Little Red Hen, 91
logic, 43–6, 123, 174, 207, 237
Look What I've Got, 118, 247
Luria, A.R., 45, 241
Lutheran church, 32

machines, 3, 24–5, 56
magazines, 53, 103, 116, 131, 219, 226–7,
    235

aid literacy, 22, 49, 73, 75, 90, 150, 175,
    184
and illiteracy, 190
Magic Flute, The, 222–3
manuscripts, 3, 19, 20, 26, 29
Map of Nowhere, A, 187, 252
maps, 32, 133, 165
Maps of Play, 85–6, 244
mark-making, 2, 18, 25, 85
Martin, Tony, 253
Masters of the Universe, 85
mathematics, 23, 43, 44, 61, 127, 135, 138,
    143, 170
    teaching, 128, 131, 133
meaning, of reading, 38
meanings,
    in early learning, 73, 91–2, 91–3, 154, 213
    and language, 140–1
    and message systems, 194–5, 221
    and sense, in early learning, 82–3, 98,
        111, 197, 200–1
    of texts, 4, 5, 35, 40–1, 70, 161, 174
    of words, 5–7, 53, 57, 124–5, 172, 173,
        186, 188, 194–5, 225–6
media, 65–6, 143, 220, 222–3
Mee, Arthur, 117
memory, 14–15, 21, 26, 65, 93, 95, 121
men, 193, 209
messages, 1, 51, 73, 74, 194–5, 213, 221
metalinguistic awareness, 47, 82–4
metaphor, 82, 110, 113, 163, 172
Milton, John, 22, 236
misalignments, 192–9
Model Making for the Real World (quotation),
    225
modern literacy, tests, 36
modules for learning, 174
monks, written records, 21–2, 241
monologues, 111, 219
Moonlight, 118, 247
Mother Goose Treasury, 116, 247
mother toungues, 13, 36–7, 57–60, 138–40,
    191, 214
Mothercare, 250
motivation, to read, 189, 198–9
Moy, Bob, 174, 224, 252
multiconsciousness, 155, 186
multiculture, implications of, 10–11, 59–60,
    97–8, 121, 136, 138–40
multilingualism, 214
music, 15, 36, 85, 87, 91, 135, 165, 222
musicians, 44, 54, 99

naming, 101–3, 112, 152
Narnia, Chronicles of, 64, 161, 219–20, 250
narrative, 65, 100–123, 184–5, 220
narrative fiction, 41–2, 84
National Curriculum, 8, 31, 54–5, 58, 63,
    134–47, 174, 184, 209, 213, 242, 248
National Writing Project, 214, 254

Index

Neighbours, 215, 219
networks of communications, 2, 56, 150
news, 56, 172, 221, 222
  dissemination in early cultures, 21
newspapers, 27, 139, 148, 162, 175, 177, 207, 216, 226–9, 231
  aid literacy, 71–2, 151
  change literacy, 3, 22, 33, 132
  rely upon literacy, 2, 5, 49
notations, 85–8, 98, 99, 152
novelists, 22, 183, 223–6, 232
novels, 3, 32, 39, 52, 103, 108, 122, 149, 181, 184, 218, 226–9
  created in play, 110
nursery rhymes, 36, 55, 83–4, 105, 112, 153
nursery schools, 74, 93, 115

occupational literacy, 11, 23
Odyssey, 15
official documents, understanding, 1, 24–5, 53–4, 190
officially literate, 161
Olsen, David, 171, 251
Once upon a time, 36, 107, 153
Ong, Walter, 16
oral cultures, 5, 14–17, 21
oral work, GCSE, 202–3
Orbis Pictus 101, 104, 246
Origin of the Species, The, 177
Ormerod, Jan, 118, 247
Owl and the Pussy Cat, The, 186

painters and paintings, 44, 117, 209–11
Paradise Lost, 22
parents,
  attitudes to children having problems, 197–8
  attitudes to teachers, 66, 130–4, 147, 156, 194
  desires for children, 50–1, 100–1, 140, 142, 155, 215, 230
  and dyslexia, 204
  early teaching by, 30–1, 55–6, 73–99
  and education system, 7–9, 126, 148
Park in the Dark, The, 155, 250
Parrot told Snake, 250
partnerships,
  early learning, 88–94
  parents and teachers, 66, 130–4, 147, 148, 156, 230
Patterns of Learning, 214, 249
Paul, sound-letter relations system, 95
Pearce, Philippa, 161, 250
personal development, 13–14, 19–20, 26–7, 30–2, 33–48
perspective, 117, 119
Peter Pan, 64
Peter and the Wolf, 250
picture books, 45, 64, 72, 74, 76, 90, 101, 115–22, 151–5, 171, 218

picture scripts, ancient writing, 18–19
pictures, 39, 45, 101–2, 150, 152, 168, 210, 221
  drawing, 94
  reading, 31, 207
Piggybook, 218
Pilgrim's Progress, The, 22, 35
Plato, 20–21, 48
play,
  early learning, 47, 55, 74, 77–88, 93, 94, 153–5
  imagination, 107–10
  stories part of, 103, 107–10
plays, 28, 38, 64, 184, 218, 222
  writing, 22, 26
pleasure,
  from new literacies, 211–29
  from stories, 98
  as motivation, 198–9
  of reading, 33, 41, 71, 118, 148, 160
  in reading stories to children, 103
Poem in the Underground (quotation), 40, 241
poetry, 15, 32, 38, 45, 93, 126, 144, 180, 182–3, 184, 187
  early learning, 80, 214
  writing, 26, 28, 72
poets, 23, 27, 89, 129, 165, 182, 183, 232, 234
politicians, 16, 24, 25, 54, 56, 104, 148, 154, 221, 231
politics, 16, 135, 150, 164, 217
  and literacy, 134
poor, the, 3, 10–11, 74, 134, 149, 189
Pop goes the Weasel, 182
popular literacy, 32, 208, 227
popular writing, dangerous concept, 27–8
Potter, Beatrix, 108
power,
  of computer technologies, 223
  of fluency, 214
  of information, 166
  of language, 54–7, 233–4
  of literates, 3, 8, 72–3, 88, 129, 192, 207
  of television, 217–8
  of writing, 2, 23, 28, 30, 65, 192, 207, 214
powerful,
  dialogues, 238
  language, 139
  languages, 37
  literacies, 136, 162–3, 211
  literacy, 10, 148
  literacy practices, 98
  literates, 11, 33–5, 238
  texts, 44
  writing, 20, 23
Primary Language Record, The, 254
primary schools, 6–7, 10, 125, 155–61, 175–7, 180
print, 75, 154, 159, 160, 190, 227, 238

printing, 3, 20, 24, 29, 63, 150, 166, 208, 226
  development of, 37–8
privileges, 8, 32, 44, 68, 114, 166
problem learners, teaching, 194–202
projects, 168–71
Prometheus Bound, 166
prose, 38, 64, 66, 152, 165, 186
proverbs, 14–15, 82, 83, 84, 105
psalms, 236
psychologists, 44, 66, 121, 122, 204, 205
psychology, 80, 230
Public Record Office, 1
publishing, 23, 26, 120, 151, 192, 223–4, 226, 231
punctuation, 185, 212, 213, 214, 224
purposes,
  of language, 140
  of literacy, 3, 10, 21, 69–73, 126–30, 138, 149, 165, 179–80, 225
  of reading, 31–2, 128
  of schooling, 126–30
  of study skills, 176–9
  of writing, 23–30, 128

quality of literacy, 149
questions, 158, 159, 167, 176, 178, 215, 216

radio, 2, 15–17, 53, 65, 184, 216, 235
Radio Times, 116
Raleigh, Mike, 174, 252
rap, 106
readers, 23–30, 54, 65, 109, 218
readership, 38, 116, 120–1
reading, 30–48
  ability levels, 161–2
  adults learning to, 28, 189–92
  attainment targets, 142
  benefits to progress, 200–2
  created by writing, 23–30
  development of, 14, 30–8, 133
  early learning 6, 75, 88–94, 124–8, 154–5, 194–5,
  early teaching of, 130–4, 156–61
  and gender, 61–2, 183–4, 193
  as labour, 137–8
  other than the written word, 4–5, 14, 207, 210–11, 217
  problems with, 189–206
  sources other than those usually accepted, 50, 58, 69–70, 71–2, 73–4
  television, 216–17
  and thinking, 42–8
  types of, 27, 151, 161, 228
  ways of, 22, 28, 33, 64, 159, 175–9, 180, 182, 190
reading to, 36, 70, 88–97, 107, 110–15
records, 18–23, 26, 39, 124, 165, 208, 227
  ancient writing, 20, 21
  official, understanding, 1, 24–5, 53–4

in school, 132, 133–6, 145–6, 148
recreation, part of literacy, 9, 39–40, 103, 181–2, 211–29
recursive progress of language, 143–5, 148, 158–9, 199, 201
Red Riding Hood, 91
reference books, 161, 175, 176
reflexiveness, 159
Reformation, The, 22, 37
regional speech, 17, 58–9
remedial teaching, 193, 200
remembering, 14, 26, 65, 95
research, learning to, 176–9
resource centres *see* libraries
rhetoric, 41, 106, 112, 122, 125, 163, 164, 225, 236, 237
riddles, 82, 83, 93
risks, early learning, 195
role playing, children, 108–10
Roll of Thunder Hear My Cry, 187, 254
Roman literacy, 20, 25
Rosemary Conley's Hip and Thigh Diet, 219
Rosetta Stone, 18–19, 240
Rosie's Walk, 122, 151, 186, 245, 248, 250
rules,
  for expert literacies, 173–4
  of games played by literates, 5–6, 238
  of language, in early learning, 79–88
  for language interaction, 236–7
  of play in early learning, 78–88
  for reading, 111–2, 236
  of school learning, 125–9, 155–7
  of speech, 236
  of stories, 92, 105–7, 108–10, 153–5
  of television messages, 216
  of thinking, 43–4
  of writing, 96, 152, 188, 236

sagas, 106
St. Gall, monks of, written records, 21–2, 241
Sand, George, 184
Satanic Verses, The, 41, 219
SATS (standard attainment tasks), 141–7
School Boards, 32
School Library Association, 175
schooled literacy, 12, 100–1, 124–47, 141, 143, 148, 155–162, 232, 236–7
  and technological advances, 209–11
schooling, of language, 48
schools, 44
  concept of literacy 75, 97
  development of, 32
  English teaching in, 138–47
  libraries in, 175
  and reading standards, 31, 50
  reception classes, 74
  responsible for literacy, 7–12, 58–60
  teaching practices, 66, 155–62
  television in, 126, 220

science, 126, 127, 133, 135, 138, 171, 197
scientific literacy, 23, 27, 43, 44, 45, 61
Scollon, Ron, 86–8, 222, 244
Scollon, Suzanne, 86–8, 244
Scollon, Tommy, 86–8, 95, 96, 99, 244
Scots literacy, 15, 59, 88–9, 106
Scott, *Sir* Walter, 234
scribes, 3, 19–20, 21, 22, 23, 32, 208, 212, 215
scripts,
    ancient writing, 18–19
    national differences, 4–5
scrolls, 3
secondary orality, 15–17, 164
secondary schools, 125
    identifying literature, 180
    pupil's capabilities, 214–5
Secretary of State for Education, 138
seeing,
    language, 14, 84
    in learning, 196
    picture books, 117, 118, 119, 121–2, 218
Sendak, Maurice, 121, 248
sense, and meanings, in early learning, 82–3, 157, 196
sense and nonsense, 55, 187
sensory contact, for early readers, 69–70, 152
sentences, 102–3, 111, 181, 213
sermons, 104, 105, 236
Shakespeare, William, 22, 29, 70, 119, 182
shopping lists, 2, 48, 73, 75
signs, 35, 38, 39, 73–4, 103, 210, 221, 238
singing and songs, 14, 83–4, 105, 152, 182, 183
skills, 72, 151, 201, 212
Smith, Frank, 194, 253
Smith, Norman Kemp, 234
Snowman, The, 118, 119, 247
soap operas, 17, 84, 215, 219
social activities,
    early literacy, 73–5, 194, 234
    reading, 41, 175
    reflected in stories, 100–23
    thinking, 45
    watching television, 216, 221
social attitudes to literacy, 3–4, 31, 32, 43, 49–68, 129, 130, 189
social class, effects of, 8–9, 10–11, 136, 139, 204
social needs, for literacy, 7–9, 11, 24, 28
society,
    attitudes to literacy, 49–51, 97–9, 122, 163, 230
    changed by television, 221–2
    changes literacy, 6–7, 37–8, 49–50
    cultural changes in, 10–11
    pre-literate, 14–15
Socrates, 20–21, 48
sound, 13–17, 84, 95, 153

special needs, 203, 205
speech, 13–17, 58–9
    (see also) talking
spelling,
    emphasis on, 29, 142, 185, 208, 233,
    learning, 94–6, 153, 202, 212–4, 234
Standard Attainment Tasks, 141–7
Standard English, 59, 135, 138–47, 163, 213
State of the Language, The, 226
status, of writers, 30
Stevens, Harry, 250
Stevenson, R.L., 88–9
Stoll, Clifford, 255
Stone Book Quartet, 187, 252

stories, 17, 29–30, 64, 65, 72, 100–23, 148, 152–5, 181, 234, 235
    (see also) fiction
    children telling, 79, 237
    children's early writing, 214
    early learning, 45–8, 74, 80, 84, 88–94, 161
    early literacy, 75, 98, 167
    as literature, 180
    and television, 17, 216, 218
storytellers, 171, 184, 218–9
Street, Brian, 192, 241
study, 165–88
styles,
    of speech, in early learning, 80
    of television productions, 218
    in writing, 22–3, 105, 125, 172, 185–6, 227–8, 236
success,
    associated with literacy, 8
    in early learning, 76, 78, 130–1, 167
    and literacy, 11, 73, 148–52
    as motivation, 198–9
    not subject of research, 193
    and school, 31, 50–1, 128–9, 130–47
Sunshine, 118, 247
Sweden, 32
Switzerland, monks of St. Gall, written records, 21–2, 241
symbols, 39, 44, 73–4, 87–8, 95–7, 133, 210, 221, 224

talking, 17
    (see also) speech
    adolescent competence, 215
    development of, 13–17
    early learning, 54–7, 76–7, 79–88
    easier than writing, 26
    as part of study, 170, 173
    and reasoning, 46
    school conventions of, 127
    and stories, 104–6
    and thinking, 44
Task Group on Assessment and Testing, 142, 248

Taylor, Mildred, 187, 252
teachers,
    attitudes to adolescents, 215
    attitudes to literacy, 58, 93, 94–5, 97–9,
        155–62, 208, 232
    need acknowledgement, 129, 132–3,
        135–6, 174
    partnership with parents, 66, 130–4, 147,
        148, 156, 230
    of reading, 31
    responsible for,
        literacy, 7–9, 126–30, 148, 166–74, 193
        results of National Curriculum, 138–47
teaching,
    beneficial to reading progress, 200–2
    gifted children, 194
    and its obligations, 129
    and learning, 66–8, 70–3
    literacy skills, 29, 176–9
    methods, and relations to success, 7–8,
        151, 156–62, 168–74, 183
    and the National Curriculum, 138–47
    problem learners, 194–202
    remedial, 193–4
    writing, 22–3, 28
Teberosky, Ana, 254
technological advances, 10, 15–17, 28, 37–8
    aid literacy, 3, 134, 175–8, 184
    change literacy, 49–50, 85–8, 191, 192,
        208–11, 216–26
    change literature, 181
    control of, 56, 167
television, 150, 151, 164, 216–22, 231, 236
    aids confidence, 29, 56, 73, 214–5
    aids literacy, 75, 84, 85–6, 91, 104, 114,
        115, 169, 185, 186
    changing literacy, 7, 15–17, 37–8, 54, 60,
        64–5, 99, 107, 178, 207, 227
    and illiteracy, 131, 132, 190, 192
    and picture books, 118–19
    relies upon literacy, 2, 49, 53
    in schools, 126
Television is Good for your Kids, 220, 255
television literacy, 38, 216–22
tests, 11, 143, 149
    (see also) examinations
    for dyslexia, 205
    of modern literacy, 36
    National Curriculum, 135, 137
    reading, interpretation of, 50–1
    in schools, 128, 131
    Standard Attainment Tasks, 141–7
textbooks, 171–4, 175, 220
texts,
    ancient writing, 20, 21
    and changing literacy, 35–7, 99, 190–1,
        219
    early writing, 22, 213–14
    of first books, 100–2, 107, 115–22
    interpretation of, 32, 140, 141, 164

as literature, 28, 62–5, 183
in school, 125, 145, 157–62, 237
story telling, 111, 153
studying, 165–88
The House That Jack Built, 14
thinking, 23, 26, 35, 42–8
Thomas the Tank Engine, 218
Time Out, 116
Times, The, 227
timetables, 29, 42, 74, 180
Titch, 93
Tizard, Barbara, 76, 80–1, 104, 111, 244
Tommy, early learning game, 86–8, 95, 96,
    99
Tom's Midnight Garden, 250
tools,
    for investigation, 41
    for learning, 166–74
    for literacy, 223–6
    literacy as, 71–3
    for writing, 3, 6–7, 18, 19, 28, 152, 212
traditions,
    of cultures, 107
    of literacies, 37, 57–60, 97, 180
    of literacy, 233
Tripp, David, 216, 254

United Nations, 231
United States, teaching in, 171
universal literacy, 32, 63–5, 205, 208
universities, 8, 17, 129, 188
Up and Up, 119, 248
uses,
    of language, 140–1
    of literacy, 3, 11, 48–68, 71–3, 77, 100,
        135, 162, 165–88, 190–2
    of reading, 38–48
    of storytelling, 122–3
    of texts, 33, 233–4
    of writing, 1–4, 21, 23, 29
utilitarian literacy, 10

values, of literacy, 136–8, 162, 190, 207
Vedic hymns, India, 15
verse, 14–15, 83–4, 186, 235
Very Hungry Caterpillar, The, 105, 247
videos, 49, 118–19, 184, 202, 221
Vietnamese literacy, 5, 191
visual literacy, 115–22
vocabulary,
    for computer culture, 209, 225
    of dyslexia, 203, 205
    early learning, 111–2, 197
    for expert literacies, 161, 173–4, 226–9
    television criticism, 220
    and thinking, 47
voices,
    behind words, 186, 219
    early learning, 70, 80, 92
    radio, 235

of texts, 34, 65, 107, 171, 237
Vygotsky, L.S., 48, 112, 241, 244

Waddell, Martin, 250
Warnock Report, 205
*Watching Media Learning, making sense of media
education*, 255
Way to Sattin Shore, The, 250
Welsh literacy, 5, 15, 135, 144
When the Wind Blows, 116, 247
Where the Wild Things Are, 45, 64, 98, 112,
121, 248
Where's Julius, 119–20, 248
Where's Spot, 74
Williams, Raymond, 210, 241, 254
Winnicott, D.W., 88, 245
Wizard of Oz, The, 112
Wolf, Joanna, 212
Wolf and Seven Little Kids, The, 92
Woman Warrior, The, 183, 252
women, 193, 209
word processors, 10, 18, 20, 28, 49, 66, 86–
8, 150, 208, 223–4
words, 46–7, 101–2, 105, 159–60, 161, 221
worksheets, 174, 176
writers, 89, 182, 192, 223–6, 231
for children, 91–2

enjoy language, 54
habits of, 109
power of, 30, 65, 207
and readership, 116, 161, 162–3
subjectivity of, 177
writing, 2–3, 18–30, 162, 202, 210
accurate, 140
attainment targets, 142
development of, 133, 151
early learning, 75–7, 85–8, 94–7, 102,
152, 213–14
experiments, 150
and gender articulation, 62
as labour, 137–8
learning, 70, 124–8, 155, 170, 223, 229
power of, 2, 28, 192
and reasoning, 46
social uses of, 1–4
styles of, 22, 25–7, 105, 125, 153, 172,
185–6, 227–8
systems, 4–5, 18–20
and talking, 17
and thinking, 48
Writing in Society, 254
Wuthering Heights 41

Yeats, W.B. 70
Young Children Thinking (quotation), 81